THE DIVINE PASTIME

THEATRE ESSAYS

by

Harold Clurman

Macmillan Publishing Co., Inc.

NEW YORK

Collier Macmillan Publishers

LONDON

792.082
C64d

Library of Congress Cataloging in Publication Data

Clurman, Harold, 1901-
  The divine pastime.

  1. Theater—Collected works. I. Title.
PN2038.C5   792'.08   73-10561
ISBN 0-02-526150-9

m N

Macmillan Publishing Co., Inc.
866 Third Avenue, New York, N.Y. 10022

Collier-Macmillan Canada Ltd.

FIRST PRINTING 1974

Printed in the United States of America

TO

Ellen Adler Oppenheim

The theatre—"the most divine pastime that cultivated men and virtuous women can enjoy when more than two of them are gathered together."
—Voltaire

Contents

xii   Contents

Contents   xiii

Introduction

"CRITICISM IS, has been and eternally will be as bad as it possibly can be." Thus spake George Bernard Shaw, the best theatre critic in the English language in at least the past hundred years. What he meant was that critics will never satisfy everyone concerned, that they will always make horrendous "mistakes," that they are bound occasionally to cause damage, and that the degree of their benefactions will always fall under the shadow of serious doubt.

What is a critic anyway? For the reader of the daily newspaper he is one who issues bulletins in the manner of a consumers' report. He is a sort of advance man, a freeloading publicity agent charged with the duty of instructing the prospective theatregoer as to what he should or should not buy. He is to tell his readers in no uncertain terms, "I like it" or "I don't like it."

If the reader were as careful in his perusal of printed matter as he is admonished to be about his diet, he would realize that in most cases the inference contained in the declaration "I like it" is of little value, in fact, is nearly meaningless. All three words are vague!

First: who is the "I" that speaks? Why should his assertion carry any particular weight? For him to exercise any decisive influence over me, should I not take the measure of the man, learn something of his intrinsic qualifications, his human disposition, his beliefs, his personal complexion? There are critics whose most emphatic encomia fill me with misgivings.

Second: what does the critic mean by the word "like"? In what way does he like it? I like pretty girls and I do not particularly "like" Samuel Beckett's work; yet I do not rush to a show which boasts a cast of pretty girls (I can meet them elsewhere) and I hope never to miss a Beckett play.

Above all: what is the "it" which the critic likes or dislikes? I like candy and I like meat, but before consuming either I should be able to distinguish between the two. The primary obligation of the critic is *to define* the character of the object he is called upon to judge. The definition itself may constitute a judgment, but insofar as they are distinct from each other the definition should precede the judgment. It is perfectly proper to rave about *Barefoot in the Park* as candy, and I can well understand the critic who damns Wedekind's *The Awakening of Spring,* but I can have little respect for him if he does not recognize that it is meat. It is certainly true that one man's meat is another man's poison, but the manner and reason for the choice may characterize the man.

To put what I have said another way: the reviewer whose reaction to a play is contained in some such ejaculations as "electrifying," "inspired," "a thunderbolt," "a mighty work," "a dismal bore," may in each instance be right, but his being right does not by itself make him a critic. For these epithets only indicate effects: pleasure or displeasure. The true critic is concerned with causes, with the composition of human, social, formal substances which have produced the effect. Strictly speaking, it is not even necessary that the critic name the effect; it is imperative that he take into account the sources from which it springs. In doing this the critic is faithful to the work he treats of, while at the same time he affords the reader some idea of what manner of man the critic himself is—which is a crucial consideration.

In estimating Shaw as a critic it does not upset me that he was captious about Wilde's *The Importance of Being Earnest*—he was wrong—and that he was much more receptive to the same author's *An Ideal Husband,* a play for which I have less regard. In both cases he said things of great interest and moment; I am more impressed by him in my disagreement than I am by the critic who pronounces *Any Wednesday* a "wow"—a statement which brooks no denial.

Theatre having become a luxury commodity with us, the person in quest of entertainment demands instantaneous guidance, and the daily critic is there to supply it with the necessary dispatch. His columns tend to make the pronouncement of opinion a substitute for criticism, so that very few of his readers have any idea of what criticism really is.

Newspaper editors are not especially interested in the theatre. Their views are generally similar to that of the ordinary playgoer. There is, thus, little inquiry into the qualifications of the person who is to occupy the post of theatre critic. If he is a competent journalist, is not so eccentric in his tastes that his recommendations are likely to disappoint or offend readers, the editor is satisfied. If, in addition, the critic can wisecrack and shape his opinions into formulas as efficient as an advertising slogan, the editor is delighted. What concerns him is circulation.

The daily critic is actually responsible to no one but his newspaper. In the context of our present theatre situation the critics of at least three or four of our dailies (the columns themselves even more than the people who write them) exercise far more power than anyone desires them to—power, that is, which affects sales. The critic may himself be embarrassed by the commercial influence he exerts. He will even go so far on occasion as to disclaim that he is a critic, protesting that he is simply a reviewer, that his word is hardly more important than the next fellow's. After all, as has often been remarked, he is usually constrained to write his review immediately after the performance in less than an hour. While such defenses are largely sincere, they contain some unconscious hypocrisy. The fact remains that most of the daily reviewers mistake their opinions for criticism. They are as much in the dark on the subject as their readers.

Criticism, to paraphrase Anatole France, is the adventure of a soul (or a mind) among presumed works of art. Just as the artist seeks to communicate his experience of life through the use of its raw materials and the specific means of his art, so the critic, confronting the resultant creation, sheds a new light on it, enhances our understanding of it, and finally ends by making his own sense of life significant to his readers. At best, the critic is an artist whose point of departure is another artist's work. If he is a truly fine critic, he will make his reader something of an artist as well. It is not essential that he also make him a customer!

Let us agree that the daily reviewer is rarely a critic of this kind because, for one thing, he has no time to be. One notices, however, that he infrequently has more to say about a play after a week's reflection than he said immediately after the performance. Some reviewers do not even desire more time. They trust that the rush from playhouse to typewriter will furnish them with the impetus to convey hot-off-the-griddle reaction.

For my part, I often do not know what I really think about a play as I leave the performance. Momentary satisfactions and immediate irritations frequently warp my judgment. My thoughts and feeling become clear to me only when I read what I have written! And then, I must confess, I sometimes alter my view, in the sense that I see plays—as I do people—in many different perspectives according to time and circumstance. The critic ought to proclaim the right to change his mind, just as an art work itself changes even for its own creator. Our relation to art ought not be static; it is a very human business.

To be candid, however, let us assert that most daily reviewers are not critics because they are not richly enough endowed with sensibility, thoughtfulness, personality, knowledge of art and life or literary skill to hold our attention for much longer than it takes to read their reviews.

It should not surprise us that great theatre critics—Lessing, Hazlitt, Lewes, Shaw—and even lesser ones of the same line are rarely employed as daily reviewers because men of this rank have prejudices about which they are as explicit as possible—prejudices, moreover, which are rarely those of the casual reader. And one of the authentic critic's main purposes is to enunciate or construct an attitude toward life—if you will, a "philosophy"—and to make it as cogently relevant as possible. This must necessarily scare a newspaper editor whose publication is designed to please "everybody," that is, from 400,000 to a million readers daily.

Criticism can never be wholly objective—though the critic should keep the "object" well in view—but our basic complaint is not that certain daily reviewers are too subjective but that too often they are themselves such puny subjects.

Critics of the mass-circulation weeklies are usually men who write in the vein of the daily reviewer except in that they employ a more specialized or more "pointed" vocabulary. The men who write for the smaller (usually liberal) weeklies aim to fulfill the requirements of true criticism, though too often—as sometimes in the case of George Jean Nathan—they believe they will attain this goal by defiantly reversing the daily reviewers' coin. To thumb one's nose at Broadway values is not in itself an artistic gesture. Still there is a value in upsetting settled and stupid habits of mind.

In the monthlies and the scholarly quarterlies, criticism generally becomes aesthetic debate or exposition, frequently valuable instruments in criticism. (Aristotle's *Poetics* is the classic model for this sort of criticism.) Often this proves to be drama, rather than theatre, criticism. It is necessary to make the distinction because criticism of drama is a branch of literary criticism (though to be sure drama, like poetry and the novel, has its own laws), while the theatre critic, who must be thoroughly aware of literary values, looks upon drama as it historically came into being—as a part of, but not the whole of, the theatre, which is an art in itself. There are men of sound literary judgment who are unattuned to the theatre, just as there are cultivated folk who have little real feeling for music or the visual media. One has only to compare Max Beerbohm's essay on Duse with Shaw's corresponding piece to become aware of the difference between a brilliant commentator on the drama and a complete theatre critic.

In the introduction to my earlier collected volume of theatre reviews and essays, *Lies Like Truth* (Macmillan, 1958), I said: "My notices in the weeklies tended to be milder than those I wrote for the monthly, and I suspect that I should be more careful to be kind if I wrote for a daily."

One may well ask how this statement can be reconciled with "honesty" and high standards. "My years of work as a producer and as a director," I went on to say, "taught me many lessons about snap judgments and the dangers of a too proud or rigid dogmatism . . . I would conduct myself in criticism . . . with due regard for immediate contingencies without ever losing sight of the larger issues and aims. Do not, I tell myself, squash the small deeds of the theatre's workers, trials and errors with an Absolute."

Can a person professionally engaged in the theatre also be a reliable critic? The simplest answer is to cite—I have already indirectly done so above—the names of some of the best critics of the past who have been craftsmen and critics in their respective artistic areas—a list I might extend further to include poets, musicians and painters. But I shall once again call upon Shaw to speak for me: "I do my best to be partial, to hit out at remediable abuses rather than at accidental shortcomings, and at strong and responsible rather than at weak and helpless ones . . . A man is either a critic or not a critic . . . He cannot help himself."

I shall go further. The fact that I am engaged in active stage work does not render me either timid and indulgent or resentful, malicious and vindictive. It makes me scrupulous and responsible. I am convinced that a critic of contemporary effort owes it to his job to be responsible to everyone in the theatre: the audience, to begin with, as well as to the dramatists, actors, directors, designers. In doing this he becomes responsible to the Theatre as a whole.

George Jean Nathan once cavalierly said that he did not care if every box office in the country closed. I do care. For the closing of the box office bespeaks closing of the theatre, and this would mean that we would end by being more culturally maimed than we are with the theatre in its present deplorable state. There can be no "masterpieces" where there is no production, no routine theatre activity. Even in Elizabethan times, without a box office, no theatre; without a theatre (and inevitably many bad plays), no Shakespeare to write for it.

I would encourage playgoing. (Do not lift your brows too high; it makes you look idiotic.) I would encourage it not by rave reviews of mediocre plays, not by discovering "genius" in every promising talent, but by being wholly committed to saying, with due regard to all the complexity of the elements involved, what I feel at each theatrical occasion I am called on to attend. Such treatment, which arises from a devotion to talent howsoever modest, will arouse interest in the theatre. Making extravagant claims for entertainment which one knows will prove remunerative, with or without critical ballyhoo, depresses such interest as much as does the neglect of promising, but not yet wholly ripe, efforts. I regard the writer to whom the practical economic, social and professional aspects of the theatre are totally alien as at best a curator of the drama, not as a true critic.

As to my own "philosophy" of life and the theatre: it must become apparent with the continuity of my progress as man and critic. It is for that rather than for my incidental recommendations—when I take the trouble to make them—that I write. Just as opinions, yours are as good as mine.

Recently I was introduced to a gentleman as a person about to stage a new play. "What do you think of it?" I was asked. "It's a good play," I answered. "Ah, I notice you are careful not to say it's *great*," he remarked.

I then explained that in the history of the theatre from Aeschylus to Axelrod there were probably less than a hundred plays I would call indisputably great. Not all of Euripides, Shakespeare, Molière, Ibsen or Chekhov is great. Shaw, Pirandello, O'Neill, Brecht, Beckett, Genet are important but I hesitate to call them great.

The use of the designation, needless to say, depends on one's frame of reference. If one believes a play may retain its efficacy for, let us say, fifty years, one may reasonably call it great—though that is not the yardstick by which I measure. In contemporary American theatre criticism the word has come to signify gushing enthusiasm, similarly indicated by such a phrase as "the best play of several seasons." With us, the superlative is largely an implement of first aid to the box office.

Our theatre and its status among us are in such a sorry plight that when a reviewer labels a play "good" or "interesting," we take it to mean mediocre—hardly worth the expense of seeing it. Only a "money notice" is considered a favorable review—something having at least the force of a full-page newspaper ad. Criticism in such an atmosphere is perilously difficult. Theatre managers who complain about the reviewers do not want criticism; they want praise verging on hysterics. This generally holds true for playwrights and actors as well.

The reaction on the part of some critics to this journalistic inflation is to reverse the process: to preserve their critical chastity they assume an attitude of absolute severity. They will have nothing but the "best"; they insist on "the highest standards." One cannot be too extreme, they feel, in defense of Excellence.

Such a posture strikes me as no less false than the promiscuity of those addicted to raving about any presentation that can decently be commended at all. For while some absolute standard must be latent in the critic's mind if he is to give any play its proper place, it is not at all necessary or desirable to judge every new play on the basis of that ideal. There is even something inimical to art in such a practice.

"Masterpieces," says the poet W. H. Auden, "should be kept for High Holidays of the Spirit." That is certainly not to deny that we need organizations to keep masterpieces perennially in view. But what we must demand above all in plays is that they *speak* to us, stir us in ways which most intimately and powerfully stir our senses and our souls, penetrate to the core what is most truly alive in us. To do so plays do not have to have the stamp of universality or impeccable inspiration, or signs of top-flight genius. They have to be the consistent and persuasive expression of genuine perception, individual in origin, social in application. If Aeschylus, Shakespeare, Molière are prototypes of dramatic greatness, it must be evident that many second-, third-, fourth- and fifth-rate plays may also fulfill the function of usable art.

It is no special feat to determine greatness retrospectively. The critic who implies that nothing less than the absolutely first-rate will do is usually more pedant than artist. Immortality awards are best conferred by our descendants. "A 'high standard,' " said Henry James, "is an excellent thing, but we fancy it sometimes takes away more than it gives." We live more fully on what we create now than on what was created for us in the past. That is as true for audiences as for the makers and doers.

Since we are speaking of the total phenomenon of the theatre, rather than of drama alone, we must remind ourselves that masterpieces badly produced or produced at the wrong time and place cease to occupy their exalted position; in fact, they no longer serve the purposes of art. Under the proper circumstances, on the stage and in the auditorium, plays of more modest literary pretentions may excel them. I am often given to understand that Sophocles was a greater dramatist than O'Neill. I need no such instruction. It is nonetheless true that most productions of Sophocles (and of other Greek masters) have struck me as singularly empty, while certain O'Neill staged plays have impressed me deeply. To make this crushingly clear, on a recent radio program I informed the manager who sponsored both the 1964 Broadway *Hamlet* and *Beyond the Fringe* that I believed the latter contained the greater artistic value.

We have also learned that some dramatists of unquestioned stature—Goethe, Kleist, Racine, Strindberg—do not have the same impact in one country as in another, or make the impression they presumably should, even upon their own people at all times.

Talent of every kind, even small talent, must always be credited. That is particularly so of talent close to us in time and place. I do not suggest that we follow Herman Melville's injunction "Let America first praise mediocrity in her children before she praises . . . the best excellence in children of other lands." I submit, however, that a sense of the present and of presence are factors which it is unwise to overlook or underestimate. But the critical faculty does not consist only in recognizing talent; there must be also an ability to evaluate it. The American theatre is richly supplied (I almost said lousy) with talent, but too often talent not worthy enough to put to the best uses.

This raises an aspect of theatre criticism in which we are decidedly at fault. Our praise is usually the response to an effect, a register of stimulation. We applaud the person who produces the effect in an acclaim which ranges from a compliment to cleverness to the proclamation of genius. But what counts in talent is its specific gravity, its meaning, how and in what way it affects us, the human nourishment it offers us. Potassium cyanide is tremendously effective, but it is not food.

Everything—even the damnable—must be expressed in the theatre. I cannot hold anything to be true unless tested by its opposite. I need Beckett's negations if for no other reason than that they fortify me in my affirmations. I need Genet's "decadence" to sustain my health. I embrace the madness in certain modern dramatists to find my balance. To be sure, there is authentic "far-out" writing and there is fashionable simulacrum; it is the critic's task to distinguish between them. He must sift the stuff which composes each particular talent in relation to himself as a person representative of a certain public. "Entertainment," "good theatre," "beauty" are not enough. We must know what these virtues actually do, how they work. The critic's main job, I repeat, is not to speak of his likes or dislikes as pleasure or distaste alone, but to define as exactly as possible the nature of what he examines. And it is best to do this without the use of tags intended for quotes to be read on the run.

What I have said about the judgment of texts applies equally to acting and to those other ingredients which go into the making of a play in the theatre. ("To see sad sights," Shakespeare tells us, "moves more than to hear them told/For the eye interprets to the ear . . .") Most criticism nowadays is even more meager in regard to acting, direction and design than in evaluation of the texts themselves. Merit in acting is weighed chiefly by the degree of personal appeal it exercises. The actor is rarely judged for his relevance to the play as a whole since the play's meaning to begin with is frequently un-specified. To speak to the point about acting, the critic must judge the texture and composition of the role as the player shapes it through his natural endowment and through the authority of his craft.

Perhaps critics should not be held to too-strict account for neglect or oversight in the matter of acting, direction, etc., since most acting and direction on our stage today is rarely better than competent. In such cases a consideration "in depth" becomes supererogatory when it is not pretentious. Still, even with actors as eminent as Laurence Olivier, Alfred Lunt, Paul Scofield, Jean-Louis Barrault, or with directors as accomplished as Tyrone Guthrie, Peter Brook, Orson Welles, what our critics have to say usually comes down to little more than catchphrases, a bleat of unreserved enthusiasm or regretted dis-approval. In this connection I must cite a fact first called to my at-tention by Jacques Copeau, the actor-director who strongly influ-enced Louis Jouvet, Charles Dullin and a whole generation of Euro-pean theatre folk from 1913 to 1941: there have been fewer *great actors* in the history of the theatre than great dramatists.

No doubt I have often made hash in my reviews and essays of many of my own prescriptions. In extenuation I can only urge that while I am not sure I agree with an admirable literary critic I heard lecture many years ago in Paris who said, "The artist has every right; a critic only obligations," I always bear it in mind.

1

Tennessee Williams

[1948]

THE NEWEST WRITING talent in the American theatre is that of Tennessee Williams. His *The Glass Menagerie* was a lyric fragment of limited scope but undeniable poignancy. Tennessee Williams' latest play—*A Streetcar Named Desire*—stands very high among the creative contributions of the American theatre since 1920. If we had a national repertory theatre, this play would unquestionably be among the few worthy of a permanent place there. Its impact at this moment is especially strong, because it is virtually unique as a stage piece that is both personal and social and wholly a product of our life today. It is a beautiful play.

Its story is simple. Blanche Du Bois, a girl whose family once possessed property and title to position in the circle of refined Southern respectability, has been reduced to the lowest financial estate. She has taught English in a high school, but when we meet her she has apparently lost her job and has come to stay with her younger sister Stella in New Orleans. Blanche expects to find Stella living in an environment compatible with their former background, but finds instead that Stella is in the kind of neighborhood that playgoers call sordid, though it happens to be no worse than any of the places inhabited by the majority of American people. Blanche is shocked at these Elysian Fields (literally the name of this particular spot in New Orleans, just as the streetcar she took to reach it is actually called Desire). She is even more shocked by her sister's husband, an American of Polish origin, an ex-sergeant, a machine salesman, and a rather primitive, almost bestial person. Her brother-in-law resents and then suspects the girl's pretentious airs, particularly her obvious disdain of him. Slowly he (and we) discover the girl's "secret": after an unfortunate marriage at an early age to a boy who turned out to be a homosexual, the boy's suicide, her family's loss of all its property, and the death of the last member of the older generation, Blanche has become a notorious person, whose squalid affairs have made it impossible for her to remain in her home town. She meets a friend of her brother-in-law whom she wants to marry because he is a decent fellow, but her brother-in-law, by disclosing the facts of the girl's life to her suitor, wrecks her hopes. Drunk the night his wife is in labor, the brother-in-law settles his account with Blanche by raping her. She is ordered out of Stella's house, and, when Blanche tells the story of the rape she is thought to be mad and is finally conducted unprotesting to a public institution for the insane.

Some of the reviewers thought Blanche Du Bois a "boozy prostitute," and others believed her a nymphomaniac. Such designations are not only inaccurate but reveal a total failure to understand the author's intention and the theme of the play. Tennessee Williams is a poet of frustration, and what his play says is that aspiration, sensitivity, departure from the norm are battered, bruised and disgraced in our world today.

It would be far truer to think of Blanche Du Bois as the potential artist in all of us than as a deteriorated Southern belle. Her amatory adventures, which her brother-in-law (like some of the critics) regards as the mark of her inferiority, are the unwholesome means she uses to maintain her connection with life, to fight the sense of death which her whole background has created in her. The play's story shows us Blanche's seeking haven in a simple, healthy man and that in this, too, she is defeated because everything in her environment conspires to degrade the meaning of her tragic situation. . . . Her lies are part of her will-to-beauty; her wretched romanticism is a futile reaching toward a fullness of life. She is not a drunkard, and she is not insane when she is committed to the asylum. She is an almost willing victim of a world that has trapped her and in which she can find "peace" only by accepting the verdict of her unfitness for "normal" life.

The play is not specifically written as a symbolic drama or as a tract. What I have said is implicit in all of the play's details. The reason for the play's success even with audiences who fail to understand it is that the characters and the scenes are written with a firm grasp on their naturalistic truth. Yet we shall waste the play and the author's talent if we praise the play's effects and disregard its core. Like most woks of art the play's significance cannot be isolated in a single passage. It is clear to the attentive and will elude the hasty.

Still, the audience is not entirely to blame if the play and its central character are not understood. There are elements in the production—chiefly in the acting—that make for a certain ambiguity and confusion. This is not to say that the acting and production are poor. On the contrary, they are both distinctly superior. The director, Elia Kazan, is a man of high theatrical intelligence, a craftsman of genuine sensibility. . . . But there is a lack of balance and perspective in the production of *A Streetcar Named Desire* due to the fact that the acting of the parts is of unequal force, quality and stress. To clarify this I must digress here and dwell a bit on the nature of acting in general. What is acting? What is its function in the theatre? How does it serve the goal of art, which is at all times to give flesh to essential human meanings? The digression, we shall see, may lead to a greater insight into the outstanding theatrical event under discussion.

A pedant might characterize the actor as a person endowed with the capacity to behave publicly and for purposes of play as though fictional circumstances were real. The actor knows that the lines he speaks and the action he performs are merely invention, just as he knows the objects he deals with on the stage—scenery, properties, lights—are parts of an artificial world. His acting consists of his ability to make all these things take on a new reality for himself and for his audience. Just as the first step in painting is the "imitation" of an object, so the actor "imitates" a series of human events that in terms of real life are no more true than the apple or flower or horse that we see in a painting.

The actor is himself an instrument, and, if he is able to look right in terms of what he is "imitating," his very presence on the stage is already an accomplishment. Yet we know that an actor of a convincing presence who merely reads his lines intelligibly offers us little more than information, which is the small change of the theatre. The actor who adds visual illustration to what he is saying (beating his breast to indicate anguish!) provides a sort of lamp whereby we read the play more comfortably, although at times the illustration if well chosen may give special illumination. The actor becomes creative only when he reveals the life from which the play's lines may have emerged, a life richer perhaps than the lines' literal significance. The creative actor is the author of the new meaning that a play acquires on the stage, the author of a personal sub-text into which the play's lines are absorbed so that a special aesthetic body with an identity of its own is born. . . . Just as the painter who merely sets down the image of an apple that looks like one is not an artist, so the actor who merely "imitates" the surface impression that we might gather from a perusal of the play's text—an actor who does not create a life beyond what was there before he assumed his role—belies the art of the theatre.

The new meaning that the actor gives to the play emerges from what is popularly known as the actor's personality—not alone his physical "type," but the whole quality of his skill, emotion, insight, sensibility, character, imagination, spirit. These have an existence of their own, which the actor with the aid of the director must shape to the form of their interpretation or understanding of the problem they have set themselves for the play.

There are two things to be considered in any judgment of acting: the material of the actor himself and the use that the material has been put to in relation to the play as a whole. A very fine actor may utterly distort the intention of a play—that is, transform it with as much possibility of happy as of disastrous results. Bernard Shaw tells us that Duse was superior to Sudermann; it was her acting of that dramatist's play *Home* that made it a work of art. In Paris I saw the Laurette Taylor part in *The Glass Menagerie* very ably played in a way that robbed the character of all poetry. In my opinion, most of our highly regarded Hamlets are simply *readings* of the part but rather inferior acting or not acting at all. Katharine Cornell's Cleopatra may be said to have certain attractive aspects (no one need debate Miss Cornell's natural endowments), but, even aside from the question of physical qualifications, she creates nothing with the part, not only in the Shakespearean sense but within her own orbit. On the other hand, I have read that Michael Chekhov's Hamlet was not Hamlet (in the sense that there might be an "ideal" Hamlet) but that it was a true creation, albeit a very special one.

In *A Streetcar Named Desire* all the actors are good, but their per- ✓
formances do not truly convey Tennessee Williams' play. By virtue
of its power and completeness the play pretty nearly succeeds in
acting the actors, but the nature of the play's reception indicates a
prevailing sentiment of excitement and glowing enthusiasm disassociated from any specific meaning.

Jessica Tandy's Blanche suffers from the actress' narrow emotional
range. One of the greatest parts ever written for a woman in the
American theatre, it demands the fullness and variety of an orchestra. Miss Tandy's register is that of a violin's A string. The part represents the essence of womanly feeling and wounded human sensibility. Blanche lies and pretends, but through it all the actress must
make us perceive her truth. She is an aristocrat (regardless of the
threadbare myth of Southern gentility); she is an aristocrat in the
subtlety and depth of her feeling. She is a poet, even if we are dubious about her understanding of the writers she names; she is superior by the sheer intensity and realization of her experience, even
if much of what she does is abject.

If she is not these things, she is too much of a fraud to be worthy
of the author's concern with her. If the latter is true, then the play
would be saying something rather surprising—namely, that frank
brutality and naked power are more admirable than the yearning for
tenderness and the desire to reach beyond one's personal appetites.
When Blanche appeals to her sister in the name of these values, Miss
Tandy is unable to make it clear whether she means what she says
and whether we are supposed to attach any importance to her speech
or whether she is merely spinning another fantasy. It is essential to
the play that we believe and are touched by what she says, that her
emotion convinces us of the soundness of her values. All through the
play, indeed, we must be captured by the music of the girl's martyred
soul. Without this there is either a play whose viewpoint we reject or
no play at all—only a series of "good scenes," a highly seasoned theatrical dish.

Marlon Brando, who plays Stanley Kowalski (Blanche's brother-
in-law), is an actor of genuine power. He has what someone once
called "high visibility" on the stage. His silences, even more than his
speech, are completely arresting. Through his own intense concentration on what he is thinking or doing at each moment he is on the
stage all our attention focuses on him. Brando's quality is one of

acute sensitivity. None of the brutishness of his part is native to him: it is a characteristic he has to "invent." The combination of an intense, introspective, and almost lyric personality under the mask of a bully endows the character with something almost touchingly painful. Because the elements of characterization are put on a face to which they are not altogether becoming, a certain crudeness mars our impression, while something in the nature of the actor's very considerable talent makes us wonder whether he is not actually suffering deeply in a way that relates him to what is represented by Blanche rather than to what his own character represents in the play. When he beats his wife or throws the radio out the window, there is, aside from the ugliness of these acts, an element of agony that falsifies their color in relation to their meaning in the play: they take on an almost Dostoevskian aspect.

For what is Stanley Kowalski? He is the embodiment of animal force, of brute life unconcerned and even consciously scornful of every value that does not come within the scope of such life. He resents being called a Polack, and he quotes Huey Long, who assured him that "every man is a king." He screams that he is a hundred percent American, and breaks dishes and mistreats his women to prove it. He is all muscle, lumpish sensuality and crude energy, given support by a society that hardly demands more of him. He is the unwitting antichrist of our time, the little man who will break the back of every effort to create a more comprehensive world in in which thought and conscience, a broader humanity are expected to evolve from the old Adam. His mentality provides the soil for fascism, viewed not as a political movement but as a state of being.

Because the author does not preach about him but draws him without hate or ideological animus, the audience takes him at his face value. His face value on the stage is the face of Marlon Brando as contrasted to that of Jessica Tandy. For almost more than two-thirds of the play, therefore, the audience identifies itself with Stanley Kowalski. His low jeering is seconded by the audience's laughter, which seems to mock the feeble and hysterical decorativeness of the girl's behavior. The play becomes the triumph of Stanley Kowalski with the collusion of the audience, which is no longer on the side of the angels. This is natural because Miss Tandy is fragile without being touching (except when the author is beyond being overpowered by an actress), and Mr. Brando is tough without being irredeemably coarse.

When Kowalski tells his wife to get rid of Blanche so that things can be as they were (the author is suggesting that the untoward presence of a new consciousness in Kowalski's life—the appeal to forbearance and fineness—is a cruel disturbance and that he longs for a life without any spiritual qualms), the audience is all on Kowalski's side. Miss Tandy's speeches—which are lovely in themselves—sound phony, and her long words and noble appeals are as empty as a dilettante's discourse because they do not flow from that spring of warm feeling which is the justification and essence of Blanche's character.

One of the happiest pieces of staging and acting in the play is the moment when Kowalski, having beaten his wife, calls for her to return from the neighbor's apartment where she has taken momentary refuge. He whines like a hurt animal, shouts like a savage, and finally his wife descends the staircase to return to his loving arms. Brando has been directed to fall on his knees before his wife and thrust his head against her body in a gesture that connotes humility and passion. His wife with maternal and amorous touch caresses his head. He lifts her off her feet and takes her to bed. . . .

This, as I have noted, is done beautifully. Yet Brando's innate quality and something unresolved in the director's conception make the scene moving in a manner that is thematically disruptive. The pathos is too universally human (Kowalski at that moment is any man); it is not integrated with that attribute of the play which requires that Kowalski at all times be somewhat vile.

If Karl Malden as Blanche's suitor—a person without sufficient force to transcend the level of his environment—and Kim Hunter as Blanche's sister—who has made her peace with Kowalski's "normal life"—give performances that are easier to place than those of the two leading characters, it is not because of any intrinsic superiority to the other players. It is simply due to the fact that their parts are less complex. Miss Hunter is fairly good, Mr. Malden capital, but both appear in a sense to stand outside the play's interpretive problem. They are not struggling with a consciousness of the dilemma that exists in the choice between Kowalski's world and that of Blanche Du Bois.

As creative spectators, we cannot satisfy ourselves at a play like *A*

Streetcar Named Desire with the knowledge that it is a wonderful show, a smash hit, a prize winner (it is and will be all of these). It is a play that ought to arouse in us as much feeling, thought and even controversy as plays on semipolitical themes; for it is a play that speaks of a poet's reaction to life in our country (not just the South), and what he has to say about it is much more far-reaching than what might be enunciated through any slogan.

I have heard it said, for example, that Tennessee Williams portrays "ordinary" people without much sense of their promise, and reserves most of his affection for more special people—that minority which Thomas Mann once described as life's delicate children. I find this view false and misleading, but I would rather hear it expressed than to let the play go by as the best play of the season, something you must see, "great theatre."

If the play is great theatre—as I believe—it is precisely because it is instinct with life, a life we share in not only on the stage, but in our very homes by night and day. If I have chosen to examine the production with what might seem undue minuteness, it is because I believe that questions of the theatre (and of art) are not simply questions of taste or professional quibbles, but life questions. I can think of no higher compliment to the director and actors of such a production than to take their work with utmost seriousness—even to the point of neglecting to make allowance for the difficulties attendant on the realization of so original a play on Broadway.

[1948]

It is comforting to realize that Tennessee Williams is not a writer of hits, but a writer with a problem. His problem rises from the conflict between the quality of his sensibility and the objective material of his plots.

In *Summer and Smoke* (written at about the same time as *A Streetcar Named Desire*) Williams appears torn between a character and a theme. The character is observed with delicate sympathy, but the theme—too consciously articulated without being mastered—disturbs both the characterization and the play's dramatic clarity. It remains nevertheless a play whose very faults are interesting.

Alma Winemiller, the daughter of a Mississippi minister and his insane wife, is a spiritually energetic girl in love with her lifelong neighbor, Dr. John Buchanan. The young doctor is attracted by the girl's idealism, but he expresses his tenderness toward her by a harsh insistence on its sexual aspects. Shocked, the girl tries to pit her idealism against the boy's boastful sinfulness. ("You're no gentleman!" she cries—and she is right.) Alma wins the "argument" only when John's father is killed in an accident brought about by John's soiled companions. Now redeemed from his carnal course, John does not turn to his savior Alma, but instead marries a buxom little female of coarser background. Alma, in turn, converted to the doctrine of the senses (reversing the pattern of ladies from Thaïs to Sadie Thompson), now seems prepared to indulge in casual affairs.

One of the springs of Williams' inspiration is his fascination with the opposition between the old Adam which tends to keep us mired in a kind of primitive inertia, and our impulse to transcend it. In *A Streetcar Named Desire* this fascination led him almost unconsciously to a social theme: the "animal" in that play is identified with the "ordinary" American. The naturalistic details of portraiture in *Streetcar* are so right that the audience accepts and enjoys them on their own terms whether or not they follow the author's ideological intention, which, to begin with, is intuitive rather than analytic. In *Summer and Smoke* so much time is given to a conscious exposition of theme that Williams loses the specific sense of his people and to a dangerous extent our concern as spectators.

The thematic base of *Summer and Smoke* is rendered ambiguous by being stated through characters that do not properly embody the forces the play is supposed to pit against each other. Is Alma Winemiller "sexually repressed" because of her overreliance on her spiritual nature? Not really, for she loves John Buchanan with an eagerness and a shyness that are both entirely normal in themselves. That she should be repelled by his crudity is also normal. That she should be presented as the champion of the "soul" and he as advocate for the "flesh" is a confusion that derives from the author's inability to know when he is creating character and when he is interfering with the characters by talking—sometimes a little foolishly—in their stead.

The ancient dispute about the polarity of body and soul is mostly a Puritan obsession and a consequence of the abuse of words induced by faulty religious education. Of the two characters in the play, the man, who rationalizes his promiscuity on intellectual grounds, is surely the more Puritan, one might even go so far as to say the more "repressed" and the less normal. His sexual activity does not strike one as a manifestation of natural exuberance but of moral defiance.

It would have been perfectly proper for Williams to present the situation in this light. In that case the play might have suggested that so many American men are Puritans in revolt against themselves that they drive their women to licentiousness. But perhaps a residue of Puritanism in the author prevented him from knowing this.

As a result the play alternates between psychoanalytic hints (never artistically convincing) and what becomes—aside from several fine passages which reveal his natural endowments as a poet–playwright —an almost trite and at moments badly constructed plot line. Fragments of true feeling have been attenuated and vitiated by the author's failure to find a proper form for them, to think his problem through.

It is the function of the director of a play as subtly difficult as *Summer and Smoke* to articulate a coherent interpretation which the audience can actually *see*. It is evident that such an interpretation never existed in regard to this play. The production, in fact, provides an example of how a group of talented people, when there is no firm hand to guide them, may contribute to a play wholeheartedly but without valid effect. As Alma Winemiller, Margaret Phillips, an actress of considerable quality and ability, has been permitted or encouraged by the director, Margo Jones, to overstress such secondary characteristics as a nervous laugh, an affected speech, super-refinement of manner, at the expense of the main motive of the character, which should be her innate womanly instincts. Tod Andrews as John Buchanan is earnest as well as handsome, but he has been given no real characterization.

Jo Mielziner's setting is not only as pretty as can be, but an honest attempt to capture the play's special style. The setting is none the less dramatically unsuccessful because it restricts the free movement essential to the play, and its stylization ends by being almost more confining to the imagination than a realistic set. What would be best would be practically no set at all.

Whatever the precise moment of its composition (the copyright date of the one-acter from which the present version was made is 1948), Tennessee Williams' *Camino Real* should be regarded as a work of the author's nonage. Though this is what I sensed immediately as I watched it in the theatre, I could not help feeling irritated with it. As I sit down to write about it a day later, I am inclined to view it more sympathetically. The "history" of this change may constitute the main point of my notice.

Being essentially a youthful work, *Camino Real* is immature. But like the youthful and immature work of most artists, *Camino Real* is significant of its author's seed thoughts, impulses, and ambitions. Far from being obscure, the play reiterates its intention and meaning at every point. In fact, it is too nakedly clear to be a sound work of art.

Kilroy, typical of the "natural" young American of little education, is presented more or less out of time, though the language is sharply contemporary, and out of space, though the atmosphere is the sultry one of Latin American "bohemia" with its ambiguous tone of varicolored lights, strange intoxicants, hybrid excitements, roguish pursuits, and appetizing danger. With this there is a kind of literary afflatus characteristic of the man who feeds his dreams with the color of foreign cultures. Kilroy is bewildered and innocent, seeking a haven in a world corrupt to the core, grasping for security and love in places where he can find nothing but humiliating adventures. The rich are smug and cruel; officialdom is heartless and blind; all, except the heroic poet who is willing to take action, shrink from the nobler exploits of the spirit. Kilroy is doomed to die young because he is honest, ignorant and without guile. His redeeming feature is aspiration—not without a touch of Puritanism—an unconscious idealism which makes him brother to other errant knights who have sinned, suffered, and still believed in the inherent magnificence of life. "The violets in the mountain will break the rocks"—the dream will conquer crass reality. Don Quixote bids the boy not to pity himself, forever to seek the uncharted paths of the more exalted quests even if the ultimate destination is never to be known.

This is the mystique of romanticism, with a special stress on pity for the insulted and injured, the persecuted minorities, the victims and outcasts. Considering the times we live in, I am entirely cordial

to these sentiments—particularly since they are no longer intellectually fashionable. Williams also hankers for an unfettered theatre,
a theatre free of the bonds of workaday naturalism, a theatre where
the poet in him can speak more personally and with a greater degree
of self-revelation than the usual prosy play permits. Thus *Camino
Real* discards the routine props of logic, exposition and straight story
line. Though there is a certain juvenile impatience in this, I can embrace Williams on this count too. His crimes have a healthy source.

What is less fortunate is that his play, instead of being the sur-
realist phantasmagoria it intends to be, is far too literal—in almost
every respect far less poetic than *The Glass Menagerie* or *A Streetcar Named Desire*. To say, "We're all of us guinea pigs in the laboratory of God," or to have street cleaners represent death or an
airplane named Fugitiva stand for escape, is far less imaginative than
to have the hapless Blanche Du Bois of *Streetcar* go off to an insane
asylum depending on the kindness of strangers. The most successful
moments of *Camino Real* are the sardonic vaudeville of the gypsy-
fortuneteller scene and, even better, the boy-and-girl love scene—a
sort of wryly sentimental comic-strip ballet of courtship—which is
almost as specific as the Gentleman Caller scene in *The Glass Menagerie*. In other words, Williams, like Sean O'Casey and many
others, is less suggestive and poignant when he aims point-blank at
his aesthetic, poetic or symbolic target than when he employs the
concrete means of a real situation. Poetry cannot be captured by direct assault; beauty cannot be won unless we woo it first through the
beast.

As with the play's poetry, so with its "philosophy." It is too blunt.
It does not matter in art whether or not one is a pessimist or an optimist. To say that life is lovely is no more correct, convincing, moving or significant than to say that it is horrid. It is the substance—
not the conclusion—of an argument that gives it validity. Its *living
matter*—the images, forms, characters, incidents, evocation of experience, life-content—give a work of art its power, meaning and value.
If these are rich, then the work is creative no matter how white or
black the summation of the whole may be. When Kilroy repeats, "I
am sincere, I am sincere, I am sincere," he is touching even in the
poverty of his speech, but on the ideological level *Camino Real* is
negligible because its fabric, for all its fancy patterning, is "general
issue."

Yet I am loath to be harsh with it. When people on the first night are puzzled because the play seems cryptic to them, I am astonished at the paradox which makes them believe they understand the much subtler *Streetcar*—the theme of which they are hardly ever able to state; when people at the second night "love" the play in protest against what they consider a backward press, I am distressed that they are not really seeing or thinking about it so much as expressing an ill-defined and frustrated resentment against something.

That "something" is not the press. The sad fact of our theatre is that a play like *Camino Real* with all its faults ought to be produced, listened to, criticized with measure and affection, but that this is difficult when its production costs a fortune, when it is forced to become part of the grand machinery of investment, real estate, Broadway brokerage and competition for reputation. A play like *Camino Real* should be produced—as it might be in France, for example—with modest means in a small theatre where it would be quietly seen, enjoyed, and judged for what it is—a fallible minor work of a young artist of important talent.

Elia Kazan's production adds to the script's flaws by being conceived in a major key. It is scenically too heavy; it is vocally too noisy. It is too punchy, forthright and "realistic." It stampedes where it should float; it clamors and declaims where it should insinuate. It has much less humor than the text. There are, none the less, good actors in it—too many to list here.

2

Audrey Hepburn

[1954]

THE NATURE of my reaction to *Ondine* makes it seem proper for me
to address an open letter to its star. Therefore:

Dear Audrey Hepburn:

Perhaps it will strike you as unkind if I say that the response of the
audience—including, of course, that of the reviewers—to your performance in *Ondine* is more a private manifestation than a critical
judgment. It is as if everybody were asking for your telephone number.

You are enchanting. (How tired you will soon become of hearing
this!) You must forgive me if I begin this way, because, though apparently self-evident, it is a statement that cannot be addressed to
many actresses of our day. The stage at present has only a few really
beautiful women, and most of the screen beauties resemble posters
rather than people. Yours is truly a face. It is a face that has fineness,
breeding, grace, and in the large lovely dark eyes there is something
that appears to withhold part of yourself for yourself, as well as something that seeks to behold the fascinating world outside. This is rare
and precious, and our ecstatic clamor is a cry for the uncommon.

Your delicate apartness shows itself in your choice of vehicle. Giraudoux was a poet and an aristocratic wit: most of his plays are spar-
klingly veiled proclamations against the crassness of contemporary
civilization. The attraction of *Ondine* for an actress like you and for a
good part of the public relates to our deep need to get away from the
kind of realism that merely mirrors what is ugly to begin with. We
are a little like those Frenchmen who at the end of the nineteenth

24

century got so fed up with the naturalism of the *théâtre libre* that they took refuge in tiny theatres where Maeterlinck's hushed and misty symbolism was being revealed or went jubilantly mad when Rostand's *Cyrano* was first brought to them. For somewhat the same reasons there is nowadays a growing appetite for the mood play as differentiated from the plot play.

But young as you are, dear Audrey, you must guess that that is not the whole story, for it is clear that you are as bright as you are sensitive. The audience, while adoring you, coughs a little too much as your play unfolds. For my part, while admiring Giraudoux and enraptured by your presence, I still found that I ceased following the play's text about halfway through the second act, and could never, despite all possible good will, get with it again. It was not that I was bored—how could I be with you on the stage in the third act, modestly weeping and cutting so exquisite a figure?—it was simply a feeling that what the stage was offering no longer engaged my interest.

Ondine is not the best of Giraudoux's work. Charming spirit though he was, Giraudoux was no romantic. His style is opulent impressionism, playful irony, common sense and intellectual paradox appareled as whimsy. Giraudoux's vein is that of a high sophistication, mental refinement, and the ultimate of an ancient—I almost said attenuated—culture, decked out in very light attire. All this is heady and delicious as a wine of superb vintage, but it has little to do with the gravity and thick sentiment of the Ondine legend. Giraudoux can be sportive with Hellenic fable, sparkling about the crazy quilt of France suffering the taint of the twentieth century, but he loses some of his natural grace when he tries to shape the foggy mood of Germanic yearning into a Parisian pattern. There is a basic discrepancy here between manner and matter, and the result is only intermittently harmonious.

The bridge between the two elements can only be effected by the most original and imaginative sort of production. The production you shine in is expensive and old-fashioned fashionable; it is not creative. Instead of evoking a new or different world, it gives the impression of a ballet setting in a post-Ziegfeld musical. It is more pedestrian for all its fancy but essentially conventional air than a bare stage might be.

Still, it is you I am most concerned with now. You are not only beautiful, you are gifted. You have vivacity, your body is trained as well as trim, you are capable of dedication—you follow the director as unselfishly as an actress should—you are, in short, a wonderful instrument with a soul of your own. But, said old Grandpa Ibsen, talent is not just a possession, it is a responsibility. You are at the beginning of your career; because this beginning is so dazzling you must not allow—as so many others do—the beginning to become the end. Your performance in *Ondine* as acting is sweet, young, technically naïve. Your training as an actress is still in its early stages: you do not yet know how to transform the outward aspects of a characterization—the water sprite you play—into an inner characterization. For this reason your performance actually lacks mystery, a dimension beyond your own entrancing self.

You can learn to be a real actress if you do not let the racket, the publicity, the adulation and the false—that is, ignorant—praise rattle you away from yourself. Most young people on the stage have the problem of how to gain an opportunity; for you and all the brilliant youngsters of the present generation the problem is to make something of your opportunity. Keep on acting, studying, working—and not always at your greatest convenience. Play parts that are risky, parts that are difficult, and do not be afraid to fail! Above all, play on the stage—though I do not suggest that you give up films. Do not trust those who tell you that screen and stage acting are the same species or of equal artistic value: it is simply not true even when Jean-Louis Barrault says so.

Devotedly yours,
Harold Clurman

3

Laurette Taylor

[1946]

THE DEATH of our finest actress—Laurette Taylor—should not go without comment. The perfunctory tributes of the press were dismaying. Perhaps little more could be expected from a theatre which has lost all sense of tradition and all ambition beyond that of profit—and consequently all dignity.

It is not enough to speak of Laurette Taylor's triumphant performances in the manner of a romantic novel or a publicity blurb. What distinguished Miss Taylor just as much in her failures as in her successes was the quality of her talent. She expressed a constantly tremulous sensibility that seemed vulnerable to the least breath of vulgarity, coarseness or cruelty without ever wholly succumbing to the overwhelming persistence of all three.

She was staunch even when she appeared broken. She suggested a kind of mute devotion and loyalty to what she loved even when everything conspired to batter her. In her this hurt loyalty took on a particularly womanly significance. Without being especially identified with "mother roles" or the generally disagreeable type of "good woman," she became a symbol of the enduring woman, the very modesty of whose suffering is more personally touching than the martyred mother of heroic myth.

Laurette Taylor seemed to be the victim of a thousand unkind cuts so minute that no word could describe them, no poet make them pathetic. She seemed always to be weeping silent tears, and her slightly bent head or averted eye were unspeakably moving because they were gestures so brief as to appear wholly imperceptible. Her voice was like buried gold whose value we could not guess; her speech flowing and ebbing in strange unequal rhythms was like a graph of her soul in its bursts of tender feeling and recessions of frustration and confusion. A luminous confusion composed her aura. It shone brighter for its ambiguity and its refractions. It warmed us deeply because it was generated from the unrhetorical sources of an ordinary woman's being rather than from any studied glamour. There was always something surprising about it, and no one appeared more surprised by what she sensed and experienced than Laurette Taylor herself. Her face was always suffused with a look of startled wonder, at once happy, humorous, frightened and innocent.

Laurette Taylor's life was tragic. Her appearances in the past fifteen years were so infrequent that when she arrived in *The Glass Menagerie* most people spoke of her as a discovery. She had made a "comeback." But Laurette Taylor's fate in this regard is very similar to that of many other players—particularly actresses—beaten by the brutal anarchy of our stage. It would be dolefully instructive to draw up a list of the really talented actresses—living and dead—who have been unconscious sacrifices to our mindless theatre. To speak of their personal vices in order to explain their destiny is to mistake the effect for the cause. Most of the actresses who do survive our system of theatrical production, so that at the age of fifty they may be considered at the height of their effective powers, are endowed with a kind of toughness that rarely accompanies the most sensitive kind of talent.

4

Judy Garland

[1956]

As for the triumphant, adored and adorable Judy Garland, she is in the grand line of those American singing actresses—Helen Morgan, Fannie Brice to name but two—whose talent is so close to the great masses of their countrymen that they are at once hugely successful and never developed to their fullest extent.

Everything about Judy Garland touches me. When she appeared here in 1951 I became somewhat irritated by little admixtures of salesmanship—her management must have called them showmanship—which tainted the essential purity of her performance. Her present program (subject to slight changes at every appearance) seems to me more direct in presentation. It contains fewer of the songs in which I believe she most excels: the heartbreaking ones.

Miss Garland's singing is technically consummate, but what she brings to it goes beyond skill. On the surface there is a kind of contented showgirl geniality. When I saw Miss Garland while she was still a kid in a silly football movie, I was struck chiefly by the impassioned energy of her delivery. To this the years have added profoundly pathetic elements.

She is professionally *bound* to be "happy." The free-and-easy style which she mentions in song is more akin to frenzy. She is wholly feminine in a robust and at the same time melting sense, but to put herself over she feels constrained to behave a little boyishly. She has the freedom of spirit of the old-time troupers (or troubadours), but to fit our up-to-date entertainment business she allows herself to be slightly "industrialized." (This does not happen to Edith Piaf, because in an expensive Parisian nightclub she is permitted to remain the same tragic gamine that she had been on the public square.) Miss Garland escapes this "industrialization" with a humorous cuteness, but the marks of pain it has caused her are evident in her every glance.

Her songs are often slushily emotional—that is, empty of specific feeling—but she informs them with the anguished lyricism of a heavily laden personal experience. She is at bottom a sort of early twentieth century country kid, but the marks of the big-city wounds of our day are upon her. Her poetry is not only in the things she has survived, but in a violent need to pour them forth in vivid popular form, which makes her the very epitome of the theatrical personality. The tension between the unctuously bright slickness which is expected of her medium and environment and the fierceness of what her being wants to cry out produces something positively orgastic in the final effect.

In Helen Morgan we beheld the body and soul of a true woman slowly expiring in a world too tough for her; in Fannie Brice that woman shrewdly forgoing her major gifts. In Judy we witness the inspiring bravery of a woman expressing her realest self though everything seems to conspire to seal her mouth with the commercial smile of show business.

5

The Threepenny Opera

[1954]

KURT WEILL's and Bertolt Brecht's *The Threepenny Opera* is a masterpiece; in its present production at the Theatre de Lys it very nearly misses fire. Such is the paradox of the theatre: the presentation is almost as much of a part of a play as the material itself.

The Threepenny Opera—called that because it is so oddly conceived that it might be a beggar's dream and so cheaply done that it might meet a beggar's budget—sums up a whole epoch and evokes a special state of mind. The epoch is not just the Berlin of 1919–28; it is any epoch in which a lurid rascality combined with fierce contrasts of prosperity and poverty shape the dominant tone of society. The state of mind is one of social impotence so close to despair that it expresses itself through a kind of jaded mockery which mingles a snarl with tears. Such in a way was the England of John Gay's *The Beggar's Opera* (1728), from which the Brecht "book" derives, and certainly the Germany which preceded Hitler. No wonder the one period produced William Hogarth and the other George Grosz.

We do not live in such a time—though people who remember the Depression days between 1930 and 1935 will appreciate the mood of *The Threepenny Opera* most readily—but it makes the mood irresistibly present and, strangely enough, induces us to take it to our hearts with a kind of pained affection. There is, despite

31

the sharp sense of period that permeates it, a universal quality in *The Threepenny Opera*. It fosters a bitter sense of regret that we live so scabbily in relation to our dreams and also a kind of masochistic attachment to our wounds, as if they were all we have to show as evidence of our dreams.

This effect is achieved through Brecht's brilliant lyrics rendered with remarkable intuitive insight and witty skill in Marc Blitzstein's adaptation—and through the one score Weill composed which places him on the level of an Offenbach. What bite and tang, what insidious irony, in the clean thrusts of Brecht's verses; what economy and lightness in Weill's songs and orchestration! How poignant is the sullied lyricism of this work with its jeering bathos, its low-life romanticism, its sweetly poisonous nostalgia, its musical profanity, and its sudden hints of grandeur, godliness, and possible greatness! Here in contemporary terms and with a strange timelessness is the ambiguous, corrupt seduction of a submerged half-world akin to that which François Villon sang of long ago.

How disappointing, then, to have so unique a work—acclaimed practically everywhere since its premiere in 1928—reduced to a minor event by so ill-prepared a performance as the one we now see! Except for Lotte Lenya, who appeared in the original production, the cast ranges from the amateurish to the adequate. Lenya's nasally insinuating whore is superb for its incisiveness and triple-threat innuendo. But the fault is not the actors'—most of whom could do much better—but the director's. Everything seems labored and awkward instead of sprightly and bright. The miracle is that the inherent superiority of the material survives all hazards.

6

My Fair Lady

[1956]

My Fair Lady, a musical adapted from Bernard Shaw's *Pygmalion* by Alan Jay Lerner and Frederick Loewe, is a good show; in fact, a very good show—adult entertainment. Yet why, I wonder, are musicals when they are good greeted with more rapturous acclaim and a greater noise than almost any good play? Is it because applause is the natural response to the high spirits of a musical, whereas the reflective nature of drama induces a certain quiet within the marks of approbation? Or are we delighted beyond our knowing when things are made easy for us? We are intrinsically lazy.

These are some of the things which passed through my mind as I watched *My Fair Lady*. What musical does not permit time for our minds to wander?

The show is good, I said to myself, not because of any single element but because of the intelligent integration of all its elements. Shaw's dialogue—much of it has been retained—his basic good humor, health and self-respect cleanse the air. Lerner's lyrics have a certain crispness and quality of urbane banter. The idea of making a triumphant little song and dance when Liza progresses from "The rine in Spine falls minely on the pline," to "The rain in Spain falls mainly on the plain" is theatrically brilliant.

Oliver Smith's sets are festive with a kind of refreshing neat-

33

ness, and Cecil Beaton's costumes radiate an unoppressive cheeriness. Loewe's music serves—we are glad the music is there; it does not come as a relief but as an extension of the scenes.

How truly Shaw lends himself to musical comedy! (Have any of us seen *The Chocolate Soldier,* which was the musical of *Arms and the Man*?) It took the authors and producers of *My Fair Lady* to remind us that Shaw never was a realist. He often is taken for one, but almost all Shaw productions clinging to a literal representation of the environment in which his plays presumably unfold are as wide of the mark as are most productions of Shakespeare.

Shaw is Punch and Judy, vaudeville and rhetoric informed by paradoxical common sense and joyous wisdom. His speeches are comic tirades (consider Doolittle's contrast of lower-class morality with that of the wealthy) or virtuoso arias in the grand manner—full of humanitarian passion and robust conviction. Shaw's quips, gags, handsprings and somersaults derive from the oldest of old theatre—which is one reason they endure. Shaw's lineage is the "classic" theatre from the street harlequinade to grand opera. That is why he seems very much himself in the new framework.

The cast of *My Fair Lady* is predominantly English. Rex Harrison is a first-rate light comedian. Julie Andrews' face and manner are adorably cameolike in the manner of the musical-comedy heroines of an earlier and happier period when stage faces had a quality of tinkling romance about them. Stanley Holloway as Doolittle is English musical hall with its homey familiarity.

What makes me enjoy all these players most of all is a quality of *bravery,* a certain professional sturdiness and reliability which are characteristic of the English actor at his best. They are disarmingly impudent, self-confident and modest at the same time. They are entirely immersed in the fine task of being entertaining. They are our humble servants and have a grand time at the job which they have taken pains to learn thoroughly. What they bring to the stage is not their private selves, but a craft which has somehow ennobled them for our pleasure and admiration. The total effect is in the honest sense wholesome. It is strange—but that is how I would finally describe the show.

7

William Shakespeare

ANYONE CAN STAGE a bad production of a Shakespeare play, and in our theatre virtually everyone ambitious enough to try has succeeded in doing so. It should therefore surprise no one that the first production of the recently founded American Shakespeare Festival Theatre at Stratford, Connecticut, is a wretched piece of work. I shall not review the production, because what is significant about it is not its badness but the reason it was doomed before the first rehearsal was called. The flaws were in thinking and theory—in approach.

Americans have created no style for the playing of Shakespeare, the directors of the new enterprise have said, because we have not trained any group of actors in Shakespearean *speech*. It is a crucial error to assume that the playing of Shakespeare is essentially a matter of speech. Certainly, the actor who undertakes a Shakespearean role should speak well—but this ought to obtain for all actors.

It is unfortunately true that in the past twenty-five years American actors have neglected their studies in voice and diction, have lost an awareness of beauty in spoken language. But this loss affects all of the theatre, not merely the playing of Shakespeare. The fact that slovenly speech may be less distressing or noticeable in *Lunatics and Lovers* than it would be in a play by Congreve does not make sloppiness of speech acceptable in any play. Stanislavsky,

35

whose Moscow Art Theatre reached its characteristic style in the plays of Chekhov, was as severe on the score of fine speech in these plays as in that of the more formal plays of his repertory.

Many American actors in the teens laid so much stress on the "externals" of acting (carriage, diction, deportment, and so on) that they seemed ill prepared for the interpretative demands made by the plays of O'Neill and later on by those of Odets, Williams, Miller and others. Because of these new plays, greater stress has lately been put on the psychological, emotional, "real-life" aspects of acting. But most of us now understand—if we never did before—that undue emphasis on either aspect of acting—"inner" or "outer" —to the detriment of the other must cause a fatal distortion. The actor needs sensibility, observation, imagination, as well as an expressive body, a good voice, an ear for language. Insofar as he is deficient in any of these respects, he is a deficient actor—for all plays.

Shakespeare wrote *plays*—not exercises in speech. Plays have to be acted—not recited. Every play contains an idea, a world view, a specific quality of feeling, a weight and an impulse, in a word, a nature of its own—of which plot, characterization, movements, atmosphere and language form an organic whole. It is the function of a company of actors (under a director) to find the core and to form the theatrical body of each specific play in a specific way, so as to move the audience with the stirring vision of life which the play is supposed to convey.

In the Stratford, Connecticut, production of *Julius Caesar* the setting—so the program informs us—aims to reproduce the Elizabethan picture of Rome as the historians and artists of that period conceived it. Why was this approach chosen? Is the play intended as an archaeological study? Does the play have some relevance for us now or is it simply an essay in scholarship? Why the Elizabethan costumes? (I leave aside the fact that even as such they are cumbersome and unsightly.) Do the sets and costumes help the actors convey a sense of the play's basic structure, drama or human validity? There is no reason for doing Shakespeare on the stage today unless he is to mean more rather than less than the good "commercial" play.

Julius Caesar at Stratford, Connecticut, is a misbegotten effort not because the actors don't speak well (generally, their speech is not bad) but because even if they all were to speak like gods or at least like Gielgud, Redgrave, Olivier and so on—the production would still be less than commonplace, because it has no creative idea: the play is not seen freshly as something which possesses an immediately exciting substance. There is little point in discussing Shakespeare apropos this production because in the last analysis there is no play there at all.

In London, I recently saw *Henry IV* (Parts I and II) at the Old Vic. The production was not remarkable for its "originality," the acting was not "great," but the play was given with a conviction, a zest, a kinship to the dramatist's overwhelming abundance. It was the "wow" of the season. And years ago, was not Orson Welles' *Julius Caesar,* for all its lack of fundamental coherence, a grand show because so many scenes reflected the sparkle of an alert mind and a vivid theatre sense. These are some of the things needed for the successful performance of Shakespeare. They are present in some of the productions in Stratford, Canada, where neither the actors nor the director are specifically trained "Shakespeareans." And I have seen wonderfully alive Shakespearean productions in Europe where English was not spoken at all—so that I couldn't judge the speech! One realized, however, that one was confronting the greatest dramatic genius of all time.

Othello

No wonder there are so many fantasies about the authorship of the most beautiful plays in the English language. Impossible that a single Shakespeare could have written all those masterpieces! When Shakespeare is done in a manner that makes each scene intelligible and permits one to hear the torrent of words as part of a human action, one is led to marvel and conjecture about the magnitude of such genius. No one man could have created all these riches: it must have been a committee!

Let others cavil at the Brattle Shakespeare Players' production of *Othello.* The cast reveals no exceptional players—they are almost all young, able, devoted and intelligent—but the line of the play is so well articulated that a sense of what the play means to communicate is rendered. We should be grateful for this: I have seen more elaborate productions with acclaimed actors in which there were greater effects but less play.

Othello is Shakespeare's tragedy of sensuality. The chief fault of the Brattle production is that it misses this crucial element of Othello's character. Here, as in most productions of this play, the emphasis is largely on Othello's "nobility," which is mainly the mark of his simplicity and massive forthrightness. Othello is not noble in any truly moral sense: he is demoniacally possessed by that sort of fierce lust which always contains within it the seeds of destruction, a violence of passion that must ultimately consume and shatter both the lover and the beloved.

A psychologist has recently described love as the ability to connect oneself with a second person in a unit which still preserves the integrity of both partners. It is a sound definition. It explains why love is so rare and why the capacity to achieve it is one of the human goals most difficult to attain. But amorous passion by itself—and this too is not as common as we suppose—can never be altogether satisfied. While it rages, it must create chaos in the person who experiences it, as well as ravage and annihilate the person who is its object. For what passion tends toward is the elimination of both the selves involved in the mating. That is why Tristan and Isolde must dissolve in a love-death, and Othello, who at the play's peak speaks of "that whiter skin of hers than snow/And smooth as monumental alabaster" must do away with both Desdemona and himself. "I kissed thee ere I killed thee: no way but this,/Killing myself, to die upon a kiss." That is what he (and Shakespeare) mean when they speak of "one that loved not wisely but too well."

The play is not so much about jealousy—as such it might be considered trite—it is the tragedy of the flaw within love as sheer desire. Othello needs his jealousy; he needs it, so to speak, to fulfill his passion, needs it, in fact, to make it reach its highest point of ecstasy.

Because of this theme and the agonized violence of Shakespeare's expression of it, Othello is a part very few actors have succeeded in portraying successfully. That is why the flashier part of Iago, which requires mere skill and personality, is usually sought by stars and applauded by audiences. The part of Othello is so physically and emotionally demanding that Stanislavsky once said no actor could do it justice more than twice a week—very few have been able to play it at all. I have seen only one actor who approached a realization of the part, and he was aided by the support of Verdi's music.

I shall not discuss the detail of the performance at the City Center. I will only repeat that since the performance succeeded in making me think of the play's theme—usually in the production of Shakespeare's plays, I take the theme for granted, which means I do not think of it at all—I was stirred by it, and elated to have some contact with its greatness.

8

T. S. Eliot

[1950]

THE POINT OF VIEW is all: most of the reviewers, who generally tend to be more sanguine about the state of the theatre than I, have been fairly glum about it this season. Now I find that, while I do not always share the reviewers' enthusiasm for certain popular plays, I have had more sense of adventure going to the theatre in recent weeks than I have had for some time previously. The reason for this, I suspect, is that while a play like *The Cocktail Party* does not seem to me to be the "masterpiece" it has been called, the fact of its production is something unusual in itself, and therefore a thing to excite interest whether or not one actually admires it. A play like *The Enchanted* leaves much to be desired, but Broadway is much better with Giraudoux than without him.

One was able this season to see such plays as Emlyn Williams' *The Corn Is Green* with Eva Le Gallienne and Bernard Shaw's *The Devil's Disciple* with Maurice Evans and Dennis King at the City Center. I thought the production of *The Corn Is Green* rather stock stuff, and I do not believe it to be an important play, yet I was glad to see it again, and even more pleased that those who had not had a chance to see it before could see it now at reasonable prices.

The Corn Is Green is well made in a simple way; it has a certain honest sentiment and idealism; it provides its leading actors with good parts. The play's shortcoming is that it is basically conventional, that its insights and sense of character lack the savor of genuine individuality.

The Devil's Disciple has a somewhat dull first act, a pedestrian preparation to the meat of the matter—the brilliant court-martial scene in which Shaw introduces one of his wittiest creations in the person of General Burgoyne. This is Shaw at his best—full of bright-brained fun—the point of which is the debunking of military heroics by a sharp intelligence.

The play sounds another variation on one of Shaw's key motifs— the idea that many people who seem aggressive, cynical, subversive, are really sturdy and devout Puritans whose message is one of love, forbearance and the good life in almost the most traditionally respectable sense, while there are professional moralists who are fire-eaters, heroic but not necessarily Christian men of war. The "devil's disciple" Dick Dudgeon (like Shaw himself) has something of Androcles in him, while Reverend Anthony Anderson is a man who believes in "an eye for an eye" and the devil take the hindmost.

The event of the season in the sense of a play that will make people discuss it most—even though they may not enjoy it—is T. S. Eliot's *The Cocktail Party*. The play, as I have noted, has already provoked many admiring epithets, though, in my opinion, for all the wrong reasons.

What is best in *The Cocktail Party* is the attempt to write a verse play about contemporary life. The fact that it is in verse— hardly distinguishable from a cadenced prose—is not in itself remarkable, but the use of verse in T. S. Eliot's hands bespeaks an effort to give his poetry a dramatic directness and to give the dramatic form the intense meaningfulness of poetry. This effort, I say, is in itself a virtue—for the theatre is at its best when it becomes poetic. The whole bent of modern drama, since the heyday of naturalism, is to find a means of recapturing and renewing the poetic essence of the older drama in terms of modern symbols and conceptions. Brecht in Germany calls his work "epic theatre," but what it is at bottom is a form of poetic drama— in this instance patterned to some extent on the Japanese theatre— to serve what Brecht believes to be present-day needs.

It is important, therefore, when an eminent poet like Eliot essays the dramatic form not simply as a new departure in his literary activity, but to provide material for the living theatre.

Even more important is the fact that such an effort should be crowned with an unusual degree of success. There is an element of snob appeal in *The Cocktail Party*'s success, but to leave it at that would be to underestimate the shrewd job Eliot has done.

Perhaps "shrewd job" is too gross an expression to use in this connection, but it seems to me unmistakable that what Eliot had in view with *The Cocktail Party* was an assault on and victory in the realm of the fashionable theatre. He wanted to write a play that would both convey his attitude toward life and be as chic and popular in its way as Noel Coward's plays were in the twenties. He has succeeded. *The Cocktail Party* is thoroughly modish and, though this will strike many as a kind of blasphemy— it is modish in a manner not so far removed from that of Coward as one might suppose.

A careful examination of its structure will prove that *The Cocktail Party* is not properly a drama. The first act shows some typical modern figures of the moderately prosperous middle class whose marital lives have gone on the rocks. There is the husband who deceives his wife and feels guilty about it, the wife who has deceived her husband and has failed to enjoy the experience, the mistress who realizes that her affair is sordid because her lover is as devoid of real feeling for her as he is for his wife.

The second act shows these characters at a psychotherapist's office. The psychotherapist (I cannot call him a psychoanalyst without arousing the justifiable ire of that respected calling) is not really a doctor in any precise sense but is used as a convenient mask—since the psychiatrist is now as familiar a type in popular entertainment as the cowboy of the old movies. Eliot's "doctor" is really a disguised Anglican minister—worldly, literary, and socially adept—who enunciates Eliot's convictions. The doctor tells his patients off, gives advice with a certain amount of epigram and intellectual sanctimoniousness. The "patients" agree with the doctor's analysis of them, and decide forthwith to do his bidding.

The third act is a report on the results of the doctor's advice. There is hardly any conflict at all—not even within each of the characters. The doctor preaches, the patients are immediately edified, and everyone proclaims satisfaction with the cure in a series of highfalutin testimonials.

All this is nevertheless interesting on the stage—the first act with its revelation of domestic and erotic entanglements, inoffensively indicated with a rather debonair wit; the second act with its excellently articulated truisms and near profundities; the third act with its symbolism, moral commentary and slick nobility. The manner throughout is light—even polite.

The Cocktail Party, though stageworthy, is hardly drama, since none of the characters, though they are presumably in a mess, is ever really in trouble. We must now ask ourselves whether the play is poetry. If accomplished writing and mastery of certain modes of versification employed on behalf of a serious theme is poetry, then *The Cocktail Party* certainly is poetry. But if poetry is the expression of an original sense of life carried to the point of being truly individual music, then *The Cocktail Party* is hardly poetry.

Poetry can only arise out of a depth or perfection of feeling and sensibility which is rooted in a real experience of the spirit. There is something fundamentally hypocritical, false and even empty about *The Cocktail Party.* I spoke of Eliot's psychotherapist as a mask. Everything in *The Cocktail Party* is masked. Religion and the church are never named, but are referred to obliquely as a "sanatorium"—so that, for one thing, no member of any particular church need take offense. There is a kind of flattering bow made to psychoanalysis, but in a way no enemy of psychoanalysis could object to. A strange trinity is suggested—one of the three is the "doctor"—but only a close study of the text would enlighten us as to how Eliot's trinity relates to the classical one.

None of this would necessarily be wrong, if what Eliot was trying to say was sound or inspiring or simply moving. But *The Cocktail Party* is nothing but a pessimistic defense of the status quo, that can be acceptable to nobody if it is to be taken seriously for one moment—not to the Catholic, the existentialist, the psychoanalyst, the practical man of common sense, although there is a vague appeal to everybody—except the radical left. The play is all evasion.

The pith of Eliot's play is that the world being a foul and bloody chaos, the ordinary life of the average middle-class citizen, though it is full of delusion, disappointment and frustration, is still a good life if one accepts it as such, and does not lie about it or become destructive because of it. There is another way of life—the way of *faith*—though Eliot does not specify what one is to have faith in—for he even eschews the mention of God. The way of faith is for the saints, and is perhaps the most painful of all, but we are at once assured that neither way is better and that both are necessary. The saint apparently may dedicate himself to a cause (although the chief characteristic of the saint is the capacity to make peace with his aloneness) and all causes are apparently equal except those that lead to violence or disgraceful change. Eliot tries to find room for all, embrace all—even Hollywood scenarists who write trash, since the mastery of a métier, he points out, is also respectable.

I am pleased to find Eliot so benign—conservatives often have a way of becoming quite as malicious as leftists—but I cannot say I get any comfort, even of the metaphysical sort, from his benevolence, since his philosophy—such as it is—not only lacks fervor, but strikes me as thoroughly joyless, spiritless and, if you will pardon the expression, gutless. As far as I can discern from *The Cocktail Party*, at any rate, Eliot cares only for a quiet life and good books. It is not enough; indeed, it is very little.

9

Christopher Fry

[1951]

IF, LIKE HAMLET, I were questioned as to what I had been reading after leafing through Christopher Fry's *The Lady's Not for
Burning*, I might also answer, "Words; Words; Words." The answer
in this case would not only be ambiguous but unfair.

In the first place, Fry's words were meant to be spoken in the
theatre, and the theatre has not for a long time heard so dazzling
an arrangement of words as Fry has made. Second, Fry manages
to mean something, though to read the reviews of his plays one
wouldn't guess it. Fry will ultimately have to stand by what he
means as well as by his manner of speech, although, it is true, the
style of Fry's statement is as much part of what he means as any
abstract formulation of his meaning can be.

There is wit, grace and a touch of tenderness in Fry's work which
make him an exquisite minor poet. A minor poet on our stage today
may be regarded as a major dramatist. My reservations about Fry—
which are merely an attempt to define him—must by no means be
construed as a denial of the pleasure we take in having so rare a
writer in the contemporary theatre.

Though a note of autumnal melancholy and an elegant heartbreak are very nearly constant in Fry's plays, his is an essentially
comedic talent. Now the comic may be defined, from a certain
angle, as the tragic in reverse. To make comedy, one must observe

45

the same facts the tragic artist sees, but so present them that our spirit takes refuge in mirth. Tragedy confronts reality; comedy bounces off it. In the greatest comic artists, the sense of a tragic content is present even at the moment of heartiest laughter. Where the tragic content is slight, and where the bridge between such content and the resultant comedy can only dimly be perceived, we have a light comic artist. Fry is such an artist.

In *The Lady's Not for Burning,* a young man asks to be hanged because he is disillusioned with life. Man is petty; the world a fraud. A girl is condemned as a witch, but she does not want to die: she represents the irrational force which finds in life its own reason, in the love of life its own justification. The young man offers to save the girl because her death would be brutally unjust. He falls in love with the girl, despite himself, and consents to go on living—without renouncing the sense that this determination is a kind of folly. It may be that Fry regards the two differing impulses—the boy's and the girl's—as two sides of the human coin.

What motif is most frequently stressed in Fry's presentation of his story? Fry's doubting Thomas says:

> The heart is worthless,
> Nothing more than a pomander's perfume
> In the sewerage. And a nosegay of private emotion
> Won't distract me from the stench of the plague-pit,
> You needn't think it will.

Almost immediately after, he says:

> Make this woman understand that I
> Am a figure of vice and crime—
> . . . .
>   Guilty
> Of mankind. . . . .
> Half this grotesque life I spend in a state
> Of slow decomposition, using
> The name of unconsidered God as a pedestal
> On which I stand and bray that I'm best
> Of beasts, until under some patient
> Moon or other I fall to pieces, like
> A cake of dung.

The girl answers:

> . . . . Something compels us into
> The terrible fallacy that man is desirable
> And there's no escaping into truth.

Alfred de Musset, the nineteenth-century French poet and dramatist, said things to the same effect. But it cost the Frenchman blood to say it. Fry spills ink. He spills it as prettily as you please, and he makes smiling sad patterns with it, but he does it as a delicate pastime; and aside from the study and pains needed to make an excellent craftsman, he pays very little for it—and neither need we.

The significance of Fry's success—apart from the fact that he has reintroduced the "magical" note into the English-speaking theatre— is its relationship to the existentialist mood, which, make no mistake about it, represents a state of mind characteristic of a large part of the educated middle class. Most of the French existentialists, however, are in dead earnest, and desperately cry out that they must act and take responsibility for their acts, no matter how philosophically "unguaranteed" they may be. Fry is not desperate at all: he is, on the contrary, extremely comfortable. His "pessimism" is half poetic pose, half accommodation to the mournfully uncertain philosophy of his coevals.

This does not mean that Fry is insincere, only that the hurt his work centers on is less crucial to it than the charming conceits he draws from it. The intellectual tone of the day has supplied Fry with his material, and he employs it to fashion an art that is chiefly decorative.

John Gielgud's production of *The Lady's Not for Burning* is a satisfactory one insofar as the company is composed of charming people, speaks well and understands the basic dramatic significance of the frequently intricate lines. Pamela Brown has an intriguing personality. Eliot Makeham is delightful as the most engagingly conceived character of the play (perhaps an unconscious projection of Fry himself), an old chaplain who is a mixture of a pure aestheticism with kindliness; and Richard Burton plays with an almost ingenuous emotional directness that comes close to exposing the artificiality of the others, so that at moments his performance seems like a mistake, as if he were giving the whole show away.

I can imagine and might prefer a very different sort of production. John Gielgud has taken Fry at his word, and does the play as a "romantic comedy" set against a more or less fifteenth-century background. The result is conventional: a production that might just as well have been applied to a verse play of fifty years ago. But Fry is essentially contemporary, and he is "romantic" in the ornamental sense which enables an expert couturier to make an ultra-smart modern gown from a medieval model. What *The Lady's Not for Burning* requires is a production which would make visible exactly how Fry's style differs from that, let us say, of Rostand.

[1952]

DECORUM leads to decoration. The motifs of decoration may be similar to those of tragic art. A thorn in decoration loses its sting; a dagger may become as pretty as a flower. There is something of this transformation in Christopher Fry's work. Its material is often brackish, but the manner is always sweet. If one listens closely to *Venus Observed*, for example, one hears some fairly gloomy sentiments, but the total impression is always *agreeable*—almost delicious.

"The note is loneliness," says the Duke in *Venus Observed*. "So much I delighted in is all ash," he continues. And further:

> . . . I forgive
> Both us for being born of the flesh,
> Which means I forgive all tossing and turning,
> All foundering, all not finding,
> All irreconcilability,
> All the friction of this great orphanage
> Where no one knows his origin and no one
> Comes to claim him. I forgive even
> The unrevealing revelation of love
> That lifts a lid purely
> To close it, and leaves us knowing that greater things
> Are close, but not to be disclosed
> Though we die for them.

All this, as far as sense goes, is in the existentialist vein. But Fry turns it into something elegant, witty, exquisitely sentimental. Better still is a certain gentle, almost tenderly humorous forbearance. Fry's mood is autumnal ("The landscape's all in tune, in a falling cadence/All decaying"). It is autumnal not only in this play, which is an allegory of the passing of old (aristocratic, imperial) England, but even in plays presumed to reflect the atmosphere of brighter seasons.

That is why Fry's plays, even when they contain "strong" action (a pistol shot, arson, a rescue from fire, threatened imprisonment) seem placid and passive. The best days are over; the struggles ahead, we know from the past, are not worth the burning. Let us embrace civilization and forget progress. Since it is their way, the young may toss and turn; the wise will contemplate the universe with an affectionate nod. It all comes to a snore in the end.

Let no one say that Fry's work consists of playful, euphonious words and no more. The meaning is clear to anyone who will pay attention. (The continuous verbal coruscation sometimes makes attention difficult, so that the line of the play—which is usually as pointed as a fable—is obscured.) And the meaning, no matter how one reacts to it, is historically (or socially) revealing. Fry's plays are poems of resignation in which tragic substance is flattened into lovely ornament. The French existentialists (most of whom are poor as creative artists) have a more vigorous intention and an activist temper. Fry confesses here through his leading character, who dwells in the high air observing the stars, "I like to conform."

The challenge of Fry's plays is seldom met by directors because they seem to appreciate him only in terms of quips and fine speeches, and not in terms of feeling, atmosphere, significance. *Venus Observed* is done as a romantic drawing-room comedy rendered limp by literature. Rex Harrison, who is an admirable light comedian—his delivery suggests intelligence—seems miscast in this play. His manner is brittle and worldly in a tripping sort of way, whereas Fry's duke "dances" to a graciously regretful tune. Harrison stoops and fumbles to convey age: there is no sovereign tiredness or melancholy anywhere in him.

The rest of the cast is careful or valiant—smiling bravely through the hazard of words they have respectfully learned. John Williams, who plays a faltering representative of mercantile England, seems to be having fun—this helps us to enjoy his performance.

10

London

[1950]

THE BEST PRODUCTION I saw in London was that of a French play, Jean Anouilh's *Ring Around the Moon* (originally *Invitation to the Palace*); the best play, Chekhov's *Ivanov*. This is not to suggest that nothing good is being written by English playwrights: it is impossible to overlook the meteoric appearance of Christopher Fry. What is notable, however, is the rarity of good plays reflecting contemporary England.

There is a certain kinship in mood between the best work being done in England and in France. Anouilh and Fry (who did the superb translation of *Ring Around the Moon*) tend toward a poetic and quasi-satiric playfulness. The Frenchman is the more authentic playwright, the Briton the more consciously literary personality. The Frenchman has more hurt in him, more acid, more immediate social relevance. The Briton is a virtuoso of words, and one guesses that he is sufficiently happy in the pleasure of their use. Fry's themes serve chiefly as occasions for his brilliant rhetoric. Anouilh hates the past, is tense and suspicious about the present. Fry simply neglects the present by wrapping it in a dazzling fabric wrought from stuff in which strands of ancient pattern predominate. Both men are highly cultivated, but neither appears spiritually vigorous. I doubt that there is any new birth in either of them.

Anouilh writes plays he calls "black," and others he calls "rosy." The "rosy" plays are ornaments based on the material of the "black" ones. The bright plays remind one of the kind of eighteenth-century art in which a sparkling prank may be interpreted as a sign of disease. *Ring Around the Moon* is about an exquisitely weary society in which the nobility deplores the present mess (shades of Giraudoux!), rich young men toy with love, millionaires are wretched and pure young girls are buffeted around by everyone. Yet Anouilh's play is jolly—a charade or "comedy-ballet." He gives it a happy ending, because, as he says, "it wouldn't be decent" to do otherwise.

The English production, infinitely superior to that given *Thieves' Ball*, a similar Anouilh play I saw in Paris, emphasizes everything romantic, pretty and gay in the material. There is no hint of bitterness. It is right that this should be so, since the British public is much less cynical than the French, hardly aware (in the theatre at any rate) that the contemporary world is thought by many artists to be thoroughly rotten. The cast of *Ring Around the Moon* is well-nigh perfect, Oliver Messel's settings enchanting, and the direction —by London's new find, Peter Brook—prodigiously clever.

Laurence Olivier's production of Fry's *Venus Observed* is, on the whole, rather mediocre. Yet one cannot be sure that it is only Olivier's presence in the cast that has made the play a success. Though generally obscure, it has an elegance, a wit and a mood of lofty, smiling sadness which appease and bemuse the London audience—just as New York is lulled by *The Cocktail Party*.

No one appears to know exactly what *Venus Observed* means. Fry has said that it is a mood play, and just as his earlier comedy, *The Lady's Not for Burning,* is springlike, *Venus Observed* is written in an autumnal key. The theme, Fry adds, is loneliness. Perhaps only a reading of its profuse and flashing text will disclose what it contains and reveals, but, as I watched it, the play seemed to me an allegory on the state of England today.

The central character is an aging aristocrat who in his youth was quite a fellow. Now that he is turning mellow, he has taken to studying the heavens and being generally understanding and benign. His agent (or chief employee) cheats him in order to gain the riches necessary to the kind of civilization or dignity which his employer possesses, and the latter (the duke) sympathizes with the reasons for which he is being despoiled. (He has had so much that it doesn't really matter to him that he is now being robbed.) The agent's daughter is a young firebrand who has been to America and to prison for having joined a society devoted to the destruction of ugly monuments. The aristocratic duke falls in love with her. When danger threatens the girl and her elderly admirer, she clings to him —but it is not love, only fear. The girl will marry the duke's son, who, always in awe of his father, has been awaiting his chance. The old man and his equally passé agent sit down in the night in a kind of satisfied and calm retirement from the world, which they leave to their children, having done all they can to protect, instruct and inspire them.

Closer examination of Fry may show that the less serious one's approach to him, the more his work improves. Perhaps the caliber of the fireworks that erupt from his moldy mansion should suffice us and teach us that it is a mistake to look, in their light, for the outline of a new architecture. On this score, however, the critic must reserve the right to change his mind at any time without notice. But I could not help thinking, as I watched *Venus Observed*, that one English poet today is spinning a dry wisdom, while another is just spinning.

[July 6, 1970]

The sensation of the late London season is the National Theatre's production of *The Merchant of Venice*. The main attraction is Laurence Olivier's Shylock, though there are other novelties in the occasion.

The play has been staged by Jonathan Miller, who was one of the stars of *Beyond the Fringe* and who has recently been marking time by refurbishing Lewis Carroll and Shakespeare with contemporary conceits. The revue touch is especially effective in the casket scene in which the Prince of Morocco is played as a modern African potentate, and the Prince of Arragon is burlesqued as a senile and purblind idiot. But there is less humor in the rest.

Miller mitigates the anti-Semitic aspect of the play. Thus when Bassanio witnesses Shylock's extreme humiliation, he is markedly affected and does all he can to stop his friend Gratiano from viciously guying the suffering Jew. Even Antonio, played as a respectable Victorian British businessman, is shaken when he hears Shylock's terrible sobbing immediately after he has left the court in defeat. The play begins and ends with what sounds very much like a traditional Hebrew chant of lamentation.

I have always thought of *The Merchant of Venice* as an ironic comedy about "capitalist" hypocrisy. Antonio and his companions— their whole society in fact—live on unearned income. Most of them are wastrels parading as gentlemanly gay blades. They hate the Jew for being a moneylender which was virtually the only profession open to one of his religion in the sixteenth century. But they require his money when they have been profligate in the use of their funds. After they escape the consequences of their improvidence and bankrupt the Jew, they turn once more to their thoughtless fun and games. This explains the last act, which is superfluous, even fatuous, unless the play is so understood.

Something of this comes through in Miller's production, but hardly enough. Still I suspect that the interpretation I have suggested is based on the assumption that every one of Shakespeare's plays is a coherent whole. I am not at all convinced that this is so. Shakespeare was a giant among poet-dramatists, but he was also a popular playmaker, and when he wrote *The Merchant* he was dealing with a tricky theme. He planned to write a play with lots of laughs and pretty diversions, a melodramatic comedy which would also contain the menace of a fantastic creature, a *Jew,* who in the England of his day was an unknown phenomenon, since the Jews had been banished many years before.

But because Shakespeare was a genius he could not create an entirely false character, and Shylock became a highly complex one: an ogre to the groundlings, a man of fierce and understandable passion for the more aware. He has been denatured by the cruelty of his situation as an "alien" in a corrupt society. On several occasions I have referred to him as "the poisoned conscience of Venice." He is no "hero" and just as certainly not the laughable villain the Elizabethans must have taken him to be.

What I saw at the National Theatre is a clever show with hints and overtones of contemporary significance and a *reasonable* portrait of the pivotal character. Except for the late nineteenth-century English mode in which the play is set, the production marks no startling departure from previous interpretations of recent years.

As performance, Olivier's Shylock is superb. His beardless makeup possesses a striking resemblance to some Anglo-Jewish tradesmen of Austrian or German origin often seen today in London. His delivery and readings are wonderful in their clarity and eloquence. With great conviction he conveys the justified resentment of the persecuted. The famous "Hath not a Jew eyes," is not special pleading but the exasperation of a man fed up to the teeth with injustice. Storming about the stage his protest rises tempestuously from within him but is not addressed to anyone in particular.

Shylock here is reduced to middle-class proportions. The slight Germanic accent conspires to enhance this impression. (There is in the whole idea of making Shakespeare a man of our day, whether in a "Marxist" or "existentialist" vein, something basically middle class.) What is lacking in Olivier's Shylock—and the production generally, more a thing of good and less good bits and patches than a satisfactory whole—is a sense of *grandeur*. Without it Shakespeare's stature is diminished.

I was an interested observer, even at moments an admiring one, at this *Merchant*. But it did not move me nor did it cause me to see the play in a new light. Intelligence and skill had gone into its making, but I felt less involved than I did in the ephemeral pieces I saw on some of the other evenings.

Just as there hardly exists a truly tragic drama in the contemporary theatre, there are virtually no genuine tragedians. The last one I can remember seeing was Chaliapin, and between 1916 and 1922 John Barrymore struck me as having that potential. Laurence Olivier is not essentially a tragedian. He is a romantic actor, a brilliant delineator of (often comic) characters. He has extraordinary power, scope and charm, and he is certainly the most dazzlingly accomplished player today on the English-speaking stage.

11

John Osborne

[1957]

JOHN OSBORNE, an actor still in his twenties, wrote a play two or three years ago, *Look Back in Anger,* which knocked at the door—this time at the door of British drama. The knock reverberated momentously through the English theatre, and its echo, slightly muted by its ocean passage, may now be heard on our Broadway shore.

I saw the play at its opening in London, where it was received by the leading critics with an excited gratitude which astonished as much as it pleased me. What the play represented to its English audience was the first resounding expression in the theatre not only of troubled youth but of the tensions within large segments of the middle class in England today. The play is contemporary in a way in which Rattigan on the one hand or Eliot and Fry on the other are not.

The play brings before us two young men of working-class origin in the English midlands who have a candy-stand concession in a local cinema. One of them—Jimmy Porter—has had a university education and acts as a self-appointed protector to his Welsh buddy, an uncomplicated person happily free of metaphysical anguish.

Jimmy is married to a pretty girl whom he feels he almost had to steal away from her family, the kind of family whose strength and graces were grounded on England's 1914 Empire. Jimmy not only resents his wife's family and all the institutions that bred them because they led to nothing but the dust and ashes of 1945; he also berates her for having lost the stamina presumed to be characteristic of her background, without having replaced it with any new values of her own—even romantically negative ones like his.

A fourth character, a young actress, represents that middle class which obstinately holds on to its customary traditions; and there is also the wan figure of Jimmy's father-in-law, bewildered and impotent in an England he no longer recognizes.

Jimmy Porter, then, is the angry one. What is he angry about? It is a little difficult at first for an American to understand. The English understand, not because it is ever explicitly stated, but because the jitters which rack Jimmy, though out of proportion to the facts within the play, are in the very air the Englishman breathes. Jimmy, "risen" from the working class, is now provided with an intellect which only shows him that everything that might have justified pride in the old England—its opportunity, adventure, material well-being—has disappeared without being replaced by anything but a lackluster security. He has been promoted into a moral and social vacuum. He fumes, rages, nags at a world which promised much but which has led to a dreary plain where there is no fiber or substance—only fear of scientific destruction and the minor comforts of "American" mechanics. His wife comments to the effect that "my father is sad because everything has changed; Jimmy is sad because nothing has." In the meantime Jimmy seeks solace and blows defiance through the symbolic jazz of his trumpet; while his working-class pal, though he adores Jimmy and his wife, wisely leaves the emotionally messy premises.

Immanent reality plus a gift for stinging and witty rhetoric are what give the play its importance. It is not realism of the Odets or Williams kind, nor yet poetry, although it has some kinship to both. It adds up to a theatrical stylization of ideas about reality in which a perceptive journalism is made to flash on the stage by a talent for histrionic gesture and vivid elocution. While the end product possesses a certain nervous force and genuineness of feeling it is also sentimental, for it still lacks the quality of an experience digested, controlled or wholly understood.

Someone asked me if I didn't believe the play might achieve greater dimensions if American actors were to play it in a manner now associated with the generation influenced by the Group Theatre. The question reveals a misunderstanding of the play's nature.

It calls for the verbal brio and discreet indication of feeling which it receives from the uniformly excellent, attractive English cast— Kenneth Haigh, Mary Ure, Alan Bates, Vivienne Drummond.

Jimmy Porter, "deepened" in another vein, would prove an intolerable nuisance, a self-pitying, verbose, sadistic jackanapes. He is a sign, not a character. We accept him because in the final count he is more amusing than real. We can look beyond him and the flimsy structure of the fable in which he is involved and surmise some of the living sources in the civilization from which he issues.

That John Osborne is attached and attuned to those sources is the virtue and hope of his talent. It may take ten years for him to achieve what most people have declared he already has.

12

Jean Giraudoux

[1949]

A PAINFUL EXAMPLE of the inadequacy of our producers' and directors' approach to plays of quality is the current production of Jean Giraudoux's last play, *The Madwoman of Chaillot*.

Here is a play that may well deserve being called a masterpiece. It is a socially keen comic fantasy. It is a model, in one special vein, of what I believe the contemporary theatre should aim for: the discovery of concrete symbols whereby a vision of modern life can be conveyed through poetic and picturesque dramatic imagery. Our theatre today needs intense, sharp and dynamic expression of the artists' truly personal reaction to the spectacle of life as they actually witness it. Contemporaneity is important, imaginativeness crucial. The universal must be sought in terms of the immediate. *The Madwoman of Chaillot* is a poet's reaction to the corruption of Paris between 1939 and 1944. Yet it speaks not only of France but of Europe, indeed of the whole Western world and of its dominant product in this era: the profiteer, the man who thinks only of how he may convert everything into capital. These people, Giraudoux says, are machines: they don't "smell"; and they are turning the world into a flavorless, soulless place which will die of dry rot before it explodes altogether.

Giraudoux imagines a woman who represents the romance of another era, when birds flew and flowers bloomed and people had manners, and love was something that people believed in. This mad-

woman and her cronies live like relics in obscure seclusion where
they continue to dream of the past because the present offers very
little for them to cherish. But when the madwoman sees a young
couple threatened with extinction by the evil men of the modern
world she comes to the rescue of the jeopardized pair. The only
ones who understand the madwoman are the ragpickers, the itiner-
ant peddlers, the discarded artists; they explain to her that there is
little hope of saving anyone. The machine men are too numerous,
too powerful, and they are joined in a great conspiracy in which
all the forces of society are conjoined and interlocked. The madwoman realizes that the weakness of these monsters is their greed.
She pretends to have found oil—which she hears they are seeking
—found it underneath the very floor of her cellar dwelling, and she
leads the evil ones to their doom: she drowns them all in the un-
speakable and mysterious sewers of Paris.

Giraudoux relates all this with the irony and fancy of a man who
does not believe he is describing a possibility, but merely expressing
a wish. Giraudoux (who died in 1944) was a conservative, not a
revolutionary, and he spins his yarn with the gay unconcern of a
hawker of magic baubles. But his tongue is not only glib, his eye
is sharp, and all his wild paradoxes and frothy palaver are a
laughable distortion of what is literally true. He only pretends not
to be serious. He tosses his ideas, like a juggler's clubs, helter-
skelter into the enchanted night of his fantasy, in the hope that
somehow or other they will end as a pattern of prophecy when they
land before our eyes.

The play is replete with wonderful fun that makes us see the
world through tears of laughter, enhancing rather than blurring
our vision. How witty, for example, is the moment when the president (chief of the financial malefactors) advises his companion, the
baron, not to buy shoelaces from the peddler who sells them at the
café terrace since such shoelaces are only bought by people who have
no shoes, just as neckties are sold by similar peddlers to people who
have no shirts. How saucy is the scene in which the president is
trying to find a commodity to set as a basis for the corporation for
which he is ready to issue stocks, but which he cannot properly
launch until he has found a name for it! And what Voltairean eloquence in the great defense of the monied class which the ragpicker
delivers as a means of condemning it. The play is an unbroken tissue

of delightful improvisations contained within a master conception of happiest inspiration.

The Madwoman of Chaillot is a play that might be done in any number of unforgettable productions by a variety of talented directors. But in New York it has fallen prey to that commercial destiny whereby one of the production units least equipped to present it adequately has been bequeathed its treasures. Aside from the near indestructibility of the script itself, nothing holds the present production together except for Christian Bérard's sets from the original French production. These sets are wittier than they are glamorous, more picturesque than they are theatrically serviceable. The set in the madwoman's cellar is entrancing as idea and design, but not wholly successful in its arrangement for purposes of ingenious staging. In any case, the sets are an attempt to match the playwright's gifts. For the rest, the production is a disaster of flatness—amounting to something close to sabotage.

The disgrace of this vandalism is that it is not deliberate. The producer-director undoubtedly loves the play and appreciates its beauties as much as anyone else. He simply hasn't the slightest understanding of how such a script should be translated to the stage. Indeed, he could not have realized that a production of such a play must be a *translation*, that is, a transference of material from one medium (the written word) to another (the theatre).

One of the reasons for this ignorance is that, aside from a few consciously trained theatre craftsmen, most of the audience—including a majority of the reviewers—is equally in the dark on the subject of what constitutes stage direction. Most comments on *The Madwoman* indicate that its present production is either regarded as an acceptable one or that the play itself is considered tedious! It is as if the manuscripts of the Mozart symphonies still existed but no one was left to play them except the musically semiliterate.

For example: the play opens with one of the most scintillating speeches in any modern play since the early Shaw, a speech in which the president gives a commandingly epigrammatic summation of his career and his philosophy as a financial wizard who has learned to turn unreal values into gold. The speech is read with ponderous complacency as if the author intended to portray a smug fool instead of a creature of electric intelligence and drive. The gendarme who sits down to drink beer at the café terrace and bets the gold button from his uniform against the madwoman is a type that must be played by a character actor like one of the men who surround Raimu in the *Marius* series. Instead he is played by an actor who is embarrassed at his own curious behavior, as well as by his proximity to the play's star! The life of the café is not created; the café gives the impression of being empty and one that is not much frequented, whereas it is supposed to represent a teeming center of prosperity around which the suppressed people, like inhabitants of a marvelous underworld, flit about to trouble the conscience of the evil ones on their sidewalk thrones. This calls for a series of Daumier-like impressions; what we get at the Belasco is a collection of small-part actors who have been made to feel that they are hardly anything more, because they have been given no specific image or outline to fulfill.

Finally, the madwoman herself is conceived as a kind of trim but musty elegant with a greenish tint, like a mask, around her eyes, as if she were a character out of some English Gothic romance. Giraudoux's madwoman is romantic in the sense that she is old and as real as Paris itself, with its dirt, its decay, its accumulation of ancient memories, traditions, defeats, wisdom. The madwoman shouldn't be played with that movie glamour which reveals a once-famous beauty upon whom an eerie shadow is thrown; she is glamorous because above the misfortune of her abject neglect rises the pride of age-long human experience—complex, majestic, triumphant. It is the essence of Giraudoux's conception that the spirit of the old Paris buried beneath the surface of the smart city must win out for a human order to be restored. In his sets—the first with its series of empty window frames rising and spreading in endless monotony like a throng of featureless faces; the second with its moldy riches thrown haphazardly in all directions like exploded and unheeded treasure—the designer has attempted to suggest some of this meaning. But our producers no longer know even how to read a play in terms of the theatre. In its transformation into show business, the theatre has become a dead language.

[1950]

Jean Giraudoux was no philosopher and has never exercised an influence even on his own countrymen comparable to Eliot's influence in England and America. Giraudoux was a conservative, but his work has love—a very simple kind of love for the fundamental things of life—and his love informs his best efforts with captivating brightness, color, charm. The love that we find in Giraudoux often gives his work a special creative connection with the contemporary scene. For it is Giraudoux's love that leads to a peculiar provinciality (his image of the good life is the life of his native village), a provinciality which often makes him a sharp and engaging critic of modern society. In such a play as *The Madwoman of Chaillot*, for example, Paris is shown debased by money, and graciousness is made to dwell in mad exile in the subterranean passages of the city.

Giraudoux's *The Enchanted* is, I am told, more admired in France than *The Madwoman*. If this is so, it can only be because the literary texture of *The Enchanted* (in the original) strikes the French playgoer as more exquisite than that of *The Madwoman*. In France the words or writing of a play are deemed almost more important than the plot or characters. There are very fine passages of writing in *The Enchanted* and, as usual in Giraudoux, considerable wit. In *The Enchanted*, the life of the unfettered imagination—a form of poetic naïveté—is seen in constant danger of being victimized by the rationale of officialdom and trite expediency. The play is a smiling song of regret that high-spirited maidens grow up to become canny French housewives. *The Enchanted* is at once simpler than *The Madwoman* but more abstract: its subject matter is so general that its story becomes almost shapeless, with the result that much of it tends toward a sugary preciosity—the reverse side of Giraudoux's gift.

13

Samuel Beckett

[1956]

I WAS utterly absorbed by and thoroughly enjoyed Samuel Beckett's already famous *Waiting for Godot*. It is necessary to begin this way —it is not usually important for a reviewer to express so bald a reaction—because much abstruse and quite simple nonsense will probably be written apropos this play.

But even if I did not like the play, I should still admire it. I have my reservations, yet I think it a masterpiece. But should it prove not to be a masterpiece, I should still insist on its importance. This is no paradox; I am merely suggesting that there are various ways of viewing the play—all of them relevant.

It is a poetic harlequinade—tragicomic as the traditional commedia dell'arte usually was: full of horseplay, high spirits, cruelty and a great wistfulness. Though the content is intellectual to a degree, the surface, which is at once terse, rapid and prolix in dialogue, is very much like a minstrel show or vaudeville turn.

The form is exactly right for what Beckett wishes to convey. Complete disenchantment is at the heart of the play, but Beckett refuses to honor this disenchantment by a serious demeanor. Since life is an incomprehensible nullity enveloped by colorful patterns of fundamentally absurd and futile activities (like a clown's habit clothing a corpse), it is proper that we pass our time laughing at the spectacle.

We pass the time, Beckett tells us, waiting for a meaning that will save us—save us from the pain, ugliness, emptiness of existence. Perhaps the meaning is God, but we do not know Him. He is always promised us but He never recognizably appears. Our life is thus a constant waiting, always essentially the same, till time itself ceases to have significance or substance. "I can't go on like this," man forever cries; to which the reply is, "That's what you think." "What'll we do? What'll we do?" man repeatedly wails. The only answer given—apart from suicide, which is reticently hinted at—is to wait: "In the meantime let us try to converse calmly, since we are incapable of keeping silent."

What is all this if not the concentrate in almost childlike images of the contemporary European—particularly French—mood of despair, a distorted mirror reflection of the impasse and disarray of Europe's present politics, ethic and common way of life? If this play is generally difficult for Americans to grasp as anything but an exasperatingly crazy concoction, it is because there is no immediate point of reference for it in the conscious life of our people.

Art, someone has said, is the articulation of an experience. Beckett's experience is almost commonplace by now to the middle-class European intelligentsia and valid by virtue of that fact alone—and his expression of it is sharply witty, inventive, theatrically compact. (He uses even boredom as a means of entertainment.) Yet the play may be said to be too long, too simple, too clear, too symmetrical a fairytale, because it is an abstraction. Abstract art, it often occurs to me, is far too logical and direct as compared to the more "realistic" art. Too soon we see through to its meaning. *Hamlet* is in many ways still a puzzle to us, because its abstract significance is part of the complex stuff of its material, which being humanly concrete must be somewhat elusive. In *Waiting for Godot* almost everything is named. When abstraction is so clear, our attention weakens. As soon as we perceive the play's design everything else appears supererogatory.

Finally, I do not accept what *Waiting for Godot* says. When it is over my innermost being cries out " 'Tain't so!" We all, at times, feel as Beckett does (so much, alas, in the contemporary world gives us reason to do so), but in the sum of everyday living we give this mood the lie. Beckett is what in modern times we call a genius: he has built a cosmos out of the awareness of a passing moment. But what saves humanity is its mediocrity: its persistence in becoming wholly involved in the trivia of day-to-day physical concerns out of which arise all our struggles and aspirations, even to the most exalted level. It is this "stupid" appetite for life, this crass identity with it, which is its glory, sometimes called divine.

I can imagine a number of different ways of staging the play. Herbert Berghof's way of doing it is admirably understanding of its dual aspect: the farcical and the pathetic. I missed certain depths of feeling and poetic exaltation, a certain anguished purity which the play may have, but I am not at all sure that this lack should be ascribed to the play's direction. Even so, Bert Lahr (a true and wonderful clown with a face that conveys all), E. G. Marshall, Alvin Epstein and the others are remarkably good—and likely to improve with further playing. All in all, a memorable evening.

14

On Acting

[1949]

THE THEATRE is not a lamp by which a text may be read. The theatre, under favorable circumstances, is a creative art. To be properly understood, the theatre's parts—the dramatic scheme, words, acting, setting, music, and so on—must be viewed as a whole. As we sometimes isolate one element of a painting—composition, drawing, color, subject—as its most telling feature, so in the theatre we may regard one phase of a show—the spoken text, the acting, the general pattern of stage movement—as a production's most significant aspect. However, it is always necessary to remember that whatever we may say of the color in a painting or the plot of a play, we perceive the picture and the production as a whole. To regard the theatre as merely interpretive is to misunderstand and ultimately to destroy it.

When Chaliapin entered the coronation scene of *Boris Godunov,* the libretto informed us that he was a czar and a guilty man. Before a word was uttered, we felt that this czar was something more than a murderous king. He was a tragic figure, whose sin had a depth that exceeded the individual case. His was the guilt of Holy Russia in all her barbarously majestic splendor, religious conscience, superstition and power. Here was the very presence of something that could hold us in awe as if we were ourselves oppressed and worshiping muzhiks. A queer sense of epic grandeur was created as surely as in one of the great Muscovite cathedrals of

66

the sixteenth century. Moussorgsky's score was not only made flesh; it was transcended.

You might say that this miracle was wrought by such details as the wonderful costume, but it was the way that Chaliapin wore his costume that made it seem the spirit as well as the fabric of a world of tortuous magnificence. (I have seen other actors in the same role wear the same costume with only illustrative effect.) How Chaliapin made his Boris what it was is part of the technique of acting, part of that mystery of "personality" which is at the core of all art. My point here is that an appreciation of the opera's music or words would be insufficient to explain or even to recognize the quality of Chaliapin's Boris. Something was made of these elements through the body and soul of the actor that was new and not to be truly grasped by a separate analysis of each element.

What is true of an actor like Chaliapin is true of a director like Reinhardt. Reinhardt worked with first-rate actors such as Rudolph Schildkraut, Albert Bassermann, Alexander Moissi, Werner Kraus, as well as with plays by Shakespeare and other giants. But though these actors were marvelously projected through Reinhardt's direction without the forfeit of their particular contributions, and though the plays were given fascinating illumination, the whole of Reinhardt's creation was marked by that feeling of opulently sensuous rococo characteristic of the cultivated middle-European bourgeoisie between 1895 and 1914.

A knowledge of the texts employed by actors and directors is of course vital to the comprehension of what is being created by theatre artists, but one need not think of these texts entirely in terms of their literary excellence in order to evaluate what one sees on the stage. For example, I no longer recall the lines in the Dunning-Abbott melodrama *Broadway,* but my memory of the tawdry innocence, shimmer and tension of the speakeasy twenties is still vivid in the atmosphere, images, tempo that were typical of the Jed Harris production. When I saw Charles Mac-Arthur's revival of *The Front Page,* it had lost all the scalawag and brass-knuckle humor that it had originally been given. A play such as *Edward, My Son,* if it were to be taken at all seriously, would read like a trashy "social" melodrama, but as played by Robert Morley it is a kind of mischievously cute parlor entertainment. To suppose that Morley conveys any of the play's literal meaning is not only to be blind to acting but even to the merits of Morley's performance itself.

This leads to the conclusion implicit in my premise: that acting and direction possess a content in themselves—that is, they possess it when actors and directors are artists. Appreciation of the theatre bespeaks the audience's capacity to sense the content of what is seen on the stage; the critic's job is to define it. Once we have established that the content of a theatre production is not necessarily the equivalent of what the literary critic may find in the play's written text, we are ready to proceed to a further examination of the interrelations among acting, directing and other elements of theatre art.

Every element in a staged play is part of its direction. The director writes the "score" or "notes" of the theatrical production; the others play them. One might say that the director is the author of the theatrical production, except for the fact that in the collective art of the theatre no one can be more than a crucial collaborator. In the playing of the director's "notes," each of the collaborators— actors, designer, costumer, and so on—brings something of his own individuality or talent to bear.

In *They Knew What They Wanted* Muni is himself the director —in fact if not in name. But he is not a good director, since he plays his Italian vintner with a kind of storybook colorfulness— even to the makeup and costumes—while the rest of the cast plays with the naturalistic approach of the stock production. The result of this is that some fairly nondescript performances seem more "real" than Muni's, which is chock-full of good things. Impatient with directorial discipline and dependent on his own gifts, Muni helps make nonsense of his production and belies the values of his superior talent.

Acting and direction must themselves possess a content. Without an awareness of what the particular content of each individual performance is, there can be no valid theatrical judgment. Let us examine a detail of two performances as a study in comparative content. In *Anne of the Thousand Days*, Harrison as Henry VIII looks into his baby's crib only to discover that the

child is a girl, not the boy he had prayed for. The same scene
was played by Laughton in *The Loves of Henry VIII*. Since
both are scenes without words, our judgment of them receives
no support from the text. In *Anne* what the actor does constitutes information neatly delivered: the king is disappointed
and cold. With Laughton, the moment strikes a note of almost
animal pathos, and adds a touch to the portrait of a heroically
childlike primitiveness which Laughton drew in his Henry.

So true is it that acting has its own content—when it *is* acting—that types, modes, styles and epochs have been set—not
alone for the stage but for society at large—by actors. ("They
are the brief and abstract chronicles of the time.") Rachel made
the French of the 1840s aware of a new attitude toward love
through her romantic transformation of Racine's classicism;
George M. Cohan for many years typified the American as a
shrewdly jaunty optimist; John Drew gave New Yorkers in
the late nineties and early twentieth century a fresh sense of their
increased urbanity in the Anglo–Continental manner; Pauline
Lord introduced to our stage a special feeling for womanhood, akin
to that to be found later in the plays of Tennessee Williams.

The art critics tell us we cannot understand painting if we
look at pictures in terms of the subjects they depict. Somewhat
the same thing is true in the evaluation of acting. Volumes have
been written to direct our eyes to what is significant in the graphic
arts. For similar training in the appreciation of acting, the first
step would be to differentiate among the actor as material, the
nature of acting as function (what it is *to act*) and the meaning
of acting as interpretation.

* * *

Speaking of actors, the other day I came across a statement
by Samuel Johnson in connection with David Garrick. "The
player," Johnson said, "only recites." Charles Lamb said much
the same thing in a famous essay on Shakespeare. Both these
eminences were wrong. Being an elocutionist is not being an actor.
Acting is not primarily related to words at all.

To act on the stage means to behave under "unreal" or imaginary
circumstances as though these circumstances were real. In this

definition the word "behave" is crucial. Mimic ability or a capacity to imitate is valuable to an actor, but acting is not imitation. When I speak of "behavior" on the stage I mean that the actor must bring to each moment of his role a sense of fully experienced truth—physical and spiritual—within the circumstances of that moment: he must see, hear, move, react and feel with organic completeness and definite intention. This has little to do with "realism." The actor "forgets" himself in his role, yet always knows that he is playing, and that the object of his performance is to entertain.

There are people of engaging presence on the stage who though they have acquired facility in public deportment are not in my sense actors. They are not transformed by the imaginative reality of the circumstances which the stage calls upon them to face. The play's words and situations and our will-to-believe make them seem to be acting. They are sometimes referred to as "personalities."

Personality in an actor is of two kinds. The first relates to what might be called social personality—such as we remark in a pretty girl, a charming man, a funny fellow, and so on—characteristics which may or may not contribute to acting talent. The second kind of personality has to do with the actor as an instrument. A person of fluent emotional nature, quick sensory reaction, mobility of inner constitution, a person with an expressive voice, striking mask, natural grace, commanding figure, imagination, impressionability and temperament, ought to provide the best acting material.

When Tallulah Bankhead and Charles Boyer are called "superb," what is meant is that they do indeed act, and that they are, in addition to this, striking media or instruments for the stage. For final distinction in acting still another element must be present— illuminating interpretation.

"Interpretation" is a word often loosely used to indicate almost anything the actor happens to do with his part. More strictly, it should apply to what the actor chooses his part to mean. We call a writer "good" not simply to compliment his skill in the use of language but to approve his content. One may agree that an actor shows interesting skill and yet find in him a lack, or a falsity, of interpretation. Boyer's Hoederer in *Red Gloves* seemed to me to have very little interpretation, just as the Morley of *Edward, My*

Son—part social wit and part actor—strikes me as an amusing and fortunate "misinterpretation."

I have seen actors give remarkable acting performances in plays which they virtually wrecked. Years ago Jacob Ben-Ami played the name part in Giraudoux's *Siegfried,* a play about a Frenchman who, having lost his memory in the war, gains a high post in German diplomacy. Ben-Ami gave an unforgettable portrayal of the tragedy of living one's life without memory of one's past, but the play happened to be a comedy about the delightful difference between the French and German mentalities.

The interpretation of a part may sometimes be solely the actor's work. It may even be wise to allow a player of profound intuition to make a part entirely his own. Indeed, the very choice of a certain player (Laurette Taylor, let us say) may be a sign that the director has agreed to give his production the stamp of that actor's quality. Yet in sound theatre practice the director should be held responsible for the overall interpretation of a play and its parts. The director should not only set the outline of the actor's interpretation but help him find the method for its concrete embodiment.

Critics often fail to distinguish between the acting and direction of a play because they conceive the director's function as an editorial one, concerned chiefly with technical neatness, pace, mechanics.

I should like to add that our actors have more real personality than would appear from their performances, and are usually capable of greater interpretive values in their playing than we see. The fault here may be ascribed, to a considerable extent, to our directors, but even more to the chaos of our theatre, which makes a haphazard thing of the relation between actor and director: at the beginning of rehearsals actor and director rarely know each other and are at times even leery of each other.

* * *

An actor's personality might be said to possess a certain weight. This means a certain degree or quality of human experience. If we think of José Ferrer's facile and amusing performance in *The Silver Whistle* and one that might have been given in the same role by Otis Skinner, we may discover something about the younger actor's limitations. The difference is not in the skill, but in the stuff of life out of which acting is made. John Barrymore was surely the first actor of our stage between 1916 and 1925, not only because of his physical endowment but because of a richness of sensibility, wit, mental force, artistic aspiration, aristocratic soul. Many actors cannot be judged as artists at all because they are composed of thin stuff.

Is not the "stuff" of the actor's nature something he is born with? To a large extent, yes. But I believe it a great mistake to leave it at that. To a great degree, the actor may be *made* (or unmade) by his social and theatrical environment. What surrounds the actor—his audience, company, playwright, general artistic influences and director—can contribute much to the measure of the actor's personality. I can think of no English-speaking actor with greater natural gifts than Alfred Lunt. Yet Lunt's achievement in the last ten years cannot be compared with that of Laurence Olivier, whose actual talent is not superior to that of the American actor. To understand this discrepancy, we must examine the environment both inside and outside the theatre to which both men belong.

Such an examination would take us far afield. But it is to be noted that no English actor achieves undisputed eminence whose repertory does not include several classic roles. To have played Chekhov, Sheridan, Sophocles and Shakespeare with distinction means more for an actor's prestige in England than the greatest acclaim in an ordinary box-office success. This in itself means that there is a constant challenge to the English actor to test himself in parts which make greater demands on his capacities than do most contemporary plays. It should be remembered, too, that to play Hotspur, Shallow, Dr. Astrov (in *Uncle Vanya*), Mr. Puff and King Oedipus actually serves to educate the actor more than a lifetime in plays like *O Mistress Mine*.

At this point I should like to stress the importance of the director. The director, as the active principal of a play's interpretation, works through all the elements of the theatrical medium, but primarily through the actor. Many fine individual performances are given without any assistance at all from the director; but rarely is an integrated production with a consistent interpretation by a whole cast given without a director's conscious guidance. Kingsley's *Men in White* was a well-constructed play with an interesting background, but the lofty quality given it by the Group Theatre company was not due to the excellence of its individual members but to the direction of Lee Strasberg.

The style of acting in a production is an interpretive problem which the director alone can solve. The problem is not simply a matter of taste but of meaning. What shall the play say? Is *The Dybbuk*, for example, a play of quaint folk customs regarded with sentimental affection, or a play about a ritualistic world seen as a frightening phantasmagoria of the past? It may be either. The director decides which.

In 1934 I saw a Gorky play, *Igor Buletchev*, in two different Moscow productions on two consecutive evenings. In one production the play was about the spiritual tragedy of a man who has come to doubt the truthfulness of everyone around him. In the second production, it was a play about the necessary decline of a magnificent representative of a class that could not share the needs and hopes of a new generation. There were very few textual variances between the two, but everything else—style of setting, characterizations, makeups, tempo, and so on—was radically different. Gorky said both productions were "right."

Is *A Streetcar Named Desire* a play about a healthy couple almost wrecked by the intrusion of a destructively neurotic woman, or the story of a woman of fine fiber destroyed by the brutally crude attributes of her surroundings? Whether it is one or the other does not depend solely on the ability of the actors cast for either interpretation, but on the director's choice and his craftsmanship in the realization of his interpretation. A production that achieves meaning by accident is rarely of more than momentary interest.

Shakespeare seldom has significant content in our theatre—*despite Shakespeare*—because the direction of Shakespearean productions is usually little better than smooth stage management. I could not discern any sustained line of interpretation in Orson Welles' alert production of *Julius Caesar,* but it was a memorable one because at least two scenes—the opening with its "trouble in the town" atmosphere, and the scene in which the poet Cinna was lynched—gave the feeling of a Shakespeare play seen in a time of political ferment. Without such directorial insights and/or flashes of creative acting, true theatre cannot be said to exist.

15

The Famous "Method"

[1958]

"ARE YOU in favor of grammar? Yes or no? God darn it!"

Can you conceive of people engaging in such a dispute? Do you suppose anyone could become fanatic about the subjunctive mood? In theatre circles something almost as absurd as this appears to be going on. The bone of contention is the famous Method— the grammar of acting.

Ordinarily it would hardly seem to me to be worth while to write about a matter of stagecraft for the general reader. It is not at all useful or particularly interesting for the playgoer to know how a performance he enjoys was prepared, any more than a knowledge of how pigments are mixed is helpful in the appreciation of painting. But the case of the Method has become a subject of inquiry for many theatregoers for reasons which I intend to explain.

The Method, an abbreviation of the term "Stanislavsky Method," is as its name indicates a means of training actors as well as a technique for the use of actors in their work on parts. This technique, formulated in 1909 by the Russian actor-director Konstantin Stanislavsky of the Moscow Art Theatre, and subsequently employed in the productions of that company, was introduced into this country by three of its actors: Leo Bulgakov, Richard Boleslavsky and Maria Ouspenskaya. After the Moscow Art Theatre had terminated its first Broadway engagement in 1923, these three

74

actors decided to remain in the United States. They became the first teachers of the Method, which they and most other Russians referred to as the "System."

Among the young Americans who studied with Boleslavsky and Ouspenskaya between 1923–26 were Lee Strasberg, who today dominates the Actors Studio; Stella Adler, who now conducts a studio of her own; and, a little later, the present writer.

The Method had its first real trial and success on Broadway through the work of the Group Theatre (1931–41) of which Cheryl Crawford, Lee Strasberg and I were the leaders. In such productions as those of Kingsley's *Men in White* (directed by Strasberg), Odets' *Golden Boy* (directed by Clurman), Saroyan's *My Heart's in the Highlands* (directed by Robert Lewis), the Method—rarely touted beyond the confines of the Group's rehearsal hall—proved its value as a practical instrument in production.

I go into this now familiar history to stress the fact that by the year 1937 the "battle" of the Method had been won. By that time many theatre schools had been set up (among them the Neighborhood Playhouse whose main instructor, Sanford Meisner, had been an actor in the Group Theatre's permanent company) and an increasing number of well-known players—for example, Franchot Tone, who in 1933 left the Group for Hollywood—had made the Method part of their normal equipment. The Method was no longer a peculiarity of a few offbeat or off-Broadway actors.

It is true that a few critics still spoke of the Method and the schools or studios in which it was taught as a foreign excrescence unsuited to the American temperament, forgetting that in Stanislavsky's own company many of the actors had been just as skeptical as people anywhere else might be. But critics are notoriously behind the times.

How does it happen, then, that only in the past three or four years there has been such a rush and rash of publicity about the Method? What at this late date causes the endless palaver about Method and non-Method acting in and outside the theatrical profession?

Marilyn Monroe has a lot to do with it! That sumptuous lady in her eagerness to learn had begun to attend classes at the Actors Studio. Since all Miss Monroe's movements are carefully watched, the Studio began to attract attention far and wide. Everybody wanted to know what the Actors Studio was that the phosphorescent Marilyn should be concerned with it. What went on there? Who else participated? Then it was discovered that among other people who had been more or less attached to the Studio were Marlon Brando, Julie Harris, Kim Stanley, Maureen Stapleton, James Dean, Shelley Winters, Patricia Neal—with press emphasis, of course, on the Hollywood names.

If all these people had been adherents of the Studio, then the instruction there—mysteriously called the Method—had a gimmick fascination; there must certainly be something to it. Lee Strasberg might protest all he wanted that the Studio is not a school—nearly all its members had received their basic theatre instruction at schools or classes for beginners elsewhere—that many of its members were already well-known actors before they were invited into the Studio, that the Studio was simply a place where already trained actors thought particularly promising could pursue what might be called "post-graduate" work. None of this matters to the general public or to guileless aspirants to the stage; all they knew or cared about was the glamour and mystery that surrounded this nest of genius.

Of course, there was a more substantial reason for the Studio's hold on the acting profession. The practical eminence of the Studio's directorate—Crawford, Kazan, Strasberg—led aspirants to believe mistakenly that enrollment in the Studio was a gateway to employment.

None of this would be of much consequence if it did not result in certain misconceptions and confusion both outside the ranks of the acting profession and inside. Most members of the Studio—there is always a tendency in such organizations toward clannishness and cultism—are quite sane about their activities. The damage that is done is in the vastly larger body of "onlookers"—actors and those who have a general curiosity about the theatre. This damage ultimately injures the vital elements involved.

The Method, I have said, is the grammar of acting. There have been great writers who never studied grammar—though they usually possess it—but no one on that account proclaims grammar a fake and instruction in the subject futile. A mastery of grammar does not guarantee either a fine style or valuable literary content. Once in command of it, the writer is unconscious of method. It is never an end in itself. The same is true of the Stanislavsky Method.

There was grammar before there were grammarians. Great acting existed before the Method and great acting still exists unaware of it. A theatregoer who pays to see Michael Redgrave or Laurence Olivier cannot tell by watching them in performance which of the two was influenced by the Method.

The purpose of the Stanislavsky Method is to teach the actor to put the whole gamut of his physical and emotional being into the service of the dramatist's meaning. What Stanislavsky did was to observe great actors and study his own problems as an actor. In the process he began to isolate the various factors that composed fine acting. He systematized the way actors could prepare themselves for their task—the interpretation of plays. He detailed the means whereby actors might give shape and substance to the roles they were assigned.

There were acting methods before Stanislavsky, but none so thoroughgoing for the uses of all sorts of plays—from opera and farce to high tragedy—both classic and modern. Since the Method is a technique, not a style, there is no necessary connection between realism and the Method. In Russia, more nonrealistic plays than realistic plays were done with the aid of the Method.

Why was it necessary for Stanislavsky to evolve his Method? First, because the organization of knowledge about acting which the Method represents facilitates the first steps, diminishes the fumbling, wear and tear, waste of the apprentice years; and, second, because a conscious technique aids the actor, who has to repeat a part many times at specific hours, in gaining a greater mastery over his interpretation which without some form of conscious control tends to vanish through the capriciousness and fluidity of what is called inspiration.

All this is clearly set forth in Stanislavsky's three books—*My Life in Art, An Actor Prepares, Building a Character*—which have been available to the public for years. It is true that since the first of these volumes is an autobiography and the latter two technical handbooks, no one can learn to act merely by reading them. But the information they contain is neither mystic nor mysterious.

None of the American teachers of the Method (except Stella Adler, who worked with Stanislavsky in private sessions in Paris for six weeks in the summer of 1934) has ever known Stanislavsky personally and only two or three have ever seen any of his productions. I note this because it is always important to remember that just as every actor has his own individual personality which supersedes whatever technique he may employ or aesthetic doctrine he may profess, so every teacher of the Method lends it the quality of his own mind and disposition. There is no longer an "orthodox" Method, only a group of teachers (most of them trained in America) whose lessons derive from but are not limited to the Stanislavsky sources. As so often happens, on some points most of these teachers contradict one another violently. Which of them is in the right? For the laymen, it matters very little. Only results on the stage count.

Before abandoning the purely professional aspect of the subject and advancing to what I consider from the viewpoint of the general reader to be the more significant side, I should like to dispel some false notions which have arisen apropos the Method in the past five years or so. Those who are dubious or hostile to it (usually through misinformation) often mock it by saying that "Method actors"—a noxious term by the way—have slovenly diction, undistinguished voices, and conduct themselves on the stage with a singular lack of grace.

Needless to say, neither Stanislavsky nor any of the teachers who claim him as their guiding spirit are responsible for the professional or personal aberrations—real or imagined—of individual actors who study the Method. I have never heard anyone speak as long and as dogmatically on the importance of the voice and diction as did Stanislavsky to me on the several occasions of our meeting in Paris and Moscow. As for posture, physical deportment, correctness of carriage, discipline of manner: on these subjects Stanislavsky was almost fanatic. The actors of the Comédie Française (famous for fine voices and speech) had an inadequate vocal range of hardly more than three notes, he complained. The actress I most admired in his company was guilty of rather common speech and therefore could not gain his wholehearted approbation. Most actors walk badly, he pointed out. He was not satisfied that *anybody* anywhere had developed a voice to match the inherent demands of Shakespeare's verse.

American directors who were among the first followers of the Method and who have never renounced or denounced it have done shows such as *Brigadoon* (Robert Lewis) and *Tiger at the Gates* (Harold Clurman) which betrayed none of the traits of shabbiness in speech or behavior which many people associate with the Method. Indeed, it should be pointed out that a "classic" Method production, *Men in White,* was notable for a dignity which one critic declared attained a "concert beauty."

How then had this calumny about the drabness, not to say the grubbiness, of "Method acting" arisen? And is it only calumny? Marlon Brando's performance as Stanley Kowalski in Tennessee Williams' *A Streetcar Named Desire* was indirectly a major factor in the development of what might be dubbed a dreadful Method tradition or superstition. Brando's was a brilliant characterization and made a deep impression—unexpected as well as undesirable in its consequences.

It is worth mentioning that when I first heard that Brando was to do the part I thought he had been miscast. For I had known Brando, whom I had previously directed in a play by Maxwell Anderson, as an innately delicate, thoughtful and intellectually eager young man. No matter! For an alarming number of young people in the theatre Kowalski was Brando and Brando was great! The fact that Kowalski was largely a mug who frightened rather more than he fascinated the author himself—the play was intended to say that if we weren't careful such mugs might come to dominate our society—this fact escaped the host of Brando imitators. They equated the tough guy, delinquent aspect of the characterization with a heedlessness, a rebelliousness, a "freedom" and a kind of pristine strength which the performance seemed to them to symbolize. In it, they found combined their unconscious ideal: creative power in acting with a blind revolt against all sorts of conformity both in life and on the stage.

In France this is sometimes called *l'école Kazan,* although neither the muscularly energetic Kazan any more than the more intricately wrought Strasberg has ever made brutality a tenet of theatrical art. The fact that certain Method novitiates have confused realism with uncouthness in speech, manner and dress is an accident significant of the New York scene, not of the Method.

Too many of our younger actors have come to think of the refinement or decorum of the larger part of dramatic literature as somehow remote, old-fashioned, hypocritical—and alien. Their ideal is honesty, truth, down-to-earth simplicity, *guts*. "Down to earth" eventually becomes down to the gutter, and the only truth which is recognized as authentic is coarseness and ugliness.

This distortion is socially conditioned in the actors I refer to by an impulse to destroy the discipline of a gentility in their general environment, an environment usually without true roots in a meaningful and comprehensive culture. The distortion is also an unwitting protest against the streamlined efficiency of a too strictly business civilization or, so to speak, "Madison Avenue." These young actors fear nothing so much as any identification with the stuffed shirt.

The Method has influenced no theatre as much as the American. I have suggested one reason for this. Another has to do with one particular element of the Method—"affective memory" or the memory of emotions. I need not dwell here on the artistic validity, the use and abuse of this device. Suffice it to say that in the exercise of affective memory the actor is required to recall some personal event of his past in order to generate real feeling in relation to a scene in his part of the play.

This introspective action which—to an unusual degree—rivets the actor's attention on his inner life frequently strikes the novice as a revolutionary discovery. This is particularly true of the American, who, being part of an extroverted society which makes the world of *things* outside himself the focus of his hourly concern, seems to find in the technique of affective memory a revelation so momentous that it extends beyond the realm of its stage employment.

Most young actors who come upon it eat it up. Some it tends to make a little self-conscious, melancholy, "nervous," tense, producing a kind of constipation of the soul! Those with whom it agrees not only use it but often become consumed by it. With the immature and more credulous actor it may even develop into an emotional self-indulgence, or in other cases into a sort of private therapy. The actor being the ordinary neurotic man suffering all sorts of repressions and anxieties seizes upon the revelation of himself—supplied by the recollection of his past—as a purifying agent. Through it, he often imagines he will not only become a better actor, but a better person. It makes him feel that because of it he is no longer a mere performer but something like a redeemed human being and an artist. In this manner, the Method is converted into something akin not only to psychoanalysis but to "religion."

This was not Stanislavsky's aim nor does it represent the purpose of the Method teachers in America. It is, I repeat, an accident of our local scene to be explained by the psychological pressures and hunger of our youth. Where cultural activities are a normal part of daily life—as in most European countries—where self-expression is natural and habitual, the Method is taken as any other form of technical training—something to be learned and then "forgotten"—as grammar is forgotten when we have learned to use language properly.

Culture with us is still considered something apart from the main current of our lives. This is especially true of the stage. Since we have no national theatre, no repertory companies, no widespread stock companies, no consistent employment for the actor and since, too, channels for serious discussion, examination and practice of acting as an art are rare, the American actor clings to the Method and its ever-expanding centers of instruction as to a spiritual as well as a professional boon. It becomes manna from heaven.

I am glad the Method has "caught on." It has been of enormous benefit to our theatre and acting profession. Now that it has been established I hope to see it more or less taken as a matter of course. There is very little that is intrinsically controversial about it.

What the American actor really needs is more plays and productions in which to practice what has been preached. What actors of every kind need is a broader understanding of the Theatre as a whole: a general education in its relation to the world and to art in general. Young actors imbued with the Method have become so engrossed by what the Method can do for them that they forget that the Method exists for the Theatre and not the Theatre for the Method. What they must finally understand is that the Theatre is here for the pleasure, enlightenment and health of the audience—that is to say for all of us.

16

Valley of the Jordan, Israel

[1949]

THE STORY of my life might be deduced from the causes that make it possible for me to be writing these lines on a collective farm in the valley of the Jordan not far from Nazareth of Galilee. What prompted me to come to this place so unlike all the cities I am familiar with and which, by this time, I regard as my natural habitat? Was it historical curiosity, an appetite for travel, a bent toward exploration and adventure? None of these things, I am sorry to say, has anything to do with my presence here. I am here because of my addiction to the theatre.

When the Habimah company played its season in New York in May 1948, I wrote several articles about them and made the acquaintance of their actors. They asked if I would like to direct a play for them in Israel. I said "yes" with some suspicion that the request was hardly more than a friendly gesture. Today I am in Israel, and in the midst of rehearsals for a play that is scheduled to open soon.

It has occurred to me that interested people might like to know something of the work that I am doing in Israel because the circumstances happen to be unusual, and also because, while I have discussed stage direction several times from the standpoint of the audience, I have never made any attempt to detail the process itself. Though I am inclined to doubt the value of technical information to the "layman," perhaps these notes may lead to further thought about the theatre as an art.

Perhaps the fact that the play I am directing for the Habimah is a French play, of which I can read only the French text and not the Hebrew translation which the actors use, will make some people wonder, to begin with, how a director can possibly stage a play in a language of which his knowledge is confined to perhaps fifty words. In this instance the peculiarity of the situation is further enhanced by the fact that the French play being directed by the particular American with a Hebrew-speaking company takes place in Venezuela during the time of Bolívar's uprising against the Spanish in 1812. I stress these contrasts not only because they may seem amusing but because they emphasize a certain aspect of the theatre which my critical articles often stress; namely, that the theatre is not primarily a matter of words.

Certain people may conclude from this either that I am exaggerating to make some rather esoteric point, or that I am one of those arty, anti-intellectual individuals who are concerned only with "beauty," "plastic values," "rhythm," "mime" and "scenic excitement" as abstract values. I need hardly make the issue personal and point to my career in the theatre to prove that this is not the case. I am deeply interested in drama as literature and I am convinced that the ideal of every director I know is to make his craftsmanship worthy of the finest plays that contemporary and classic writing provide. My point is simply that a play on the stage does not function as a poem or a novel does, for the sufficient reason that the minute you put an actor on a platform in front of an audience and have him do anything more than recite or "illustrate," you have introduced so many extra elements that a new "condition" has been created, not to speak of a new art.

To understand a play as a written text it is enough to be a sensitive reader. To know how to stage a play one must have some of this sensitivity, but one must know that a play on the stage is not composed of words but that the words of the play, for the stage director, are an indication of actions that have to be embodied and carried out through a medium as different from the page of a book as a man's body is different both from an anatomical chart and a poet's description of it.

For the stage director (and the audience as well—though it is unconscious of the mechanism of its activity), a play is a chain of actions which includes words but is not contained in them. When a man jumps with fright, falls on his knees and exclaims, "Oh, my Lord!" we think of the words he utters not as the essence of his behavior but as part of a whole circumstance much more complex than the words employed. No matter how explicit the playwright may be, the moment you transpose his text into terms of flesh and blood, to three-dimensional space, to canvas, wood, electricity, sound and movement, problems arise that are no longer simply questions of "understanding the play" in the library sense of the word.

It so happens that in the case of *Montserrat*, the play I am directing, an English text exists in the shape of an adaptation by Lillian Hellman which Kermit Bloomgarden and Gilbert Miller are to produce in New York this fall under Miss Hellman's direction. At the time I read Miss Hellman's adaptation, on which she has subsequently done much work, I felt it to be an honest attempt to capture the spirit of the original play and to render it as convincingly and as clearly as possible to an American audience. But after rereading it—though the changes from the French text were minor—I realized that were I to direct it, my whole conception of it, theatrically speaking, would have to be different from my director's conception of the literal translation that I am using for the Habimah production. In other words, though the story and characters in both texts appear identical, a slight difference in stress and purpose necessitates distinctly different scenery, casting and characterization for proper theatrical embodiment to convey how Hellman differs from Roblès, the play's French author.

Words are certainly important in the theatre, and the treatment of language is a vital matter for actors and directors. There can be no doubt that I am at a disadvantage in not knowing the language my actors at the Habimah speak (most of them understand English), but it excites me to discover that often I am not only able to detect misunderstandings of intention in an actor's approach to a particular scene or speech but, through a sense of the theatre, to spot even mistakes in particular readings that are part of a defective language sense in the actor.

In one respect my work on *Montserrat* here resembles that of similar work at home. It is rushed. With us in America, the director knows that he will be allowed only three and a half weeks for rehearsal with an additional two weeks of out-of-town tryout to pull his production into its final shape. For all but the simplest kinds of plays I believe this time schedule is inadequate. But this arrangement has been established in the Broadway theatre through economic necessity. In Israel a director may up to a point determine his own schedule. Unfortunately, commitments at home made it impossible for me to take more than four weeks to do *Montserrat*.

In New York the director has Equity's permission during the first three weeks to rehearse his company on the basis of an eight-hour day. I rarely rehearse more than six hours a day. The Habimah company, however, gives performances every night while it is rehearsing a new play, and considers even six hours a day excessive. The actors point out that in a semitropical climate a siesta is indispensable. Another difficulty is caused by the Habimah's tours outside Tel Aviv, such as its present five-day stay at a collective farm where it plays in an open-air theatre.

Casting on Broadway is done on an "open market" choice of types. With the Habimah you are limited to the forty members of the regular company. There are eleven major parts in *Montserrat*. Montserrat himself is a Spanish officer of perhaps thirty-five. While the part is not as brilliant as that of Montserrat's antagonist, Izquierdo, it is essential that the impassioned idealist who is Montserrat be completely convincing and sympathetic. The only younger actor in the Habimah who might conceivably have played Montserrat is a little stagy—an attribute which qualifies him for the role of the Actor in the play but not for Montserrat. I therefore chose an older actor who is not the physical type (the element of youth which is important had to be sacrificed) because he has sincerity and emotional power. There are nearly always such problems in casting a play from the ranks of a permanent company.

A scene designer was selected for me, since I had not had time to study the scene designers here as I had the actors of the company. I was a bit worried because my designer, like most of the Habimah designers, is a painter and given to overpigmentation of his sets. But my designer proved receptive and adaptable. Though *Montserrat* is a modern play both in language and in theme, it is cast in an essentially classic mold. The fact that Spanish and Indian motifs might influence the design owing to the play's South American locale is worth remembering but not of first importance. The play does not deal with an environment but with a spiritual question. An atmosphere has to be created which is bare, lofty and hot. The basic color ought to be a blue-gray white.

Though the action of the play is confined to the officers' quarters of the Spanish army of occupation—probably not an attractive place—it should have a certain beauty, richness and variety because a single setting of a realistically plain room is nothing an audience ought to be asked to look at for two hours. The problem was to make a visually interesting set that would be neither distracting nor irrelevantly handsome.

The French text calls for an entrance through which come the play's six hostages as well as another door that leads to the never-seen general's private quarters. When each of the hostages is led off to be executed—moments that punctuate the play's action like terrible heartbeats—his exit is presumably made through the same door he entered. I feel that this is rather undramatic and might become monotonous. We decided to make a room that suggested a building placed on an elevation. The hostages enter down steps that apparently connect with the exterior. The effect of this entrance is to make the room we see look like a vault built on a high place. On the other side of the stage a higher staircase leads up to the general's remote seclusion. Underneath this staircase is a wide, cavernous opening through which the hostages descend to the inner court where the executions take place. There is only a small table on the stage and a few stools; the only decoration is a rather fierce Aztec image which is part of the room's masonry, a Spanish madonna in gold where the general's staircase begins and in the stage-right corner, as if placed against the "fourth wall," we see part of a great ebony crucifix jutting out.

The Habimah company has been known to sit around a table reading for the first month of its rehearsals. We read *Montserrat* in this way for four days. (By following the French text and listening to the actors' Hebrew I was soon able to identify each speech as it was read.) The first four days of reading not only permitted us to become intimately acquainted with the text, but gave me the opportunity to begin talking about the meaning of the play.

Montserrat is a heroic tragedy on an issue that confronts every person—the choice of a way of life. In critical times—during a war, a rebellion, a national upheaval such as Israel itself, as well as Europe, recently endured—the choice is often not simply a matter of dying or escaping death but a matter of the manner in which one chooses to die. This becomes the touchstone as to the kind of life one has chosen to live. Many of us believe we have chosen a way of life because we find ourselves living in a certain way, but the test of a catastrophic moment may prove that our choice has been false or that we have not really understood the nature of our choice.

This may sound abstract, disassociated from the play's plot, but the theatrical significance of the discussion is that it leads the actors to understand a certain unity in the play which, as I conceive it, derives from the dilemma in which all the characters of the play, with hardly any exception, find themselves: they are all forced to question themselves as to their choice and to enact the passion of their failure, their justification or their delusion. Montserrat believes against cold reason that he must not only die but indirectly kill in order to fulfill his responsibility to people with whom he has come to identify himself. He must do these things without any guarantee of their ultimate usefulness. Pitted against him is Izquierdo, who is convinced only of the fraudulence and folly of man's nobler motives. His senses and mind—and he is highly endowed with both —tell him that all is vanity, except for the play of one's bare will to which one may enjoy yielding without necessarily putting any faith in it. Between these two poles, other kinds of personalities with their corresponding choices play out their tragic destiny with a significance that the author believes symbolically relevant to the world situation today.

Where does each actor fit into this scheme? What must be stressed in each case? Montserrat, the director tells the actor playing that part, is not a fanatic. He has only recently come to realize the necessity of his choice; he has no theoretical point of view. He represents no party or movement. His action arises out of spontaneous impulse and that is why he finds it painfully difficult to defend. The Actor (one of the hostages) is a person who has never considered the world except through his art; the world is both incomprehensible and terrifying to him. It is through his art at the end that he manages to raise himself to the level of a dignity greater than he ever possessed.

After these days of character analysis and a quest for the tone and mood of the play as a whole, each act is broken down into segments of small actions which dictate the movement, fragments of action ("business"), tempo of the play. This breaking down of the actions may be carried out in several ways. When one has enough time and an "ideal" cast, it is best to induce the discovery of the play's actions through a process of stimulation that makes the actors' discovery seem entirely their own. When one is pressed for time—as one generally is—one outlines the features of each scene both by a verbal statement of what the actor will be expected to do at each moment—to persuade, to threaten, to listen for an answer, as the case may be—and by the actual staging of these moments within the framework of the set in a manner that makes for a coherent whole.

There is one respect in which work with a theatre such as the Habimah is more gratifying than work at home. Because American stagehands are dependent on every job with each new production as a separate undertaking, their union will not allow directors to use any properties that are to be used in the actual production of the play unless a stage crew of at least three men is assigned to cover the rehearsal time. This entails an expense which the hardpressed producer usually cannot afford. Rehearsals are technically and artistically inadequate in New York for lack of helpful properties for the actors to work with. (Rehearsal facilities in New York are becoming increasingly dismal as well as impractical every season.) In the Habimah the stage crew is part of the theatre staff, and is employed on a yearly contract. The crew will build the needed steps for rehearsals if steps are called for—as in *Montserrat*—or procure the proper-sized table when a table is important in the staging of a play. The Habimah has both a good-sized rehearsal room for readings by the cast as well as another rehearsal room large enough to accommodate the framework of the actual set.

The majority of Habimah's actors are hard-working, extremely serious, admirably equipped with strong bodies, good voices, theatrical temperament. Their long years of experience with so many plays in constant performance have made them thoroughly professional in their ability to hold the stage and to give what is known as a reliable and even vivid account of themselves. But this experience has its negative side. The actors are both too dependent on their director and at the same time not altogether free to respond completely to him. This in turn makes the director rely too much on certain effects he knows he can easily achieve by employing the actors simply as formal instruments.

In a play like *Montserrat*, for example, there are both the values of strong melodrama—heroics, cruelties, tears of imploration—which can always be made effective by actors accustomed to similar material. But suppose the director would like Izquierdo to have lightness, wit and a philosophic tension because unless Izquierdo is something more than a "heavy" venting his spite on a group of victims the play becomes a conventional costume piece. There is a hostage in *Montserrat*, a man who makes terra-cotta jars in intricate and curious shapes. He is a sort of peon, worrying his way through life and depending on his exquisite workmanship to assist him in making a living for a large family. The pathos and horror of his dilemma as he is threatened with the firing squad for no crime whatever are easy for any good character actor to convey. But suppose the director wants to suggest through the character that he is also unsympathetic, like the equivalent of those artists whose miserable existence is devoid of any relationship to anything but their work and to the job of keeping their dependents alive through their work. For this sort of thing both director and actor have to seek extremely subtle means of characterization.

The Habimah actor will do only as much as his stage experience has taught him, and in this instance it is not enough. Most of the Habimah's directors have emphasized pictorial visualization, and the objectives in *Montserrat* are matters of the spirit and mind rather than of externals. For this the actor needs a director to stimulate his thinking and feeling, but the director in turn must have an actor who can find his own solution to the delicate task. If the actor cannot do so he will fall back on the clichés of suffering, and the director in distress will think up some clever piece of business, some bit of pantomime, some trick of makeup or costuming, which will do the job for him and the actor as well. But a play such as *Montserrat* eludes standard devices or shrewd artifices.

While in rehearsal I begin to realize both the shortcomings and the assets of American actors and those with whom I was working in Israel. The American actor doesn't always have the fullness of means that some of the actors in the Habimah have. The American actor's background and life seem to have made of him a rather meager individual. But if he is confronted with an imaginative or thoroughly aroused director who can make him realize aspects of a play or a part which had previously escaped his notice, the American actor will respond wonderfully and will eventually grow from this experience. The Habimah actor, too long trained in putting on masks that belong to the director's museums of imitations or inventions, is always waiting for the new director to hand him his particular brand of mask, which, if complete and striking enough in its details, the Habimah actor will wear with impressive confidence. But if the director believes, as I do, in serving to inspire qualities that rarely come into being unless the actor can draw them out of his deepest self, qualities which lie somewhere beyond the boundaries of his conscious technique, the director will find that in the Habimah he has chiefly a troupe of powerful performers who can cry, shout, roll their eyes, sing and generally act with greater virility than our ordinary good actor but who are, nevertheless, inadequate to some of the finer problems that serious modern drama involves.

The American actor needs greater contact with life and more employment in the theatre and with proper guidance he will display astonishing originality, as every season some new actor or actress—Uta Hagen, Barbara Bel Geddes, Marlon Brando, Julie Harris and others—demonstrates. The Habimah actor needs a more basic technique than he now possesses; not the technique of stage address which he has to a remarkable degree, but the technique of using his native emotional and physical endowments for less conventionally effective and hence more truly creative ends. Without either modesty or conceit I feel at this point that a company of American actors could get more out of me in four weeks because of their "inexperience" than the Habimah will because of their too long experience with a technique that was applied to them but which they never fully absorbed or understood. Strangely enough, what the Habimah most needs is what some of the company and most of the theatre world believes it already has—a thorough grounding in the Stanislavsky System.

17

Directing in a Foreign Language

[Tel Aviv, 1953]

THE QUESTION most frequently put to me about my work in Israel, where I am staging *Caesar and Cleopatra* in a Hebrew translation, is how a director can put on a play in a language of which he understands no more than a few words. It is not enough to reply that many members of the acting company understand English and that an interpreter translates the director's instructions for the benefit of those who don't. The question is neither an individual or a mechanical matter, but involves a fundamental problem of theatre art. How can the director know what is being said at each particular moment of the play, and how can he deal with the nuances of language and speech?

The question becomes particularly pertinent when we consider that Shaw's play is surely more important for its ideas and words than for its plot. Yet even in this case I find that because he was a playwright and not merely a pamphleteer, the problem of directing Shaw in a foreign language is not as difficult as it might seem.

This problem necessitates a discussion of the nature of stage direction. Structurally, a play is not a series of speeches but a series of actions. The first question a dramatist asks himself—and this is even truer of the director—is not "What do the characters say as they enter the stage?" but "What do they do, what do they intend to do, what do they succeed or fail to do in the course of the scene?"

Take, for instance, the first speech of Act I in *Caesar and Cleo-*

patra—one of the most literary, as distinguished from dramatic, in the whole play: "—Hail, Sphinx: salutation from Julius Caesar! I have wandered in many lands, seeking the lost regions from which my birth in this world has exiled me," and so on. It reads like the baldest sort of rhetorical exposition—a kind of exalted fanfare to set the tone and introduce the ethical motif underlying the horseplay which follows. Because the actor who plays Caesar usually thinks of his speech as a wordy introduction to the action proper, I have often found the speech not only rather boring but hard to "catch on to"—the dignified words, apparently abstract, lull the spectator into a sort of lofty lethargy.

But if we think of the speech as an action we realize that Caesar, curious, eager, energetic and always mentally alert, is studying the desert, seeking something in it to which he looks forward with the intense pleasure of a man who knows he confronts a great force with which he feels entirely capable of dealing. The riddle of life which the Sphinx represents is no profounder than Caesar's capacity to grasp it, for Caesar identifies himself with the Sphinx, sees it as something akin to himself.

Thus Caesar's speech is a self-explanation effected through an excited probing of the symbol of his own genius which he finds in the Sphinx. When Caesar asks, "Have I read your riddle, Sphinx?" he is glowing with an exultant pride and a (characteristically Shavian) sense of self-satisfaction. We almost anticipate, with Caesar, that the Sphinx will answer with a hearty "Ay!" and wink its approbation. Understood in this light, the scene is not only not oratorically static; it is all drama, that is, action.

Once the director discovers what happens in a scene, not in obvious physical terms alone but in terms of the basic human action, the spoken words become instruments of that action and can be heard as such. (Deaf people, it is said, are often much more acute judges of acting than people who hear the words of a play for their surface meaning only, because the deaf try to see what is actually going on. When actors do no more than repeat words—that is, recite their lines—nothing is going on, and the stage under these circumstances becomes dull and theatrically uncommunicative.) The director chooses actions for the actors to carry out as notes are set down for the musicians to play. If these notes are clear to the director, and the actors play them well, the director can hear as well as see them distinctly, no matter what language is being spoken. What I am describing is not a figurative truth but a literal one. As rehearsals progress and the play's actions become ever more sharply defined by the actors' performance of them, my ear becomes increasingly attuned to the exactly proper pitch which their execution requires—visually, acoustically and even phonetically. Thus, without knowing Hebrew I not only can follow practically every word but can detect wrong emphases and even peculiarities or blemishes of accent. In other words, through familiarity with the specific theatrical actions of the play I am able to tell what actors have good and what actors have bad enunciation!

The language of the theatre, in short, is not so much the language of the specific words being used as a kind of universal language of action; so that the correct use of speech in the theatre is not necessarily achieved by the person with the best diction but by the actor with the clearest dramatic intention.

18

On Audiences

[1952]

AUDIENCES at previews and at opening nights often strike me as participants in a contest. They behave as people who have either been lobbied or challenged. When they are pleased, they act wildly surprised, as if they hadn't expected this could happen; when they are displeased they are outraged, as if no one had the right to offer them anything less than the superb. Generally they sound as if the point of a theatrical performance were the opportunity it offered them to form an opinion of it. The impression made by these audiences is that of a group composed entirely of investors or those who had been asked to invest—and refused. In such an atmosphere the play always seems much better or much worse than it is. In fact, it does not look like a play at all but some sort of prize—fabulously costly or ignominious. The play under such circumstances loses its innocence and becomes a more or less perverse vanity.

All this occurred to me as I left the preview performance of George Tabori's *Flight into Egypt*. As the curtain fell someone nudged me to ask, "What do you think?" which chiefly meant would the play "go." I realized suddenly that I not only didn't care whether or not it would "go" (I wasn't an investor), but I hardly cared what I "thought" of it. While I watched it my mind registered certain objections—the uncertainly articulated theme confusing a plot line that might be considered trite; what was important to me was the fact that I was enjoying a certain relation to what I saw that could hardly be defined in terms of opinion. It was a sense of contact with a living thing—noticeably imperfect —hence an experience that was pleasurably ambivalent. Only through such contact could I *know* anything about the play.

The experience of the play—the sense of each actor on the stage, their struggle with the material which was suggestive and intrinsically absorbing—was being driven from me by something that was not essentially of the theatre. It is true that part of the pleasure of the theatre is the arena-spectacle aspect of it—the who-will-win excitement of a sports event. But what is most characteristic of the theatre experience is the joy of looking into a strange, imaginative world, and observing it with more concentration, love and curiosity than we do our workaday activities. This essential pleasure we are being increasingly robbed of by the cash-register or race-track climate which pervades our playhouses. The severity of our theatre audiences before the signal has been given them by press, rumor and gossip that it is all right for them to enjoy a play is not at all a critical severity. Criticism bespeaks awareness, sensitivity, discrimination as to the nature of one's feelings, above all and to begin with, an openness of the senses and the heart. Our critical severity is a commercial reflex: we don't want to be fooled—we must like or praise only what is accredited. That is why we have so much "criticism" in superlatives of praise or blame—both equally distorted. And the tendency of our official criticism is to imitate our practice rather than to correct it. Our practice consists in treating the theatre as a business rather than as free expression and play— even though the playgoer is not in the theatre for business.

In this way we are not only killing our pleasures in the theatre but ultimately the institution itself. When we measure the theatre mainly in terms of snobbish opinion or box-office profits (the two slowly coalesce) the need for theatre ultimately disappears: there are more rarefied pursuits to be snobbish about and entertainments that are more profitably popular. We often say that this state of affairs is due to the economics of the theatrical situation: I am sometimes inclined to believe that our approach to the theatre encourages, indeed necessitates, its ruinous economics.

The economics of our theatre and our distorted relationship to plays brings about a sharp limitation in the spiritual range of our drama. There are not enough "crazy" plays! Our theatre would be immensely enriched if there were more room allowed for angry, puzzling, impulsive, extravagant, ambitious, wrongheaded, adventurous expression. Our theatre is at once rigidly careful and ignorantly devoted to what is novel. "Old" plays—even plays most people haven't seen or read—are rarely profitable because "old" plays do not afford us the opportunity to guess or to be "curious" about them, the publicity value has run out of them—they are "known."

Because we are chiefly interested in the labels we put on plays— our orders of merit—we do not actually see or hear plays, as the sensitive person does a new acquaintance. Take the case of Christopher Fry. (For my part, I have altered my view of him on several different occasions and do not intend to come to a *conclusion* about him for, I hope, a long time.) Who, from hearing his plays described, knows anything about them? They are "poetry," "precious," "wordy," or "they give the theatre a breath of new life"; they "add a refreshing note." Fry is a "literary figure," a "real writer." But what exactly he represents, how his poetry differs from that of others, what it means, what its precise color and tone are, its significance as part of our time, how his fundamental attitude relates to our experience, belief and needs (what indeed it is)—is never stated. It is never stated because the answers to such questions do not relate to the entertainment business or to the need to give quick answers at curtain time.

19

"Scenery"

[1949]

SOME YEARS AGO Sidney Howard summed up his view of stage setting by saying, "My only rule is—get Jo Mielziner." Howard's rule has been scrupulously followed by many managers. Its chief virtue is that it confesses either ignorance of or indifference to the aesthetics of the question. Most reviewers are not so honest. It is obvious from their writing that even where they manifest good judgment on other aspects of theatrical production, their understanding of scene design is less than rudimentary. More alarming, however, is the fact that a great many theatre people are themselves vague on what they expect from the setting of a play—except that it ought to look "real" and be attractive.

The current exhibition of scene design and costume at the Metropolitan Museum of Art (*Behind American Footlights*) suggests a statement of principles in regard to the visual aspect of the theatre to supplement my "chats" on acting and direction. In the early years of this century stage settings had become a combination of academically Victorian landscape painting for exteriors with a kind of tawdry rococo for interiors. Costume plays were done with sets so heavily "historical" that Shakespeare's plays had to be drastically cut: the weight of the sets made quick changes impossible. The setting for the ordinary drawing room was a reflection of the gimcrack modishness of the nineteenth-century French theatre rather than any actual place. To give a production visual interest, producers spent money on some form of gaudy display or on special effects such as a train wreck, a great fire, a chariot race with real horses, as in *Quo Vadis?* or *The Whip.*

Later, David Belasco began to stress meticulous naturalism. A stage replica of a Childs restaurant became a famous setting; a scientist's library contained all the books that such a person might own; rainstorms and sunrises were reproduced with astounding verisimilitude.

Around 1915 Robert Edmond Jones, Lee Simonson and others became the pioneers of a new stagecraft inspired by European theorists and producers—Gordon Craig, Adolphe Appia, Max Reinhardt. The stage setting was now conceived mainly as a medium for the projection of a play's essential mood. Between 1919 and 1929 a whole new generation of scene designers who had learned from Jones' and Simonson's examples came to the fore. Reviewers began to devote considerable space to the work of these new men.

Decor, as it was then fondly called, has once more become a routine affair with tasteful and simplified decorativeness or naturalism as the norm. The reviewers' response to "scenery" has also become routine, with comments that range from the commonplace to the ridiculous. We even hear people affirm that plays might be better done without any "scenery" at all.

Here we have a glimpse of the basic misunderstanding. There is no such thing as a play without scenery. A bare stage is a setting; whatever is seen by an audience is part of the effect of the whole. The stage setting therefore is not primarily decoration, but a function of the play as an organism.

The director may wish his setting or, more accurately, stage arrangement to appear inconspicuous or he may wish it to play a prominent role in the evocation of a particular emotion in the audience, as in the case of the sensuous musical comedy. The director may feel that the place which the setting is supposed to represent must be photographically convincing in order for the play to be interesting, or he may believe that a mere indication of place is sufficient. In certain instances no actual place need be represented at all, and realistic detail is not only irrelevant but undesirable. The choice of setting depends on the director's artistic purpose, his creative idea in regard to the nature, quality or meaning of the entire production.

The director formulates the play's scenic or visual problem; the designer brings his talent to bear on its solution. Exhibitions of scenic art and most criticism of it tend to make scene design seem an adjunct of painting or decoration to be admired independent of its function in the theatre, where it is meant to serve the play as articulated by actors before an audience. That the set of *Summer and Smoke* looked pretty was of far less significance than that its playing space constricted freedom of movement. That the set of *The Big Knife*, which most reviewers thought handsome, looks like a Hollywood steak house is far less disturbing than that it makes it difficult for the audience to concentrate on the actors or to conceive of the play's action in any but the most literal terms—an approach detrimental to the play's most cogent elements. Even such brilliantly witty sets as those of *The Madwoman of Chaillot* may be criticized for a static quality that reduces their practicability for a kind of "magic" flexibility the play suggests.

It doesn't make good theatre sense for an audience to applaud a set for its abstract "beauty." A set is a utensil which cannot be judged until its worth is proved in practice by the whole course of the play's development on the stage.

20

Robert Edmond Jones

[1954]

OUR NEGLECT of the past may be one of the signs of our fundamental disrespect for the living. One of the truest artists the American theatre has known in our generation—Robert Edmond Jones—died on November 27th. Too little has been said on the occasion of his passing.

The American theatre can be said to have come of age in 1920 —with the emergence of Eugene O'Neill as our only full-fledged playwright. But O'Neill was part of a movement which began to manifest itself shortly before the First World War. The Washington Square Players (1914) and to a greater extent the Provincetown Players (1916), of which Jones was one of the guiding spirits, were early expressions of that movement. Arthur Hopkins was the first "commercial" manager to bring Jones' work to the Broadway audience.

Technically, Jones' great contribution was in the field of scene design. There is hardly a designer practicing today who has not learned something from his example. He taught "that a stage setting is not a background; it is an environment. Players act *in* a setting, not *against* it." (I quote from Jones' book *The Dramatic Imagination*.) "A good scene [set]," he said, "is not a picture. It is something seen, but it is something conveyed as well, a feeling, an evocation. . . . A stage setting has no independent life of its own. . . . In the absence of the actor it does not exist."

Jones never tried to reproduce reality or to embellish it. He reduced stage design to its barest elements of significant and usable detail for the purpose of creating an atmosphere in which the actor's and the playwright's dramatic plan might most amply fulfill themselves. The set for *The Iceman Cometh* was not a saloon; it was the place where O'Neill's meaning could be most appropriately voiced.

But Jones was more than a scene designer or a director. He was a teacher and a seer. He stood for something greater than his own talent, greater than the name he made, the "credits" that might be cited on his behalf. (Many of his imitators received more publicity and made themselves more prosperous.) When Jones said, "Keep in your souls some images of magnificence," he meant it, and his work showed it. And magnificence did not signify for him mere opulence or expensiveness. (Today, scenically speaking, we seem to put our faith in furniture.) He spoke of the theatre as a "house of dreams." He embodied the poetic attitude. He never sought to astonish or dazzle. He took technique for granted: he sought to use it in all humility for noble ends.

As a young man in the theatre I was often disturbed by his manner of address. He was not specific enough, not tough enough, or even sensuous enough. He did not appear to take sufficient account of the theatre's "kitchen"—its organizational, administrative, economic sides. But as I contemplate the theatre of today I can only ask myself, "And what have we practical ones, the hardheaded boys, the thick-skinned ones, made of the theatre?"

I do not believe there is less talent in our theatre today than in Jones' best days, but there is a less consistent devotion to it. Jones and his associates made the theatre count for more in our lives, gave it an excitement, a dignity, a force which are now greatly marred. It is not, to be sure, altogether our fault, but neither is it what is shrewd, clever, efficient in us that makes us, even to a slight degree, artists worthy of the theatre.

21

The House of Discord

[1956]

WE ALL KNOW the story: the American theatre has made great strides in the past twenty-five years. America boasts a fine corps of writers for the stage—men who choose relevant native themes and treat them with a degree of competence and honesty rare before 1920; no country commands a greater abundance of young acting talent; our directors compare favorably with and are perhaps superior to those in England and France; our designers are alert and even eager to experiment. We rejoice too that the past season has been the best in years. (Like the garment industry, we tend to speak of the theatre in terms of seasons.)

There is a certain amount of statistical worry. Whereas more than two hundred new productions were offered each theatrical year to New Yorkers in the mid-twenties, the average for the past five years has been about sixty. No matter: the theatre is in fine shape—*Tiger at the Gates, The Chalk Garden, The Lark, The Diary of Anne Frank* were or are all categorized more or less as hits. Off Broadway, we may see Pirandello, Strindberg, Shaw, Chekhov, Turgenev; and on the fringes of the town even smatterings of Shakespeare.

Yet is it not true that anyone who takes the theatre seriously either as business or art feels a certain uneasiness? We must dismiss for the moment the obvious fact that we have no state theatre, very few community theatres, no permanent companies, no repertory houses. All these lacks may be set down to the circumstances of our youth as a cultural entity. We have the talent, we have the wherewithal, many of us still have the desire to create the equivalent of the Comédie Française, the Moscow Art Theatre, the German state and city theatres, the Old Vic. Nevertheless, there is something amiss somewhere.

Consider: the theatre is a group art entirely dependent on teamwork, and our stage is run as an enterprise for individual benefits and private interests. Ends and means are at odds. Playwrights and actors today are very much more "earnest" than they were fifty years ago: they read more, do not blush to mention art in speaking of the theatre, go to symphony concerts and art galleries. They discuss Stanislavsky, have heard of Gordon Craig, know of Reinhardt's reputation, remember Stark Young and are willing to attend and work in several high-minded studios. Yet in practice—and their practice, through no fault of their own, is insufficient for the development of any thoroughgoing craftsmanship—their conduct is professionally more selfish than that of their hearty but barbarous stage forebears. The present organization of the stage makes everyone think of personal career, individual success, private glory. "The motives of our worst," Keats wrote of English political men in 1818, "are interest, and of our best, vanity." The theatre, filled today with soulful characters who are slightly revolted by the crassness of show business, is something like that.

No one is to blame. A few years ago everyone was sure that the source of our theatre troubles could be set down to stagehand unions. But now if we look steadily we see that everyone in the theatre—actors are probably the least culpable—behaves in his own way as the stagehands were accused of doing. "Brooklyn hates the Bronx," a 1935 Odets character said in his quaint way to describe the dog-eat-dog pattern of our competitive mode of life. The playwright today treats the actor, the producer, the director as instruments of his purpose—which is "to put the play over" and win him riches and renown. The playwright, who adores his actors when they are serving his aim and who looks upon his director as a kind of medicine man and magician when things are going well, is usually the first to declare (or to believe when it is whispered in venomous consolation) that the actors or the director or the producer or all three ruined his faultless play.

The fact that the actor or the director is something of a person too, that he is entitled to his own temperament problem and process of development, is at bottom something which makes the playwright quite impatient: he really wishes everyone connected with his play would perform like the fabled super-marionette Craig once conjured up.

Actors are equally eager to get ahead. Who will say they are wrong? But they will often suit themselves to the detriment of the play, their fellow actors and the audience. They frequently use their plays, directors, producers as stepping-stones to a fatter part in another play, to a movie or a television contract according to their convenience. If the play is less than a masterpiece—there is a tendency in the theatre to speak as if masterpieces were a dime a dozen—the actor will often patronize the playwright and not only suggest that he "made" the play but that he might be willing to put himself out for it—for example, keep playing his role somewhat longer than is personally convenient to him—if the play were really of a superior quality.

Toward the monied angels who supply the funds for production, playwrights and actors alike display indifference if not contempt. Someday I shall draw up a spirited brief in defense of the role and rights of backers, for no man of the theatre should allow himself to scorn the ground upon which he stands.

"Brigands are convinced of what?" Baudelaire once asked, and answered, "That they must succeed." There is a kind of sanctified racketeering in the theatre induced by the dream of success in money, in publicity, in glittering goods, in social esteem. With brigandage there is fear; from fear arises superstition. Instead of workmanlike understanding there are fetishes. There are box-office actors, name directors, hit houses, top producers, great playwrights. And who can be more frightened than one of our great playwrights?

When a great playwright (or a name director) hits a snag—and hasn't immediately left town to avoid unfortunate encounters—he is asked querulously, "What happened?" In vain does the playwright cite to himself the difficult careers of Ibsen, Chekhov, Shaw, not to mention artists in other media; in vain does he recall that one does not mount the ladder of achievement in an even and regular progression of steps. He feels, or is made to feel, that he is slipping, that he may be finished, that he may have been only a flash in the pan, that people no longer believe in him and that there may even be some awkwardness about finding money for his next play. He is no longer sure that he can or should write another play. He speaks wistfully of writing novels, of going into movies or television, or of providing the "book" for a musical.

The director, himself in the midst of the latent tug-of-war over which he is supposed to exercise a paternal and calming influence, often succeeds in inspiring a sense of creative togetherness, but this only endures while he remains in active charge—during the rehearsal period and for the first month after the opening. Since we have no permanent companies to which the director can maintain a close alliance, many a director—like everyone else—becomes a "shopper" in the theatre. Shortly after the play opens, the director becomes involved in a new deal, and tends to allow the reins of his authority to slacken. If he is a "name" director, he becomes wary of undertaking any play which seems too risky, for in case of failure he will either be tasked with poor judgment in scripts or with having been somehow shaky in his technique. It is not at all uncommon for a director to be congratulated on his superb artistry by producer, playwright and the cast immediately before the opening, and to have all of these begin to suspect his soundness the moment the press and public reactions indicate coldness. The director, then, is frequently transformed into a cagey and nervous gambler whose judgment of scripts grows warped.

Into this absurd nightmare enters the "artist's representative," the agent. Many playwrights and actors of standing today will heed their agent—perhaps because his motive is always simon-pure and not sullied with insubstantial artistic notions—beyond the advice of the most knowledgeable fellow craftsman. For many theatre people the agent furnishes the only true pattern of wisdom—when it is not the psychoanalyst.

The historian will see in this barely exaggerated account merely another symptom of our insane social structure. Surely economics has a great deal to do with the atmosphere I have described, since the same situation does not obtain to the same degree in England, France, Germany. Surely our press and our audiences by their distorted point of view contribute to the chaos, but they are more a reflection of the situation than a cause.

I was brought up in a very old-fashioned way to believe that the serious craftsman ought to be as much a leader as a follower, that there were a certain science and discipline in every craft, that these entailed a moral capacity to master one's immediate selfish interest on behalf of one's greater interest—the objective task one has set oneself. Since in the theatre that task was by definition collective, one had to view oneself and one's work in relation to the general aim.

Such an attitude is dictated by self-respect and knowledge of one's business. If one's business is simply to aggrandize oneself through success (whether it be wealth or "one's name in the papers"), it doesn't really matter much, as the aforementioned French poet pointed out, how one accomplishes it. But if one is in the theatre for the theatre's purpose, one must hold fast to its essential tenets—otherwise, even talent becomes a lethal weapon. I have never had anything but regard for the gentlemen known generically as "the Shuberts" (our stage's real estate and financial interests), but it is difficult for me not to mix some pity and contempt with my regard for those accomplished, sensitive and famous artists of the theatre who as they grow more secure in their acclaim employ it not as a responsibility and as a challenge, but as a bastion of self-indulgence —against everyone else in the theatre. Above all, it is painful to see the sophistication and superior instruction recently acquired in our best schools and studios employed to rationalize and disguise the wolfish acquisitiveness of our shivering souls.

We used to say: we must not be so mortally afraid of being comparatively poor, of setbacks, of criticism, of relative obscurity. The old moralities of the theatre which my generation and the younger now can repeat by rote are living and practical things—and are meant to be applied without a millennium or a mythical Moscow Art Theatre—against all the odds of pressures and the old Adam— right now, right here if we are ever to have something other than a seasonal theatre.

22

Edward Albee

[1960]

The Zoo Story and Beckett's Krapp's Last Tape

SAMUEL BECKETT's *Krapp's Last Tape* and Edward Albee's *The Zoo Story* have this in common: both are studies in loneliness. Beckett's play is a sort of marginal sketch in the body of his more ambitious work; Albee's play is the introduction to what could prove to be an important talent on the American stage.

Some may consider it ironic that, whereas Beckett's far more accomplished plays—*Waiting for Godot* and *Endgame*—were generally received here with skepticism, indifference or hostility, this new, rather slight piece has been greeted with considerable sympathy. One reason for this is that Beckett's reputation and the respect shown him by many European and several American critics have grown. It is no longer easy to shrug him off. A more immediate reason for the cordiality toward *Krapp's Last Tape* is that a thread of sentimentality runs through its dismal fabric. The play's "story," moreover, is simple, realistic, unelusive.

A solitary old man sits in abject poverty doing nothing but feeding himself bananas that are hoarded in drawers like precious possessions; periodically he washes the fruit down with deep draughts of alcohol. This old man was once an author. He has among the few miserable relics of his past some copies of a book he wrote, a book which sold eighteen copies at the trade rate. "Getting popular!" he mutters.

In the half-light the old man listens to tapes upon which he once recorded events now long past. One of these tapes is a memory of love—set down when he was thirty-nine—an apparently sincere love which for some unexplained reason never resolved itself into anything beyond its fugitive existence. The old man, absorbed and yet impatient with himself, listens to the tape, curses and mocks himself —we are not certain why—broods, possibly regrets, suppresses a sob and subsides into what is probably an endless silence.

The atmosphere of the play is grotesque, deeply bitter and yet tender. Beckett is here with something of his sardonic mutism, his mastery of concentrated dramatic image, the determination to wring the neck of his passion. The play is well-acted by a young newcomer from Canada, Donald Davis.

The Zoo Story is flawed by improbabilities and perhaps needless notes to provoke, shock or outrage—comic and horrifying by turn. Yet the play gives ample evidence of genuine feeling and an intimate knowledge of certain aspects of the contemporary scene, especially of our metropolitan area. If there were not some danger of being taken too superficially, I should say that in *The Zoo Story* certain tragic and crucial factors which have contributed to produce the "beat" generation have been brilliantly dramatized.

The young man in *The Zoo Story*, who intrudes on a respectable and modest citizen sitting on a Central Park bench, is isolated in his poverty, his self-educated ignorance, his lack of background or roots, his total estrangement from society. He has no connection with anybody, but he seeks it—in vain. When he succeeds in approaching an animal or a person, it is always through a barrier of mistrust and in a tension of disgust, fear, despair. When he breaks out of the emotional insulation of his life, it is only by a violent intrusion into the complacent quiet of the mediocre citizen on the park bench; and that unoffending bystander is then forced into effecting the mad young man's suicide. To put it another way: the derelict finally achieves a consummation of connection only through death at the unwitting and horrified hands of society's "average" representative.

This story is conveyed with rude humor—very New York—a kind of squalid eloquence and a keen intuition of the humanity in people who live among us in unnoticed or shunned wretchedness. We come not only to know the pathetic and arresting central figure as well as the astonished stranger he "victimizes," but through them both we also meet the unseen but still vivid characters of a lady janitor, a Negro homosexual neighbor, a dog and other denizens in the vicinity of both the West and East Seventies of Manhattan.

The Zoo Story interested me more than any other new American play thus far this season. I hope its author has the stuff to cope with the various impediments that usually face our promising dramatists.

The play is perfectly cast. George Maharis and William Daniels give admirable performances. Maharis, as the play's interlocutor, is truthful as well as intense. His acting is both economical and gripping. He seems possessed by all the hurts, resentment and compressed hysteria of the bewildered youth we hear so much about, but who is rarely made this real in newspaper reports, editorials, sermons or fictions.

[1961]

The American Dream

The importance of *The American Dream* is that it's Edward Albee's. A young playwright of genuine talent—that is, one who is not merely clever—is rare nowadays. (I hope I am wrong about this scarcity.) So everything that Albee writes should be given special attention. This should not be adulatory: it is dangerous to make "stars" of playwrights while they are in the process of growth; nor should our attention consist of slaughtering the playwright's second or third play in behalf of the hallowed first one.

The American Dream is a one-act abstract vaudeville sketch. It purports to typify the well-to-do American middle-class home in this age of automation and mechanized men and women. The excellent little set is hung with frames without pictures; the room itself has expensive furniture hideously gilded, blank prefabricated walls and above them all the Stars and Stripes—in short, no intimacy, no personality, no vibrations. Daddy, who earns the money, has had part of his gut removed and of sex there is no question. The family is childless. Grandma, who has a remnant of spunk left in her dry bones, is at once a protected and abandoned bit of household crockery—a sort of skeleton in the closet. She says all the right things at the wrong time and the wrong things at the right time. No one listens to anyone else or cares about what is said when they do listen. There is total spiritual, intellectual stasis. The child—called a "bumble" rather than a baby—once adopted by this juiceless family was smashed and dismembered by them.

Into this vacuum enters the "American dream" in the person of a tall, good-looking boy, a perfect juvenile specimen. He has no feelings, no active desires, no real ambition. Passively waiting, he is a prettily furbished shell. He is adopted by Mommy and Daddy—to undergo the same treatment as the earlier "bumble."

The play is funny and horrid, a poker-faced grotesque. It reminds one of Ionesco's one-act plays *The Bald Soprano* and *Jack,* although the Frenchman's plays are freer in their extravagance and more devastating. There is no harm in a young writer's being influenced—it is inevitable; besides, one chooses one's influence in the direction of one's sympathies. But there is a certain literalness in *The American Dream*—even at moments a flatness of writing—which makes me suspect that the French influence on Albee (Genet, Beckett, Ionesco and others) is not altogether helpful.

I mean by this that Albee's talent—as with most Americans—lies closer to realism than perhaps he knows. *The Zoo Story* had its "symbolic" side too and was also terrifyingly humorous—as well as obliquely tender—but what abstraction there was in it arose from true observation of specific people in specific environments.

Abstraction becomes decoration when it loses touch with its roots in concrete individual experience; and the word "decoration" is just as appropriate where the abstraction is satirically fierce as where it is beguiling. So while I appreciate the comment and the bitter barbs which *The American Dream* contains, I would caution the author to stick closer to the facts of life so that his plays may remain humanly and socially relevant. For it is as easy to make a stereotype from a critical and rebellious abstraction as from a conformist one.

The cast of *The American Dream* is well chosen and ably directed by Alan Schneider.

[1961]

The Death of Bessie Smith

The Death of Bessie Smith is a notably sharp piece of dramatic writing.

Bessie Smith, a famous Negro blues singer of the twenties and thirties, bled to death after a car accident in Memphis, Tennessee, because she was denied medical assistance in all of the city's white hospitals. Albee has dramatized the incident in an unusual manner. Instead of emphasizing the shameful shock of the episode he helps us understand its human sources.

One never sees Bessie. The play is focused on a nurse who is a receptionist in one of the Memphis hospitals. Her life is a tissue of fear, frustration and sadistic compensations. She loathes her semi-invalid father, whose family was once (long ago) imperiously prosperous in Dixie fashion. He is an idle, shriveled, mean man—disfigured by impotent venom and the ludicrous grimaces of racist superiority. In her own way the nurse continues the paternal pattern, for though her job is ill-paid and almost menial, she cracks the whip of her "position" over a colored orderly at the hospital, a young fellow with pretensions to self-betterment. She also teases an intern at the hospital who wants her—even offers to marry her—teases him with calculated provocation without satisfying her own or his needs. In addition, she warns him against any aspirations beyond the bounds of their town's horizon. From her inner constriction and the spite that this begets she mocks and terrorizes the two men; and she does this because she is too weak to fight her way out of the impasse of her life. She insists on accepting the constraints the community imposes. Her dominance over the men embodies the environment's stranglehold on all of them. But this power maims her as well as her victims; underneath the grinning grimness of her will she is consumed by self-abomination. It must be clear from all of this that the nurse and the others, even the death of Bessie Smith herself, are peripheral symbols pointing to a tragedy wider than that of one county or segment of our society.

The writing of the play is biting, tensely risible, euphonious—making for heightened speech which approaches stylization. It marks Albee once again as a new American playwright from whom much is to be expected.

The most aptly cast actor in the production is Harold Scott as the orderly, but Rae Allen and the others who are of a softer natural disposition play with professional authority and intelligence, though they are directed a little too "psychologically" for a play in which psychology is implicit in the incisive slashes of the dramatist's "drawing" rather than in an internal probing of mental processes. But perhaps this is only a refined quibble: the production is eminently proficient.

[1962]

Who's Afraid of Virginia Woolf?

Edward Albee's *Who's Afraid of Virginia Woolf?* is packed with talent. Its significance extends beyond the moment. In its faults as well as in its merits it deserves our close attention.

It has four characters: two couples. There is hardly a plot, little so-called "action," but it moves—or rather whirls—on its own special axis. At first it seems to be a play about marital relations; as it proceeds one realizes that it aims to encompass much more. The author wants to "tell all," to say everything.

The middle-aged wife, Martha, torments her somewhat younger husband because he has failed to live up to her expectations. Her father, whom she worships, is president of a small college. Her husband might have become the head of the history department and ultimately perhaps her father's heir. But husband George is a nonconformist. He has gone no further than associate professor, which makes him a flop. She demeans him in every possible way. George hits back, and the play is structured on this mutually sadistic basis. The first cause of their conflict is the man's "business" (or career) failure.

Because they are both attracted to what may be vibrant in each other, theirs is a love–hate dance of death which they enact in typical American fashion by fun and games swamped in a sauce of strong drink. They bubble and fester with poisonous quips.

The first time we meet them they are about to entertain a new biology instructor who, at twenty-eight, has just been introduced to the academic rat race. The new instructor is a rather ordinary fellow with a forever effaced wife. We learn that he married her for her money and because of what turned out to be "hysterical pregnancy." The truth is that she is afraid of bearing a child though she wants one. Her husband treats her with conventional regard (a sort of reflexive tenderness) while he contemplates widespread adultery for gratification and advancement in college circles. George scorns his young colleague for being "functional" in his behavior, his ambition, his attitudes.

So it goes: we are in the midst of inanity, jokes and insidious mayhem. Martha rationalizes her cruelty to George on the ground that he masochistically enjoys her beatings.

Everyone is fundamentally impotent, despite persistent "sexualizing." The younger wife is constantly throwing up through gutless fear. Her light-headedness is a flight from reality. The older couple has invented a son because of an unaccountable sterility. They quarrel over the nature of the imaginary son because each pictures him as a foil against the other. There is also a hint that as a boy George at different times accidentally killed both his father and mother. Is this so? Illusion is real; "reality" may only be symbolic—either a wish or a specter of anxiety. It does not matter: these people, the author implies, represent our environment; indeed, they may even represent Western civilization!

The inferno is made very funny. The audience at any rate laughs long and loud—partly because the writing is sharp with surprise, partly because an element of recognition is involved: in laughter it hides from itself while obliquely acknowledging its resemblance to the couples on the stage. When the play turns earnestly savage or pathetic the audience feels either shattered or embarrassed—shattered because it can no longer evade the play's expression of the audience's afflictions, sins and guilts; embarrassed because there is something in the play—particularly toward the end—that is unbelievable, soft without cause. At its best, the play is comedy.

Albee is prodigiously shrewd and skillful. His dialogue is superbly virile and pliant; it also *sounds*. It is not "realistic" dialogue but a highly literate and full-bodied distillation of common American speech. Still better, Albee knows how to keep his audience almost continuously interested (despite the play's inordinate length). He can also ring changes on his theme, so that the play rarely seems static. Albee is a master craftsman.

Strangely enough, though there is no question of his sincerity, it is Albee's skill which at this point most troubles me. It is as if his already practiced hand had learned too soon to make an artful package of venom. For the overriding passion of the play is venomous. There is no reason why anger should not be dramatized. I do not object to Albee's being "morbid," for as the conspicuously healthy William James once said, "morbid-mindedness ranges over a wider scale of experience than healthy-mindedness." What I do object to in his play is that its disease has become something of a brilliant formula, as slick and automatic as a happy entertainment for the trade. The right to pessimism has to be earned within the artistic terms one sets up; the pessimism and rage of *Who's Afraid of Virginia Woolf?* are immature. Immaturity coupled with a commanding deftness is dangerous.

What justifies this criticism? The characters have no life (or texture) apart from the immediate virulence of their confined action or speech. George is intended to represent the humanist principle in the play. But what does he concretely want? What traits, aside from his cursing the life he leads, does he have? Almost none. Martha and George, we are told, love each other after all. How? That she cannot bear being loved is a psychological aside in the play, but how is her love for anything, except for her "father fixation" and some sexual dependence on George, actually embodied? What interests—even petty—do they have or share? Vividly as each personage is drawn, they all nevertheless remain flat—caricatures rather than people. Each stroke of dazzling color is superimposed on another, but no further substance accumulates. We do not actually identify with anyone except editorially. Even the nonnaturalistic figures of Beckett's plays have more extension and therefore more stature and meaning. The characters in Albee's *The Zoo Story* and *Bessie Smith* are more particularized.

If we see Albee, as I do, as an emerging artist, young in the sense of a seriously prolonged career, the play marks an auspicious beginning and, despite its success, not an end. In our depleted theatre it has real importance because Albee desperately wishes to cry out— manifest—his life. The end of his play—which seeks to introduce "hope" by suggesting that if his people should rid themselves of illusion (more exactly, falsity) they might achieve ripeness—is unconvincing in view of what has preceded it. Still, this ending is a gesture, one that indicates Albee's will to break through the agonizing narrowness of the play's compass.

Albee knows all he needs to know about play-making; he has still to learn something other than rejection and more than tearfulness. His play should be seen by everyone interested in our world at home, for as Albee's George says, "I can admire things I don't admire."

The production—under Alan Schneider's painstaking direction— is excellent, as is the cast. Uta Hagen, with her robust and sensuously potent élan, her fierce will to expression and histrionic facility, gives as Martha her most vital performance since her appearance as Blanche in *A Streetcar Named Desire*. She is an actress who should always be before us. George Grizzard is perfect in conveying the normal amusements and jitters of the mediocre man. Melinda Dillon as his debilitated spouse is appallingly as well as hilariously effective, and though I have some difficultly in accepting Arthur Hill, in the role of Martha's husband, as a tortured and malicious personality he does very well with a taxing part.

A final note: though I believe the play to be a minor work within the prospect of Albee's further development, it must for some time occupy a major position in our scene. It will therefore be done many times in different productions in many places, including Europe. Though I do not know how it is to be effected, I feel that a less naturalistic production might be envisaged. *Who's Afraid of Virgina Woolf?* verges on a certain expressionism, and a production with a touch of that sort of poetry, something not so furiously insistent on the "honesty" of the materials, might give the play some of the qualities I feel it now lacks; it might alleviate the impression of, in the author's pithy phrase, "an ugly talent."

Tiny Alice

When Edward Albee's *American Dream* was first produced I presumed to "advise" him. Though the play was specifically American in its humor, I suggested that he eschew the abstract. After the deserved success of *Who's Afraid of Virginia Woolf?*, Albee in his latest play, *Tiny Alice*, has relapsed into abstraction.

Thirty-seven in March, Albee is still the best of our younger playwrights. Since Shaw was forty-five when Max Beerbohm chose to speak of him as "young," I do not feel it improper to refer to Albee as young and to persist in "advice." The kindest way to view *Tiny Alice* is as an honorable experiment. To be candid, the play struck me as the sort of thing a highly endowed college student might write by way of offering us a Faustian drama.

Its locale is generalized (neither England nor America), its action unreal, its speech a mixture of literate vernacular and stilted literacy. The settings (designed by William Ritman) are expensively and toweringly monumental, with a touch of the vulgarly chic. Except for the first scene, they represent the habitat of "the richest woman of the world."

I shall not discuss the plot because that might lead you to believe that I complain of its being too extravagantly symbolic or too obscure. The significance of certain details may elude one—and no harm done—but the play's intention is clear enough. It tells us that the pure person in our world is betrayed by all parties. The Church is venal, the "capitalist" heartlessly base, the "proletarian" cynical and, for all the good he may do, powerless and subservient. There remains Woman: enticing mother image and never-perfectly-to-be-possessed mate. (She may also embody the universal "Establishment.") The crisis in the pure man's life arises when, having found himself uncertain of his faith, he commits himself to a home for the mentally disturbed. Suffering from the need for tenderness and from religious anguish, he dwells in this womb of conscience to emerge after six years as a lay brother determined above all "to serve." But those who rule us—Church, the Economic Forces and Woman—bid him accept the world as it is. Being pure he cannot do so. Isolated and bereft of every hope, he must die—murdered.*

Like Picasso, who said that his pictures do not have to be "understood," only seen and felt, Albee has suggested that people need not puzzle over his symbols; they have only to relax enough to be affected by them. There is this difference, however: Picasso paintings, whatever their "meaning," are fascinating on the surface. So too are Beckett's plays, Genet's and the best of Pinter's. Their images hold us; their complexities are compact with material in which we sense substantial value even when we are unable to name the exact nature of their composition. In art, Braque once observed, "It is not the ultimate goal which is interesting but the means by which we arrive there."

The surface or fabric of *Tiny Alice* is specious. The first scene (between "capitalist" and Cardinal) has some of the comic venom of *Virginia Woolf* but—except for those exhilarated by insults aimed at the clergy—it is by no means as apt. There is a certain cunning of suspense in the play, but the clearer it becomes the less convincing it seems. Its artistic method is too generalized to wound or even to touch us. Its pathos is weak, its scorn jejune, its diction lacking in most of its author's personal flair.

I do not ask Albee to stick to realism. *The Zoo Story* and *The Death of Bessie Smith* are not, strictly speaking, realistic plays—nor, in fact, does *Virginia Woolf* belong in that category. But in those plays Albee's dialogue had a true eloquence, a refreshingly dry and agile muscularity because it issued from the concrete. Their vocabulary was grounded in a life Albee had intimately experienced in his environment and in his senses. In *Tiny Alice* all his artful devices leave one impassive. The only moment my interest was piqued, I confess, was in the ambiguously sexual scene when the pure one succumbs to the millionairess' naked body.

Even though the play's terms rather than its meaning are what disconcert me, something more should be said about the content. Though Albee's spirit and gifts are entirely distinct from those of such recent masters of European drama as Beckett and Genet (each of whom in turn is different from the other), there is

---

* Mr. Albee disagrees with this interpretation. The play, he maintains, is about the confusion of illusion with reality.

evidence of a similar "defeatist" strain. I do not share their view of life, but I recognize the aesthetic potency of Beckett's and Genet's work. They speak with genuine originality. They are, moreover, voices revealing of our day. That is their justification and their merit. (It is also to be noted once again that their work, though divorced from realism, is composed of indelibly memorable theatre metaphors.)

We often speak of their work as "negative" or "pessimistic." In a way, however, the pessimism of *Tiny Alice* has an even greater coherence, a more thoroughgoing finality than that of the Europeans. But though it is always easier to adduce evidence for a black view of life, that is, to prove the world an intolerably damned place, than to urge us in any contrary sense, one soon discovers that the conclusions of pessimism have only a minor value. For logic and proof bear little relation to the processes and conduct of reality. The more tightly one argues the futility of our life's struggle, the more futile the point becomes. It is much too simple. Thus the importance of *Tiny Alice* diminishes as our understanding of it increases.

The play is directed by Alan Schneider, and has been cast with such admirable actors as John Gielgud, Irene Worth, William Hutt, Eric Berry and John Heffernan.

23

Samuel Beckett

[1961]

Happy Days

SAMUEL BECKETT'S *Happy Days* is a poem for the stage—a poem of despair and forbearance. It is to be seen and suffered. It is painfully lucid. But because it is a work of art, its lucidity is manifold in meaning.

There are only two characters in the play: a woman of fifty and her husband of sixty. We discover the woman sunk up to her waist in a mound of scorched grass. Her husband lives out of sight behind her in his own hole in the ground. At rare moments he emerges to read an old newspaper, a recurrent item of which he mumbles: "Wanted bright boy." At the close of the play he crawls in full evening dress toward his wife; we do not know whether he has come to visit her in "the old style"—a phrase which runs through the play like a refrain—to pay tribute to her long years of married isolation, or to put her (or himself) out of misery. They look at each other in terrible silence: she with a quizzical look of amused compassion and contempt, he with a heartrending stare of impotence, regret, bafflement. Her name is Winnie, his Willie—and one guesses that either one might have been the other, by which I mean that both add up to the idea of Mankind.

What has their life been? A kind of blank; literally, stasis. They are sustained by nothing except the ground in which they are stuck. (In Act 2 the woman has sunk to her neck in the earth. "Oh earth you old extinguisher," she cries, reminding me somehow of Joyce.) Man and wife have no beliefs, faith, passion, aim or great appetite.

Winnie's life is a matter of toilet preparations and taking patent medicines, the names of which she does not understand, the purpose of which is unclear. She is nevertheless an irrepressible optimist. (The play might well have been called *The Optimist.*) For as she wakes to the bell which heralds the morning, she exclaims, "Another heavenly day." She looks on the bright side of everything. She dimly remembers and usually misquotes the consoling and "unforgettable" lines of old-time classics. She enjoys listening to a music box tinkling "The Merry Widow" waltz (the "old style" again), and at the very end of the play she hums the same song, with its wistful-gay plea for love. The bag in which she keeps all her treasured possessions contains, along with toothbrush, comb, scent and a little mirror, a revolver—just in case—but she never avails herself of its service.

Her husband sleeps most of the time: "marvelous gift that," she reflects. She has "no pain, hardly any pain—great thing that." When she learns the meaning of a single word ("hog"), she observes cheerily, "Hardly a day without addition to one's knowledge." A hearty soul, she asserts, "That is what I find so wonderful, that not a day goes by . . . without some blessing—in disguise."

Most of the time she takes comfort in the thought "That is what I find so wonderful . . . the way man adapts himself." Only once does she break, crying out in ringing anguish, "No, something must happen in the world, some change." But nothing does change—except that night follows day. "One can do nothing." One prays the old prayers. One still clings to the hope that there may be a meaning to life. "Someone is looking at me still. Caring for me still." One senses one's aliveness because one does not always speak to oneself. The "other" therefore exists. And for all the bleakness and waste there is the inextinguishable sense that "There always remains something. Of Everything."

The most pitiable thing in the play is its pity. Behind the irony of its grimace there is a sort of repressed tenderness. It is this tenderness that makes Beckett's defenders (he needs no defense) deny that his message is all negation. To wait and suffer, perhaps to hope and pray in the empty world, is to evince a trait of nobility, even of heroism. Beckett, it is suggested, is a religious playwright. And it is true that many religious teachers have spoken in accents similar to his.

I am inclined to believe that this line of defense does Beckett a certain disservice. It is precisely through his particular kind of pessimism that Beckett has made his special contribution—indispensable for an understanding of our time. We require solace and remedies hereafter (I do not refer to the "next world"), but at present it is right, just, proper, necessary and helpful that brave men cry bloody murder.

Beckett is the poet of a morally stagnant society. In this society fear, dismay and a sort of a stunned absentmindedness prevail in the dark of our consciousness, while a flashy, noisy, bumptious thickheaded complacency flourishes in the open. Nearly all the finer artists of our day are saying this (very few are capable of saying more than this convincingly), and in the theatre Beckett's voice has been the sharpest, the most penetrating, the most symbolic.

Do I believe that life is what Beckett says it ("perhaps") is or seems to be? Not at all. Even the bag which holds all that remains of Winnie's existence contains much more than Beckett has put there. Do I prefer Beckett's black report to Chekhov's (or even Strindberg's) sorrow? Certainly not. The agony of the old plays was dense with human experience. Why then does Beckett write as he does? Apart from the facts of individuality and personal environment, the answer may possibly be found in this notation in Paul Klee's diary of 1915: "The more horrifying this world proves (as it is these days), the more art becomes abstract."

Must we accept Beckett wholly? No; his work represents an impasse. But we must understand him. For he feels strongly and writes unerringly. Despite their bareness, his plays are not barren, and if the stage is to be a true chronicle of the times, they belong in the theatre. *Happy Days* grows on one.

Ruth White's performance is extraordinary in its concentration, variety, nuance and endurance. (The play is almost a monologue and almost an hour and a half long.) The director—Alan Schneider—has helped her model the great mass of the verbal material so that it rises to poignancy instead of degenerating to monotony.

[December 7, 1970]

There is no writer whose mood and "message" is more alien to me than Samuel Beckett; we are poles apart. Yet I honor him as an insidiously eloquent artist. The evening at the Public Theater— Jack MacGowran's one-man show—consists of excerpts from several of his novels (*Molloy, Watt,* etc.) his plays (*Waiting for Godot, Krapp's Last Tape, Endgame*) and other prose and poems. They are shaped to a heartrending unity, with moments of convulsing hilarity sharpening the point of its unhappiness. What a chill has fallen upon our Western world!

Out of his agony Beckett has wrought unforgettable music. His desolate song is truly a miracle. There were such writers, monks and other men of the cloth, in the early years of the Christian era. Theirs was a profoundly religious art and so too, I have come to believe, is that of Beckett, the great blasphemer. It is in the intensity of his apparent nonfaith, in his awful imprecations, in his wretchedness at not being able to come upon the absolute he seeks, in his craving for that absolute, that one recognizes the reality of his religion.

Joyce has no doubt influenced Beckett. "Words have been my only love," the younger of the two says, and he further asserts that he has perhaps suffered from "want of love." We are not sure whether he refers to his own inability to love or to love not vouch- safed him by others. Joyce too seemed to have been the victim of a similar disaffection, but there was great sensuousness in him, a physical robustness, so that he was able to overcome the gap between himself and others. More thin-skinned, Beckett's solitude is total. Joyce wrote of a shattered world re-creating itself; Beckett is a poet of the world's end.

He will not be consoled. He is often funny, but his comedy has exactly the same nihilistic significance as his lament. There is a long passage in which one of his characters describes the dilemma of sucking at sixteen pebbles and wishing to assure himself that when sucking at one he is not repeating the "taste" of another.

This goes on to maniacal lengths. Then he admits: "But deep down I didn't give a tinker's curse for it was all the same to me whether I sucked a different stone each time or always the same stone. . . . I didn't care a fiddler's damn about being without, when they were all gone they would be all gone." And everything else is like that.

The surge of passion in *Krapp's Last Tape* is dissipated by the man's sense of its futility. His mind, he says, "is always on the alert against itself." There is always a negation immediately after he has confessed to an attachment. "Great love in my heart too for all things still and rooted, bushes, boulders and the like . . . and the flowers of the field, not for the world when in my right senses would I ever touch one, to pluck it. Whereas a bird now, or a butterfly . . . no mercy! Not that I'd go out of my way to get at them. . . . Nor will I go out of my way to avoid such things, when avoidable, no, I simply will not go out of my way, *though I have never in my life been on my way anywhere, but simply on my way.*"

Why do I cherish Beckett when he feels this way? Because he is aware of the unfathomable mystery of things, their never to be discovered ultimacy, the ineffable wonder of existence. Though others extol and cling to it, even exult in it, for the very reasons that he finds to bemoan it, his consciousness of its rational or logical nullity is still a closeness to it, an entire immersion in what he appears to exclude, to turn away from. His rejection of life is something other than that. It is a vast, insatiable hunger, a yearning, an immense ache and regret which is at the core of living. This is also a way—negative and tragic—of celebrating life. Is there not something quintessentially Irish in it?

Jack MacGowran, standing solitary in a ragged, black and soiled long coat, observing his shadow on the ground, haggard with puzzlement, forms an indelible figure. He is round-shouldered, slightly bowed, with dragging gait. Behind and all around him is a gray vacancy which faintly suggests sun and clouds in a distant whirlwind: it is one of Ming Cho Lee's simplest and best designs, a dun background which promises the possibility of varicolored mutation.

The actor's long, emaciated face, at once blank and shrewd with cutting glance, at times becomes gentle, kind, almost smiling. The composition made me imagine a bone washed up on an immense strand without identifiable horizon, a bone which attests to a life that may once have been moved by a will reaching toward objects of desire. MacGowran's voice is dry yet resonant, his every word distinct with constant melody in the quick flow of his speech. Though he shows not a trace of the deliberately morose or the maudlin, even as one smiles or laughs outright one feels the yearning, the lostness, above all, the beauty.

The first-night audience rose to its feet to cheer. Awed silence, as if in the presence of an epiphany of nature, might perhaps have been a more condign tribute. Jack MacGowran is one of the truly important actors of our day.

24

Bertolt Brecht

[1959]

His Achievement

THE TROUBLE with theoretical discussion in the arts—most emphatically in the theatre—is that it often turns our attention away from the work itself and leads us into a semantic maze. A flagrant example of this is much of the writing which has accompanied or preceded the production of Bertolt Brecht's plays. Many more people have discussed Brecht and his theories than have seen his plays or read his poems.

There are several reasons for this. Brecht's plays are in German and are not easily translatable. Though Brecht himself has said that his plays do not necessarily have to be produced in the manner he himself employed as a director, I have yet to see a production in any other manner which does his plays justice.

Yet these plays, whether their language is understood or not, cannot fail to make an impression. They are "different"; they look "new." Without being in the least obscure, they strike the eye as being much more "modern" than the plays by the innovators of the contemporary French theatre. Brecht's plays lend themselves to controversy of all sorts—literary, theatrical, political.

The point so admirably made and elaborated in John Willett's

very useful and thoroughly sensible introduction to Brecht's work *
is that the only proper way to know Brecht is to see the production of his plays in the theatre he founded (the Berliner Ensemble)
or at least to read them—if possible in the original. Brecht's
theoretical writing—stimulating and instructive though it be—does
not convey the "feel" of what he has created.

It was inevitable that Brecht should become the subject of every
type of exegesis. For his is the only manifestation of a total theatre
style (text and presentation in organic relationship) since the
emergence of the Moscow Art Theatre with its climactic peak in
the plays of Chekhov and the corresponding development of the
so-called Stanislavsky System or Method.

The modern theatre has known such influences as those of
symbolism, expressionism, constructivism—impulses and tendencies
which characterize certain writers, scene designers, directors, but
hardly any of which shaped themselves into a complete body of
work with any permanent organ to institutionalize them on every
level of stagecraft. That is why no one today speaks of an opposition between Stanislavsky and symbolism or expressionism, while
there is much talk of Brecht's practice as anti-Stanislavsky.

I mention this aspect of the Brechtian phenomenon for historical reasons only; it is not really fundamental. To approach Brecht
as a stage director in "opposition" to the teachings of Stanislavsky
is as critically bright as to point out that Brecht wrote plays that
do not resemble Chekhov's. The Stanislavsky Method—as distinguished from the nature of his productions—is not a style and
does not by itself lead to a particular style. It is a craft technique
of instruction for actors. Brecht's style is intimately related to what
he had to say and is the mark of his contribution as an artist.

Brecht's plays are picaresque, poetic narrations for the stage.
They are based on brief episodes of concentrated action—most of
them almost complete in themselves—each of which makes a
simple sharp point essential to the understanding of the play's
idea as a whole. The intellectual approach is tersely factual, the
tone ironic, crisp and detached. Songs in a similar vein embody
the ideological point as in an epigram. The aim is frankly didac-

---

* John Willett, *The Theatre of Bertolt Brecht: A Study From Eight Aspects* (New York: New Directions, 1959).

tic. One play tells us that war debases everything and everyone, even those who seem to be outside its antagonisms. Another play tells us that it is virtually impossible to "do good" in a corrupt society. These are morality plays as certainly as anything ever written in the Middle Ages in behalf of the church.

If you read Brechtian manuals you will learn that Brecht espoused the aesthetics of the Chinese and Japanese theatres rather than the Aristotelian aesthetic. You will learn that Brecht eschews "suspense," that his dramatic goal is not excitement but understanding. He wants his audience, it is said, to recognize its place in society and how it (the audience) can help change that society. He tries to induce in the spectator the attitude of an alert observer rather than that of a hypnotized person who seeks to be swept away by the show. He wants his public to use its critical judgment and ultimately its capacity to act, rather than to be drugged or overwhelmed by a suffused emotionalism which can have no effect on its thought patterns and social behavior.

All this may be interesting, but if not perceived through the plays themselves it is actually misleading. For the fact is that these plays with their somewhat ribald humor—part folk canniness and part twentieth-century sophistication—their starkly naïve "stories," their rude simplicity, their dry, yet poignant songs— witty homilies or grave and austere preachments—inspire a sense of nobility, a kind of humane asceticism which is cleansing and elevating. The spareness of the plays is sinewy; their slightly astringent timbre which might easily be mistaken for cynicism is invigorating; their pathos—and they have a pathos at times bordering on sentimentality—is classically serene.

What about the antiemotionalism of Brecht's *esthetique?* It exists chiefly there. Emphasis on it was made by Brecht himself both to purify the hysterical atmosphere which choked the German expressionist theatre and to counteract the orotundity and stomachic stress of "traditional" German acting. Just as there is as much "emotion" in the Parthenon as in Chartres Cathedral, as much in Stravinsky as in Tchaikovsky, so there are very few contemporary plays which provoke as much "emotion" as Brecht's masterpiece *Mother Courage.* To define the difference of "emotion" in each case is to discover the true nature of each particular work.

The artist does what he is, he makes what he can. Brecht's productions are what they are because they constitute the visible, palpable form of what he has written. Because he found the appropriate delivery, lighting, stage design for what he had to say, he was a great master, just as the Moscow Art Theatre in its day achieved mastery by finding the right stage form for the Russian realists.

How confused and confusing most explanations of Brecht's work are (including at times his own—unless they are read chronologically and in continuity) may be judged by a quote in John Willett's book. In criticizing the German classical stage Brecht said, "There is little chance of hearing any genuine human voice, and one gets the impression that life must be exactly like a theater instead of the theater being just like life." Was Brecht then a realist—for it is presumably the realist school which aimed to make the theatre "just like life." In Brecht's productions we are constantly reminded that we are in the theatre—the electrical apparatus is exposed, the actors often address themselves directly to the audience, mottoes are flashed on a screen, etc.—all purely theatrical devices and certainly nonrealistic.

Such confusion arises, I repeat, when we substitute argument over artistic terminology for actual contact with the work of art. Brecht's theatre is theatrical theatre *and* is very real. He endeavors to avoid ecstatic, stentorian, sweating, tremulous emotionalism, *and* at the same time his work communicates an emotion as lofty as any we know in the theatre today.

Another provocation to controversy—particularly among people barely familiar with his writing—is Brecht's politics and his relation to Marxism, the East–West struggle, etc. For the study of Brecht as a man this may be an indispensable vein of inquiry. For an understanding of his plays and poems the subject is much less significant than it is presumed to be. But before entering such a discussion we should ask what corruption demands that an artist be politically "correct" in his work.

There is a duality or ambivalence in Brecht's writing, a dialectic process rooted in a deep-seated skepticism—which Brecht frequently referred to as the mainspring of knowledge. Together with this we find shrewd common sense which counterbalances his persistent moralism. This explains why Brecht changed the ending of his

Galileo several times to resolve the struggle in the protagonist's (and author's) spirit between his conviction and his "comfort."

Telling too are the lines from one of his poems: "Oh we who wanted to prepare the ground for friendliness cannot ourselves be friendly." Or examine the colloquy between Galileo and his disciple who says to the master, "I have recanted but I am going to live. Your hands are dirty, we said. You said: Better dirty than void." And finally this:

> You have two rival spirits
> Lodged in you.
> You have got to have two.
> Stay disputed, undecided!
> Stay a unit, stay divided!
> Hold to the crude one, hold to the cleaner one!
> Hold to the good one, hold to the obscener one!
> Hold them united! *

No doubt Brecht was deeply influenced by Marx and was often close to (though never a member of) the Party. As with many artists of our time, "what attracted Brecht above all was the humanism of Marxist theories." Their humanism and, I would add, their activism. He could neither remain alien to these impulses nor could he accept all that their votaries did. He would not shun them entirely, for much of what the votaries did was necessary and desirable. Thus Brecht's political "indecisiveness" lends his work a good deal of its universal relevance and value. For who today is not troubled by the society we live in and, if not a coward, is anxious to take steps to alter the course of its destructive march without always being sure of the right means? If Brecht was unorthodox both from the standpoint of the communist and the anticommunist, yet deeply involved in the tension which gave rise to the Marxist movement in general, he was, as far as I am concerned, in one of the healthiest of modern traditions. That is one of the reasons I find his work more central to our times than that of T. S. Eliot, Camus, Genet, Beckett, Ionesco, et al.

Brecht's work has already exerted a beneficent influence on the

European theatre. And even such partial and not genuinely assimilated influence as may be observed at The Theatre East and The Royal Court Theatre in London, not to speak of Charles Laughton's production of Shaw's *Major Barbara* in New York, is useful in broadening the scope of our theatre concepts and practice.

In fine, Bertolt Brecht (1898–1956) is one of the outstanding figures of the contemporary theatre and with equal certainty one of the twentieth century's most notable poets.

[1963]

Mother Courage

Bertolt Brecht's *Mother Courage* is a beautiful play. Written in 1938–39 and first produced in Zurich in 1941, it is one of the peaks of dramatic writing in this century. Its production by the Berliner Ensemble in 1951 under the direction of its author and Erich Engel ranks among the truly great works of theatre art in our time. Done all over the Continent, the play is a modern classic.

I say all this at once because I wish my readers to see the play, despite the severe shortcomings of its production under Jerome Robbins' direction.

I cannot predict what an audience unfamiliar with the play will think of it now, but I hope that the New York production will not be used as evidence that Brecht is the bore that some folk through inverted snobbism (or ignorance) have recently declared him to be, and that he was in certain unfortunate American productions. My guess is that, despite present handicaps, the play still comes through to the audience with some part of its force and grandeur intact.

It requires great artistry for a modern writer to achieve pristine effectiveness and epic scope with apparently primitive means. That is what Brecht has done. There is something almost medieval, peasantlike and penetratingly poignant in the simplicity of *Mother Courage*. Brecht possesses folk canniness and mother wit, a shrewdness of vision based on intimate experience of life's basic realities. He is both skeptical and direct; his language combines

the accents and vocabulary of street and stable with the purity
and majestic rhythm of Martin Luther's Old Testament German.
The play seems massively sculpted in wood.

Mother Courage is not "propaganda"; not an antiwar tract. It
is a comic narrative that mounts to tragedy. Its central figure is a
woman without a "soul," an earthbound creature astray in the
miserable current of history. Virtually illiterate, Mother Courage
makes a bare living, supports her three children (each the off-
spring of a different father) by supplying odds and ends—brandy
and belts, chickens and buttons—to the roving armies (Catholic
and Protestant alike) during the Thirty Years' War in the seventeenth century. She has allegiance to no cause but survival and
the care of her brood. She is a pack horse and a "profiteer" of
war. She has not the dimmest idea of what all the shooting is
about. Nor does she ever grow wiser, learn a lesson. But the war
deprives her of everything—her goods, her children, her indomi-
table vitality. The only heroic and enduringly innocent person in
the play is Mother Courage's daughter, who is a mute. Brecht's
use of her in the play is a masterstroke.

The play opens on a note of gaiety—like the exciting, hopeful,
first days of war. Mother Courage's two sturdy sons are pulling
the wagon which conveys her wares and in which she and her
family live. "Here's Mother Courage and her wagon!" the quartet
sings. "Hey, Captain, let them come and buy! Beer by the jug!
Wine by the flagon! Let your men drink before they die!" It's a
lark! Slowly, very slowly over a period of twelve years, Mother
Courage and her children cross Sweden, Poland, Germany. The
wagon ages, diminishes and ends as a shadow of itself—still a
burden to "Courage," who now all alone keeps dragging it through
the wasted towns and war-torn countryside.

Much of the play is funny with harsh humor and wry wisdom.
There are no villains, barely any sentiment, little pathos. No one
preaches, no slogans are enunciated, and even the interpolated
songs, which serve as choral comment, might be taken simply as
"entertainment." All is impersonal; yet in the end we are moved
and feel close to life.

The original text contains nine songs. I have the impression
that several of these have been cut in New York—probably because, if they were retained, the time allowed to sing and play

them might exceed twenty-four minutes and the Musicians' Union would list the production as a "musical." According to the regulations, this classification would entail the employment of twenty-four musicians at heavy cost.

My supposition strikes me as typical of the obstacles that stand in the way of a fitting production for such a play as *Mother Courage*. But there are obstacles beyond this perhaps minor one: the words of the songs—superb in the original and still admirable in Eric Bentley's translation—are imperfectly heard as they are delivered in this production.

The Brecht (Berliner) production is so intimately related to the text as to seem identical with it. (That is what I mean when I speak of "theatre art.") The actors, the direction, the sets, the props and the time allowed at the Berliner Ensemble for all these to become part of a unified fabric and meaning are what made *Mother Courage* everything I have declared it to be. Very little of this is possible in our theatre.

Anne Bancroft, who plays Mother Courage, is a charming actress with a heartwarming smile and a generous honesty of spirit. She is too contemporary, too locally urban, too young, too soft to do much more than indicate the part. (She puts on age by an obvious change of wig; the later one being much too white.) Of the land, the soil, the devastation of the world she crosses, there is hardly a trace. Most of the company is in even sorrier plight. Zohra Lampert as the mute daughter is appealing. Barbara Harris as a camp follower is an actress of exceptional gifts. Hers is the best performance, and her last scene as the gilded, disease-ridden whore turned into a puffy "colonel's lady" is, despite a note of burlesque, a treat.

The sets are simplified beyond Brecht, whose visual austerity was so artful that Parisian critics when they saw his production spoke of its several hundred shades of brown. But if Robbins wanted his sets (credited to Ming Cho Lee) bare, why did he have all sorts of journalistic photographs projected against the background to make "editorial" points where none are needed? Indeed, in view of the play's style, they are altogether pointless. A revolving stage is imperative for this play; it evokes the sweep of Mother Courage's endless trek across Europe. Pulling the wagon in circles around a stationary stage, as Anne Bancroft and the others are obliged to do, simply looks silly. The props, themselves works of art and so much part of the play's "feel" in the original production, are now Broadway routine.

The inscriptions introducing the scenes should be shown on a screen if they are to retain their fine gravity; they should not be spoken by actors with little voice or impressiveness of manner. The idea of having all the members of the company introduce themselves by name (Anne Bancroft, Mike Kellin, Gene Wilder, et al.) is a parody of Brecht, whose style, while eschewing the illusionism of the naturalistic, is more *real* as well as more theatrical than most of our so-called realistic productions.

If Robbins wanted to do an original production he should really have been original; otherwise he should have remained as faithful to Brecht as materially possible. In one respect fidelity and duplication proved a mistake: while Paul Dessau's score was ideal for Brecht's words it does not blend happily with Bentley's.

For all that, and though hardly any translation can do Brecht's writing full justice, *Mother Courage* manages to remain impressive.

25

Rhinoceros

[1961]

Rhinoceros is Eugene Ionesco's "popular" play, or, as he him-self has said, the play he wrote *pour le public*. It has been a success in Paris, in Germany, in London (in good measure due to Laurence Olivier's participation), and now it has been cordially received by a press which was generally indifferent to Ionesco's shorter works.

The play's career makes a lively bit of theatre history. In Paris an American writer of avant-garde tendencies assured me that *Rhinoceros* was perhaps the only one of Ionesco's plays which was totally without interest for him, while at the same time an English critic affirmed that it was the first Ionesco play which was not rubbish. Nigel Dennis, English novelist, playwright and critic, complained that the play was too explicit and thus lacked the imaginative piquancy of Ionesco's *The Chairs;* Kenneth Tynan, in London, where most reviewers favored the play rather than the production (directed by Orson Welles), declared that the pro-duction was good but the play bad—but I rather suspect that Tynan's seeming prejudice is dictated by his admiration for Brecht, whom Ionesco scorns. Sartre—another author about whom Ionesco is icy—deems *Rhinoceros* to be a play for the complacent, because it does not really make clear why a man should not become a "rhinoceros"!

With such a background of controversy—and having myself

seen the London production—I approach the statement of my present reaction with particular care and caution. There is no use in a critic's pretending that he is never influenced. He would be less than human—therefore a poor critic—if this were so.

I advise my readers to see the play. It requires no courage—at this point—to say that it is the most interesting play of the season. (Of course, like all comparative superlatives the remark is somewhat empty: it has been a dismal season and *Rhinoceros* cannot properly be linked with *A Taste of Honey* or even *The Hostage.*) What may certainly be affirmed is that *Rhinoceros* is entertaining and, whatever one's estimate of its underlying spirit, significant. This is sufficient today to make it important.

The play was originally a short story; it is overlong as a three-act play. Its apparent point is made at least three-quarters of an hour before its final curtain. I speak of an "apparent" point because there is something more in the play's message than is contained in the symbol of men who turn into rhinoceroses—the comedy and terror of conformism. For the play, despite the central figure's ultimate defiance of bestiality, is essentially anarchistic, bitter, very nearly hopeless.

The rational mind and logic are absurd, Ionesco tells us; they have little relation to the truth (which is the chaos) of life. Intellectuals are fools. Most organized radicals are not only clowns but robots—ready under pressure to swing from extreme Left to extreme Right. The conventional middle-class gentleman is a moron; the smooth little subaltern of the business community is a fraud; favored hirelings of the status quo are grotesque; the sweet young thing whom we regard as the sweetheart of the world is spineless. Ultimately, they all turn into monsters of blind energy, cruel forces of destruction.

A little man—confused, uncertain, without direction except for some nameless grace of disposition—will resist, though he too is probably doomed. (He acknowledges that the person who wishes to remain an individual always ends badly.) Destined to defeat or not, he does resist—all by himself—which may be described as a *pathetic* absurdity. In almost all the other Ionesco plays the counterpart of Berrenger (the helpless "hero" of *Rhinoceros*) is always done in by the Monster—the mysterious Evil which dominates all. In this sense *Rhinoceros* may be said to mark an "advance" for Ionesco, a stirring of conscience against complete despair, an anguished sign of protest against surrender.

Philosophically this is an unsound, as well as an unsatisfactory, position. Humanly, it is quite understandable: many people the world over feel as Berrenger does, both lonely and afraid of others. Historically, it is typical of the state of mind of a large part of the French intelligentsia today. At worst, its attitude is preferable to the nonawareness and spiritual inanition of, let us say, the ordinary American playgoer. Ionesco's merit as an artist is that he finds theatrically telling means to reflect this contemporary fright. His plays are brilliant statements for the stage; his, therefore, is an authentic and original theatre talent.

Ionesco has said that his work has been stimulated by Kafka and the Marx brothers: it expresses apprehension through gags. In Joseph Anthony's direction of *Rhinoceros* (more engaging than that of the London production) only the gags are effective. The first act (the most successful of the three) is generally hilarious—though there is a faint touch of college theatricals throughout. The latter impression is due to the fact that we get very little sense of how the fun and games relate to the central theme, which is not at all funny.

The slightly Disney style at the beginning is not only childlike but rather childish and when protracted makes us surmise that we are witnesses to a one-joke affair. But this is not really the case. From the outset the play's final act and particularly its crucial last speech, which approaches the tragic, should have been kept in view. What is required by the material is not so much "Kafka *and* the Marx brothers" as Kafka *within* the Marx brothers. The present production has no true style because each of its elements apes whatever farcical trick or serious sentiment seems to be indicated moment by moment, and does not convey a sense that all of the play's aspects interpenetrate to form a single idea with an indivisible meaning. Thus, the last scene of the play descends to the level of a rather flat realism.

Still the "show" makes for a good evening with, as they say, loads of laughs. Complimentary remarks might be made about everyone—Eli Wallach for his bewildered sweetness, Morris Carnovsky for his expertness at rendering innocent idiocy, Anne Jackson for her cuteness, etc.; but the outstanding performance is that of Zero Mostel, whose penchant for Rabelaisian antics of inexhaustible comic verve and inventiveness makes the conversion of his bonehead bourgeois into a roaring pachyderm seem masterfully easy, despite the perspiration. My only reservation on this performance is that the final emergence of the character as a rhinoceros should be indicated by a horn thrust through the bathroom door rather than by the actor's own gargantuan baby face.

26

Eugene O'Neill

[1959]

The Great God Brown

PRAISE THE Phoenix Theatre for producing Eugene O'Neill's *The Great God Brown* anew. George Jean Nathan thought it O'Neill's best play, an opinion I do not share, but one step toward the making of a true theatre in our country is the production of old plays of merit.

It is not sufficient, though, that such plays be seen merely as new "shows"; they should be comprehended as part of a development in their author's work and as part of our own history. It is no longer of first importance that O'Neill used masks in this play, a device considered highly "experimental" in 1926, when the play was originally presented. What is important is the play's theme and the anguish O'Neill imbued it with. The theme is the practical man's envy of the artist and the artist's jealousy of the dominant practical man—a peculiarly American theme in the period of the play's conception.

O'Neill probed further than this bald statement might suggest. He saw the American businessman—for that is what Brown represents, though O'Neill made him an architect—becoming infected with the artist's yearnings and unable finally to realize himself either as one thing or another. Brown suffers some of the inner dissatisfactions which plague and impel the artist without possessing

138

the artist's sensibility or skill. More strikingly, O'Neill portrays his artist, Dion Anthony, as a trammeled human being, really a half-artist with a gnawing sense of inadequacy in his philosophy, his personality and his adjustment to life. That is a crucial American tragedy: the incompleteness of American civilization as it focuses in the individual.

This sounds old-fashioned. Today, only a brief "moment" since the dilemma appeared poignant in the growing American consciousness, terms and circumstances have altered its outer form. The businessman of today is emotionally more complacent: if he appreciates the artist's function, collects paintings, attends concerts and reads certain books or book reviews, he expresses his disquiet otherwise than O'Neill's Brown. Similarly, the artist today seems to have taken his "proper" place in our society, so that with a little maneuvering, rationalization, psychoanalysis and publicity he can feel pretty much in the same boat as the Browns. The result is that they are both prepared to moan in monotonous chorus about taxes and the threat of atomic extinction.

The core of the matter, however, is not changed as much as we pretend; if we believe otherwise, that is chiefly because we rarely think of any "core" at all, except to indulge ourselves in a specious vocabulary of high-brow platitudes. O'Neill was no intellectual; if his play suffers in form and thought as well as in clarity, its impulse and source are nevertheless real and deep.

In O'Neill's work as a whole the theme of *The Great God Brown* recurs again and again in the most diverse guises; and if we refer even cursorily to O'Neill's life we become aware that the conflicts which made the theme urgent were rooted in his relationship to his father, his mother, his brother. A blood tie binds *Beyond the Horizon, Desire Under the Elms, Marco Millions, Long Day's Journey Into Night, A Touch of the Poet* into a single underlying meaning: the individual American has not reached fulfillment; he is not full grown; neither as a doer nor as a feeling person has he yet made peace with himself or with the world, and all the blather about the "American way of life" will not heal the sore.

Note too that O'Neill's artist, for all his mockery of Brown, is not presented as a "genius." It is always clear that O'Neill never thought of himself as a master in any way. He identified himself with derelicts and failures. He has no heroes; all his central figures yammer and yearn, curse and are as much lost as Yank the laborer in *The Hairy Ape*. Immature on the level of ultimate power, O'Neill is the dramatic poet of our own immaturity—which in his work is not merely an artistic or an intellectual flaw, but a lacerating wound.

You may be embarrassed by some of the awkwardness and feeble verbiage of *The Great God Brown*, particularly in the last act; and you can, if you wish, disparage O'Neill, in academic loftiness, by comparing his plays with the best work of the European playwrights of the past forty years. The fact remains that he is not only our most important dramatist, but one whose total product is, even in some of its faults, more truly relevant to the American people— whose "story" after all concerns the whole of modern society—than any other dramatist of this period anywhere.

The Phoenix Theatre production under Stuart Vaughan's direction is much more obviously stylized than the original production directed by Robert Edmond Jones. The new production is perhaps more lucid than the early one, or let us say less "mystic." It is intelligently executed throughout. I also believe it likely that the comparatively young actors in the present production—Fritz Weaver, Robert Lansing and the others—"understand" the play and their parts better than did those of the original cast.* Yet I cannot suppress the feeling that the emotional resources of our present generation of actors are not as rich as those of former years. The distinction is not one of talent: it has much to do with the times. Today we are perhaps more troubled and possess less actual experience. Our lesions nowadays seem to be chronic and, so to speak, automatic, whereas the older actors were more truly engaged in the world and in the living theatre. They had *earned* their neuroses.

* William Harrigan, Robert Keith, Anne Shoemaker, Leon Hogarth.

27

John Osborne

[1965]

Inadmissible Evidence

SEVERAL ENGLISH critics whom I respect were less than lukewarm about Albee's *Who's Afraid of Virginia Woolf?* but were rapturous about John Osborne's *Inadmissible Evidence*. I point this out not as a comment on the plays or on the critics, but to emphasize that art and literature are not inevitably international in value. Critics are parts of communities, each with its own particular history and need. *Inadmissible Evidence* was a great popular as well as critical success in London; it has not been well-received here and is probably destined to a brief run.

There is still a "dream" in *Virginia Woolf,* as well as a jocularity, which helps keep the play's sting from being poisonous. Though *Inadmissible Evidence* begins with and occasionally reverts to stream-of-consciousness monologue, it contains no "dream"; though it crackles with sharp phrases which startle us to a guffaw, it is not at all humorous. It is a display of English nausea.

The absence of a dream is its underlying theme. Where in our lives is there anything to rouse us to significant action, to some sort of substantial idealism, to a belief or a cause which might lead us to a struggle worth the candle? In fact, says Maitland, the man who submits evidence against himself, "I've never discovered what is [worth the candle]." Everything has gone stale, flat, acidulous.

The English see in Maitland a "hero" of their day, the present archetype of the educated middle-class Britisher. He works hard without a sense of purpose. He has little except a routine relationship to his job. He has only a nagging affection for his wife, a nervous yearning for his mistress, a spastic impulse toward every pretty girl he encounters and with whom he copulates in a fog of befuddlement. His children are slightly repellent strangers. One of the most eloquent, indeed brilliantly written, speeches in the play is Maitland's denunciation of the "cool" generation, addressed to his daughter, about whose age he is in some doubt. He is addicted to pills. A solicitor, he is losing his professional grip. He sees all his clients as one dismal, distracted creature no better off than himself. "I, myself, am more packed with spite and twitching with revenge than anyone I know of. I actually often, frequently, daily want to see people die for their errors. I wish to kill them myself, to throw the switch with my own fist." The man spews spleen.

Jimmy Porter in *Look Back in Anger* was bitter about England after the war. It had lost its ancient stature. Now, says Maitland, "I'm not the one on any side. I don't have any idea of where I am." Even more to the point he exclaims, "Britain's position in the world. Screw that. What about my position!" Because there has been this apparent change from a degree of social consciousness in Jimmy Porter to Maitland's despair about himself, it has been said by a number of English critics and at least one American critic that *Inadmissible Evidence* is the profounder, the more universal play— a modern tragedy.

No doubt many Englishmen see themselves in Maitland. They honor Osborne for articulating their inner distress. (Outwardly— and this is one of Osborne's beefs—they are much too patient.) He exposes their concealed wounds, their soul-sickness. His play is a document: it *does* reveal their wearines, their atony, above all their desire to sneer at themselves. In this, together with an extraordinary faculty for derision in passages of coruscating rhetoric, lies the strength of Osborne's play.

It is a social symptom. It is not true that Maitland embodies the condition of man. At the most, he is an Englishman, and only of one sort. To be sure, he has his counterparts in other countries— but with distinct differences. Even the morally debilitated American has more youthful zest and thus a semblance of hope, of going somewhere, getting some place. There are large areas of the world in which the Maitlands hardly exist at all. They are the product of political stagnation brought on not by fear or an intellectual incapacity to change but by a society divided within itself: one part clinging to a traditional past which has become a fading memory, the other unsettled because it does not know what the future will look like. Maitland is an image of a festering England.

I say "image" because Maitland is not a *man* at all. He exists as an idea, not as a person. He is a composite of observations, reflections, confessional epigrams. He is the spirit that denies itself. The man who supposes himself a Maitland deceives himself. Maitland is a collage of traits and effects adding up to a gigantic grimace. He is truth only as a caricature is truth. The material of *Inadmissible Evidence* might prove far more cogent as a series of sketches, pathetic-comic.

There is talent in the enterprise, but not for tragedy or great drama. Apart from the unmistakable literary flair, it is a talent for catching the mood of a period, a sense of what is in the air, the gift of the adman of genius. This is coupled by what is deepest in Osborne: an outraged disaffection, a self-loathing projected as a contempt for society. None of this is irreconcilable with an irrepressible ambition.

I admire the phenomenon; I have a sneaking sympathy with it, and for all the above reasons (not excepting my own admiration) I find it hateful. It is antibiologic. Men have a life wish far more potent than any death wish. It is the life wish which must be perceived and made sensible to us in every work of art no matter how "black." It is the quickening spark which creates whatever is real and meaningful to us in the world—including expressions of anguish. Ultimately no true work of art can be a depressant. The "downbeat" is only an outcry, sometimes a howl of affirmation.

There is too little of this in *Inadmissible Evidence*. There is barely a trace of compassion (or passion of any kind) in the play. Everything hangs fire. Actually there is no situation, only a state of mind. Therefore nothing can move or be moving. Maitland's clients are not convinced of their case; they are undecided as to whether or not they demand judgment. Maitland's last words as he remains alone in his office are, "I think I'll just stay here. Good-bye." He does not want to become other than he is. His psychologic posture is to sit contemplating a supposedly injured thumb, murmuring, "A little tumor. On the end of another." For the English audience *Inadmissible Evidence* became a formidably impressive piece of publicity, reading: Sign of the Times. In this it succeeds too well.

Anthony Page's direction is excellent; the cast on the whole is very good. This is especially so, among the lesser parts, of Ted van Griethuysen as a latent homosexual—latent in almost every aspect of thought, work, play or misdeed.

Nicol Williamson's performance as Maitland is a technical triumph. The part is exhausting because *Inadmissible Evidence* is virtually an overextended one-man show. What is especially remarkable about Williamson's performance is that he forces one to listen to and to hear every phrase of the two- and three-page speeches. Not a line or a nuance is scotched or dropped. Still, from this appearance alone, one is unable to assess Williamson's full measure as an actor. At times he is as intolerable as the character he portrays—nasal in speech with a ringing, uninflected voice except to the extent to which he is able to make such an utterance as "How are you?" an oily snarl of disgust. There is in the performance a kind of unvarying proficiency of delivery which may be required by the assignment or intended to maintain the style of heartlessness which is perhaps desired by author and director. Feeling seems largely absent, or perhaps it has been avoided as evidence of sloppy sentimentality.

28

Harold Pinter

[1961]

The Caretaker

IN ITS OWN WAY Harold Pinter's *The Caretaker* is a perfect little play. Like the work of Samuel Beckett, it is a terrifying comedy. I mention Beckett, not only because Pinter has acknowledged his indebtedness to the Parisianized Irishman, but because *The Caretaker* is a variation on the theme that has begun to haunt the stage since the younger men of the theatre began waiting for Godot. This does not mean that Pinter is not an original talent: the specific English accent of his play lends it its own stamp.

I am sure Pinter detests the reading of symbols into *The Caretaker*. It is written with so much raciness, so definite a tang of British weather that one barely notices the degree of the play's abstractness. Its three characters are named Mick, Aston and Davies; the house in West London where the action takes place reeks of the wetness, the slovenliness, the mold and decrepitude of many buildings in that neighborhood. And while the play is streaked with humor, it might appear almost meaningless were it not for the ideological patterns it suggests.

The details are graphic and striking enough to be memorably self-sufficient (which is always true in a work of art). Yet they call for interpretation, even if the author were to protest that a particular interpretation, or any interpretation, belied his purpose.

Aston, a strange young man who dwells in a run-down flat in a battered and leaky house, brings home an old derelict named Davies, whom he has saved from a beating in a pub where the old man was presumed to be doing some menial job. The old wretch (ever since the war he has been going under an assumed name: Jenkins) is a malodorous grotesque—craven, boastful, aggressive. He hates foreigners (especially blacks) and is lazy and mendacious. Yet he is pitiful in his stupid pride. Aston sees through the sham and invites him to share the disheveled quarters.

Davies shows little gratitude. He begs for new shoes but is not satisfied with any of those offered. He grumbles over the placement of the bed in which he has been put up. He groans and makes ugly sounds in his sleep—keeping his host awake at night. When he learns that his benefactor was once subjected to shock treatment (Aston was committed to a mental hospital because he was a "dreamer"), Davies abuses him for not treating him as well as he should. Davies also turns for help to Aston's brother, Mick, who actually owns the house which he has bought to keep his brother in safety. Mick hardly ever speaks to his brother, though he seems semibenevolently to watch over him. Unaccountably, Mick toys with and torments old Davies and threatens him when Davies refers to Aston as a "nut." Ultimately, Aston orders the old man to get out; his complaints, his ungratefulness, his dirtiness are insufferable. Then the old beggar cries out: "What am I going to do? Where am I going to go?"

Each of the three characters seems to dwell in a world apart from the others—and from everything else. They repeat themselves endlessly but never make themselves understood. Each on his own is cruel to the others.

Who are these people? What do they signify? One is not supposed to be entirely sure. But is not Mick, the laconic prankster with his deliberate double-talk and barbed mystifications, a kind of godhead—angel and devil in one? May not Aston, crucified for his idealistic dreaminess, be a sort of Christ figure? And could not the curmudgeon Jenkins-Davies, in search of the papers which will identify him and prove who he "really" is, stand for mankind itself? He is asked to be a caretaker, but he has neither aptitude nor appetite for the job. No one knows what his "game" is; the final verdict passed on him in the play is that he must be gotten rid of because he makes "too much noise." The house which he is asked to guard is so run down it is hardly worth the trouble of anyone's care. Aston, who had hoped to make something of it, who had tried, at any rate, to protect the poor, harmless creature whom he had invited to share his digs, now dreams only of building a new shelter of fresh, clean wood—a healthy place somewhere in the nearby premises.

Pinter's refusal to make the play as neatly (or platitudinously) intelligible as this is probably justified. Plays like *The Caretaker* owe some of their fascination to ambiguity. But this ambiguity covers what is inherently a simple—perhaps too simple—design. Hence they disturb without actually moving us. The artistic plan is narrower than it pretends to be; the ambiguity is an unconscious spiritual device whereby the author, uncommitted in his soul in relation to the bewilderment and anguish life causes him, remains congealed in his quandary—a situation which may after all be easier to bear than an outright decision as to how to resolve or change it.

It is a tribute to the talent and value of *The Caretaker*—one of the most representative plays in the contemporary Englishlanguage theatre—that it can provoke such thoughts, conjectures and perhaps controversies.

Almost as remarkable as the play itself is its production under the direction of Donald McWhinnie. He has achieved that rare thing in the theatre: a true marriage of text and performance. Donald Pleasence as Davies is funny, obnoxious, astonishing, mysterious. His manner ranges from the fiercely vulgar to the apocalyptic. (How his voice echoes when he utters his last cry of abandonment!) His flailing gestures, frightening and incoherent, seem to beat the air with nameless yet vehement queries and protestations. The emotional result is awesome rather than tragic or even pathetic —in which respect it partakes of the quality of the play itself. This is true too of Robert Shaw as the play's impotent "redeemer," caught in the vise of a pity that fails to console. There is a coldness in Alan Bates' consummate portrayal of the inexplicably good–bad "landlord"—utterly real in its English impassivity, a kind of muted familiarity which in its unyielding objectivity is as fatal as a god's final judgment. Play and production wound and adhere to one's spirit like the impress of a tattoo.

29

Crisis on Broadway

[1961]

THE ONLY CONCLUSION I can come to on reading the six reports which appeared in *The New York Times* on the Broadway crisis is: "No foundation all the way down the line." This applies not to the *Times'* journalistic efforts but to the thinking about the theatre—in the theatre—which the articles reflect.

To begin with, there is scarcely any agreement as to the facts. What are some of the matters which one might suppose to be beyond dispute? Attendance in the Broadway theatre has fallen from 12,300,000 in 1930–31 to 8,100,000 last season. The theatre's physical plant has diminished from sixty-six houses in 1931 to the present thirty-three. Forty-six new shows were produced last season, a record low, as compared to the more than two hundred produced in 1926–27. Hardly any of the better productions of nonmusical plays were of American origin. Is there a crisis? One of the reporters summed up the reaction of the theatre people he questioned as "absolutely yes–definitely no."

One producer is quoted as having said, "I think Broadway is entering a renaissance. We are on the verge of a boom." (This producer has had an exceptionally profitable year: three musical hits and an English "prestige" play.) Another producer who has lost his backers considerable sums of money in the past but who made some last season with a two-person revue goes so far as to say that "the financial plight of the theatre is exaggerated."

The crisis—acknowledged by the majority—was brought to public attention not because so few plays were produced last season but because so much money was lost. Hardly any nonmusical play, except for *Mary, Mary,* showed a real profit or even paid all its costs. It is now feared that the conduct of the "legitimate" theatre will soon become a wholly quixotic enterprise and ultimately altogether unfeasible.

The suggested remedies are, first, the elimination of federal and city entertainment taxes; second, adjustments by dramatists, stars, directors, scene designers on royalties, and, third, the abrogation of certain onerous rulings by the stagehand and musician unions. So far only the Dramatists' Guild has agreed to any concession in the matter of royalty payments—*provided* stars, directors and others follow suit.

The federal and city taxes have not yet been reduced. On the other hand, it is expected that tax privileges on expense accounts for entertainment will soon be rescinded—a severe blow to the sale of orchestra seats bought by so many businessmen whose theatre-going seems dependent on their expense accounts. What is also noteworthy is that the tax on theatre tickets is part of the *entertainment* tax, which places nightclubs on a par with the theatre.

This points to the core of the trouble. Though Senator Javits, in an honorable attempt to aid the theatre through legislation, speaks of it as "a cultural expression," almost everyone else discusses it primarily as a business. For example, one of the arguments advanced in behalf of the community's taking an interest in the theatre's prosperity is that if the theatre were to disappear, other commerce—restaurants, parking lots, garages, taxis, ticket brokers—would also suffer!

There is no question that business organization must play a vital role in the conduct of all theatrical enterprise. But if the theatre is a business chiefly aimed at a profit, then it follows that if a profit is not forthcoming it must and should disappear—unless, like the railroads, its continued life is held to be a matter of public interest and need.

Even the Broadway aphorism tells us that "show business is no business." One of the reasons for the thoroughgoing confusion and muddleheadedness of our theatre world is that willy-nilly the theatre is not *essentially* a business. Even the most hardened or money-minded showman has something of the gambler (that is to say, the artist) in him. We in America have forgotten this or were rarely obliged to remember it—as long as business in the theatre could go on as usual.

The theatre as a private enterprise has existed for at least three hundred years. But almost every country in Europe has recognized that the theatre is part of a nation's patrimony and must therefore be subject to some sort of public control through government (royal, princely, civic or national) agency. Theatres in France, Germany, the Scandinavian countries and now even in England (not to mention most of the Iron Curtain countries, even before they were converted to that metal) not only have been partially government subsidized, but are subject to regulations as to their number and their specific use. (Napoleon took time on his Russian expedition to rule that the Comédie Française must always keep low-priced—five franc—seats available for the poorer public.) Some part of the country's theatre establishment—and very often the best—was protected so that it might serve its true function as an expression of the nation's spirit, its emblem. The theatre is one of the means by which a society realizes itself.

In America, for historical reasons, the theatre has never been seriously viewed as being integral with the respectability of our social life. It has been assimilated into our business community, in which success (or profit) becomes the symbolic as well as the effective goal. In a normal economic situation this does not necessarily exert disastrous influence. But when the economic balance in the community is upset, our theatre—now ideologically as well as practically dependent on the profit or pure business motive—must be stricken with paralysis and threatened with extinction.

Talent for the theatre and an appetite for it are still abundant. And theatre folk being what they are, germinal artists, the theatre goes on in our country in a schizophrenic state—half crazy from every point of view and less than half as proficient or useful as it might be.

Let us consider one minor point among the various statements in the *Times* reports by producers on matters of settings and stagehands. Some say that settings should be simplified—to reduce costs, and perhaps also because simplified sets are more "artistic." Others, on the contrary, are entirely satisfied with huge expenditures for "scenery"—when the productions they have spent the money on *prove profitable.* The question of artistic fitness in each instance is gauged by the measure of box-office success rather than by the style of scenic investiture demanded by the text. Certain plays which demand large-scale production—many sets and numerous actors—must virtually be ruled out as prohibitively costly, no matter what their intrinsic merit.

When profit becomes the chief criterion or proof of excellence, understanding of the theatre must become distorted. Business standards replace all others. The preferred actor is the one who will sell the most tickets—if nowhere else, at theatre parties. The most important director is the one who has had the most recent hits. The best scene designers are the ones whose work has graced the greatest number of smashes. This way of thinking makes sane judgment impossible, even in *matters of business.*

No wonder then that the dramatists, presumably the pivot of the theatre organism, are among the most frightened of all show folk. To write a flop is not only an economic blow; it is moral disgrace, a loss of status. Is it possible to write in such an atmosphere? Ah, but the "real" writer will never cease writing. Of course not; the question is what will he write?

Present circumstances—inevitable from the false premises on which the theatre has been obliged to operate—poison the whole theatre: the audience, the critics, the very air of the playhouses. The trauma thus created has made the past fifteen years the age of the middleman, or agent. They are the "victors," the lawgivers. There are now agents for everyone, including the audience. This is the end result of our "realism," "practicality" and nonartiness.

Certainly I favor the reduction of taxes on the theatre. (I also favor special tax benefits, such as obtain in France, for accredited theatre folk and artists in general.) Whatever immediately practicable remedies to small specific ills can be achieved must win our unqualified endorsement. But I suspect that very little will get done through ordinary Broadway channels. The provision made by the Dramatists' Guild in regard to the curtailment of royalty payments will not be acceptable to most stars, and certainly not to their agents. The same holds true for most of the others—directors and scene designers—and with a certain justification.

One agent very sensibly says, "I am willing to gamble, but it should be a concentrated effort by everyone. Are the theatre owners ready to make concessions? The unions? The producers? Is the producer willing to let the other people participate proportionately for gambling with him?" The theatre is a collective (or corporate) art. It must be managed that way. It is perhaps the model type of organization for the industrial as differentiated from the craft union. But at present the theatre is being run as a business in which every man looks out for himself as good old-fashioned business dictates. That is why we are at the point of collapse.

Yet in collapse may lie our only hope. Health may be restored through breakdown, as to a degree it was during the thirties. The theatre may have to be beaten into sanity. Reason (or art) may return to the theatre when "business" has done almost everything possible to kill it.

Already there are signs of this even in the very chaos which *The New York Times* series exposes. Our audiences—as developments off-Broadway to some extent indicate—are becoming evermore aware of values different from those which obtain on Broadway. Community theatres are growing on a more extensive scale than before. Such projects as the civic theatre in Minneapolis and Lincoln Center in New York may be auguries of a salutary change.

Not everyone inside or outside the theatre today deems it peculiar to think or speak of the theatre in the terms I have so often employed in these pages. My "pessimism" is intended as a creative implement. Before the theatre changes there must be some "new" thinking. We will not go far, even "business-wise," if we confine ourselves to so-called practical assumptions that are incompatible with the nature of the material at hand. We must be persistent and dogged. Relief will not come overnight. In the meantime we must do the best we can. The first step may be to sharpen our theatrical *intelligence.*

30

Challenge of the New Theatres

[1964]

THE "BREAKDOWN" of Broadway, the consequent propaganda for the theatre's decentralization, the aid of the foundations, the spread of university and community stages, the "cultural explosion" have all led to the establishment of a number of new repertory or semi-repertory theatres—with more or less permanent staffs—from New York to California, in the South and the Southwest. We have reason to be pleased, but it is too soon to celebrate. As Van Wyck Brooks many years ago said (in effect): America is the land of promising first acts.

An American characteristic which may frustrate our hope in the new theatres is impatience. We must not expect miracles overnight. Time is required to mature all concerned: the directorate of the various theatres, their personnel, their audiences. We have no settled tradition to proceed from. We must learn.

The first step is to define aims. The repertory system by itself is a measure of convenience; it can prove a drawback. A permanent company should be a great asset; it may turn into a deadweight. A subscription audience is extremely useful; it has occasionally acted as a block.

It is not enough to say that the goal of the new enterprises should be to offer "good theatre." As Stanislavsky told Norris Houghton, no one has ever deliberately tried to found a bad theatre. Nor can each of the new companies strive for exactly the same ends. Much

153

depends on where each theatre is situated and the conditions under which it is obliged to operate, the audience it hopes to attract, the very structure of the building it must occupy.

The Repertory Theater of Lincoln Center will serve New York. It cannot do everything for New York which New York needs, nor can it do everything at once. (It promises a studio auditorium for special productions when its permanent quarters have been built.) New York should have several similar theatres, as London at present has three, Paris four, Moscow many. It is a sign of sanity that the organizers of the Repertory Theater of Lincoln Center recognize that even if they play at capacity for fifty-two weeks every season they cannot look forward to a profit! The theatre is not a merchandising business any more than is a library, a museum or a symphony orchestra.

Countries which have long theatrical histories may maintain theatres especially designed to preserve those traditions. That is the chief purpose of the Comédie Française, and to some extent this was and is the purpose of the Old Vic and of the Shakespeare Theatre at Stratford-on-Avon. It is largely true of the various state or municipal theatres in Germany. Most European countries have produced dramatic literatures rich enough to sustain such theatres over the years.

America has not (though there are more American plays worth revival than we suppose). Certain choices are open to the founders of the new theatres. A choice which is really no choice at all is to announce that one is going to present a series of good plays. The question to be asked is: good for what, good for whom?

A company of actors unprepared—that is, not specifically trained —to do Elizabethan, Restoration or Classic Greek plays deceives itself and its audience when it undertakes to stage them. I could list a whole shelf of masterpieces—by Strindberg, Kleist, Racine, Calderon and others—which would doom any company offering them in the wrong place at the wrong time. Their *audiences* are not prepared! Remember that Beckett's *Waiting for Godot*, eagerly received and thoroughly appreciated in scores of university theatres throughout the country, flopped on Broadway despite an expert cast. The same is true of so relatively forthright a play as Sartre's *No Exit*. The circumstances—costs of production, price of seats, the whole atmosphere and mental disposition—on Broadway are inimical to the proper reception of such plays. The audience is a theatre's leading actor!

The Tyrone Guthrie Theatre in Minneapolis made a wise choice of plays for its first season. *Hamlet,* Molière's *The Miser,* Chekhov's *The Three Sisters* and Arthur Miller's *Death of a Salesman* are suitable to any American city of like size. But note in passing that *The Miser,* performed in a sort of enlarged "revue" style, and *Three Sisters* were more popular than *Hamlet,* done by actors not wholly up to the demands of that formidable play. It is a moot point whether it is better to do a great play with mediocre means than to do a lesser but still worthy play more congruously.

It might be desirable to institute a theatre entirely devoted to "difficult" or avant-garde plays (a) if the director, actors and others are equipped to do them well, (b) if there is a sufficient number of people in the community who wish to see such plays, and (c) if the financial support at the theatre's command can be counted on for respectable productions of these plays. One must remember always that we are speaking not of the desultory production of separate plays but of a continuous program of production.

To present plays by Ghelderode, Beckett, Ionesco, Genet or even more recent examples of "adventurous" drama, in addition perhaps to plays like Büchner's *Wozzeck* and Strindberg's *Dream Play* or his *Ghost Sonata,* without reference to all the above considerations would be as much an artistic misdemeanor as a sign of organizational ineptitude. There is little point in speaking of the theatre as a social art and ignoring in practice the actual society in which the theatre finds itself.

Most of the new theatres—particularly those in cities unused to a steady regime of substantial fare—will, to begin with, have to be eclectic in the manner of the Tyrone Guthrie Theatre of Minneapolis. If a university is able to finance a professional company on any long-term basis—as has occurred to some extent at the University of Michigan—the theatre may take greater risks. No theatre may look forward to a secure future where it is expected to prove a "smash" with its initial productions.

Beyond the practical considerations of the problem there lies the root question of what constitutes a true theare. The answer once given by the great Russian director Vachtangov was couched in the special jargon of his time and place (Moscow, 1919), but it is nonetheless exact: "A theatre is an ideologically cemented collective."

This bespeaks not what we call a "policy" but a fundamental Idea. This Idea—religious, social, aesthetic, political or only "technical"—must inform the entire theatrical community from dramatist to minor player and apprentice craftsman. Such a theatre is not intended as the stage equivalent of a library (offering the "hundred best books") or a museum for the display of masterpieces. A true theatre creates from its Idea; it educates its members in the Idea and generates production methods from it. The Idea is born of an impulse in the society in which the theatre's artists live and is directed toward that society. Dramatists and interpreters are interrelated as kinsmen in a common movement immanent in the social unit of which they are at once the projection and the instrument. Thus the career of such a theatre will take on the kind of character and meaning we find in the work of an individual artist.

Such unity was more or less spontaneously achieved in the Classic Greek, the Elizabethan and the seventeenth-century French theatres by virtue of the homogeneity of their respective cultures. Unity of this kind is extremely difficult to arrive at in our day—especially in America. Still, something of this aesthetic-social concord has been attained.

Besides its purely professional reforms, the Moscow Art Theatre in 1898 declared its purpose to be the creation of serious art for the People. By the "People" the leaders of that famous institution chiefly meant the middle-class intelligentsia and the educated working class. The result was a theatre which explored many avenues of theatrical expression, though its signal contribution was consummated in the production of plays by Chekhov and Gorky. With further development along these lines the studios of the Moscow Art Theatre (virtually new theatres) veered at first toward a sort of Tolstoian mysticism and then proceeded to radical departures from realism, as well as to more pronouncedly social objectives.

By 1935, the Russian theatre had branched out into extremely diverse aesthetic manifestations. Its progress was then impeded by a politically oriented campaign against "formalism," when a very restrictive interpretation of "Socialist realism" was imposed by main force.

Though the Theatre Guild between 1919 and 1929 was hardly

a theatre in the sense I have indicated, it did make a valuable contribution in organizing audiences through subscription and in maintaining a fairly consistent program of the kind of contemporary European play which had up to that time been considered caviar to the general. The Theatre Guild represented the new cosmopolitanism of New York's middle class shortly after the First World War. In 1928, the Theatre Guild adopted Eugene O'Neill, scion of another body, the Provincetown Players.

The Group Theatre (1931-41) was the first, and so far the last, conscious effort in America to create a theatre exemplifying both an aesthetic and a "philosophic" attitude. Its first emphasis was on a unity of technique—particularly in regard to acting; its second was the enunciation of what it held to be the temper of American life of the time. The combination resulted in the emergence of a playwright from its permanent acting company: Clifford Odets. He was in effect not only the Group Theatre's typical figure but that of the decade.

What Idea will motivate each of our new theatres? That is for each of them to decide for itself, depending on the composition of the companies. Without some coherent Idea to impel it, an Idea which each group must learn to formulate for itself and exemplify in its action, none will survive beyond the flush of its first flight.

It is my personal conviction that every true theatre must sooner or later produce its own native playwrights. (The Group Theatre presented plays by Paul Green, John Howard Lawson, Dawn Powell, Maxwell Anderson, Sidney Kingsley, before it reached Odets' *Waiting for Lefty* and *Awake and Sing*.) This does not mean that all other dramatists are to be considered "alien"; it means that somehow all the plays produced by a true theatre must more or less serve as "original" expressions of the group (directors, actors and others) who compose its membership.

Such a theatre does not follow fashion, however attractive, up to date, "advanced"; it bodies forth its own spirit. It should be conceived, not as an interpretive vehicle, but as a creative organism. It may find material in old plays of any period from any land, but in this kind of theatre such plays become its own plays, a facet of its own "message." This implies no distortion of revered texts in the manner of certain early Soviet productions. (Though I confess a preference for Meyerhold's staging of Gogol's *Inspector General* or the Jewish Chamber Theatre's mounting of *King Lear* in Moscow in 1935 to most of the "faithful" or faceless Shakespeare productions in America and England.) Classics are produced in my "ideal" theatre, not solely on account of their literary stature but for their relevance to its audience. The outstanding example of this sort of theatre for the past decade or more has been the Berliner Ensemble, whose guiding spirit was Brecht but whose productions have not been confined to his plays. A large community may have several such theatres with differing Ideas. If they are truly theatres each will create its own identity.

For these theatres to exist and flourish, more than a collection of expert professionals is required. The theatre as it develops must *school* itself for the tasks it envisions. We have as yet no single body of theatre craftsmen capable of coping with the wide range of styles which the perspective of our dramatic heritage offers. We must be modest even as we are ambitious. The theatre must not regard itself simply as an arena for the exhibition of a prize "product," but as the ground for the cultivation on the broadest possible basis—technical and spiritual—of the artists and world view it hopes to have emerge.

There are enormous resources of talent in our country, but little coordinating discipline or formative enterprise. That is why the theatre has become a hand-to-mouth business instead of what it was destined to be: a vital expression of adult concern. We are too concentrated on sensations, names, electrifying phenomena, bewitching personalities, and not enough on organic growth. We are eager for the fruit; we do not care about the tree.

With the establishment of the new theatres we have our best chance for a transformation. But we shall miss our opportunity if we think of the new theatres in the light of the old. These new theatres must not be as good or better than Broadway but altogether different. They must forge new paths for actors, dramatists, directors, audiences and the monied patrons. This cannot be done in a hurry. One, two, or even three seasons will not be enough.

31

Britain's National Theatre

[1964]

THE BRITISH had to wait till 1963 to establish a national theatre for which the first concrete suggestion was made in 1848. Now that it has been set up we see that it is good. Since its opening, ten plays have been presented. Of these I have seen seven. All of them, despite the reservations I shall make, are good. I shall not speak of *Saint Joan,* transferred from the repertory of the theatre in Chichester (a sort of summer annex of the main enterprise), nor of *Hamlet,* Frisch's *Andorra* and a double bill of Sophocles' *Philoctetes* and Beckett's *Play,* which, failing to attract a sufficient audience, have been dropped.

The first play I saw—the company's latest—was *The Master Builder.* The critical response to this production has been negative. The play was held to be "dated" and fault was found with the casting of Maggie Smith as Hilde Wangel. I thought the play fascinating and Maggie Smith, one of England's best actresses, though certainly not a conventional choice for the part, quite interesting. I am exasperated when a play like *The Master Builder* is called "dated" because certain of its characters refer to trolls and Hilde speaks of hearing "harps in the air." It was as normal for Norwegians of 1892 to speak of "trolls" as for us to talk of "traumas." A trauma is no more material than a troll! And for an enthusiastic young girl of the time to speak of hearing "harps

in the air" is no more odd than for a girl today to say that listening
to Thelonius Monk "sends her."

The theme of Ibsen's play remains vital. It concerns the fear
and frustration which often agitate the aging artist (or anyone of
signal achievement) that he may be superseded by a rising generation and be found "dated"! The temptation of such a man is to
suppress or deny the new voices clamoring to be heard; frequently
he harbors a sense of defeat, the suspicion that he has not accomplished all that he might have done or dreamed of doing.

The Master Builder is Ibsen's confession, an avowal of the contrary pulls of his nature. The protagonist, the architect Solness,
began his career by building churches, but made his reputation by
putting up ordinary homes for well-to-do families. Ibsen aimed at
creating great epic drama—*Brand, Peer Gynt, Emperor and Gali-
lean*—but the world came to honor him for *A Doll's House, The
Wild Duck, Hedda Gabler.* Ibsen foresaw the time when his
"middle-class" art (his realism) would no longer serve our needs.
He denounced the old "ideals"—the God or gods of his fathers—
but felt a deep hunger for some inspirational force with which to
replace them.

The dialectic of the generations, with its concomitant psychological tensions, is real enough and constant. What brings all this to life
in *The Master Builder* is Hilde Wangel, a character who, for all the
nineteenth-century and Scandinavian innocence of her vocabulary,
is as vivid, sharp, contradictory, virtuous and amoral as any impatient young girl anywhere today. To this aspect of the role—the
bubbling will to mount to the heights—Maggie Smith, with her
irrepressible humor, adds a tangy contemporary touch that emphasizes what is enduring in the play.

Michael Redgrave may be a little soft for the ruthless, egocentric
Solness (though "soft" men—particularly artists—in such circumstances are often unconscionably tough, even petty), but he has a
certain grandeur, he is thoughtful and he knows very well what the
part is all about.

The result is a production—all of it well cast—very much to the
point. What is missing is *mood;* the spiritual atmosphere which must
inform a play's structure. This fault, as we shall later note, is perhaps
symptomatic of something in the artistic makeup of the National
Theatre company.

Next I saw Farquhar's *The Recruiting Officer* (1706), in which love intrigues typical of eighteenth-century English comedy are combined with a shrewd commentary on the army's ugly devices of recruiting. The play is richly written, utterly beguiling in its characters, as well as delightfully funny in its scenes.

With a perfect cast, the production is in every way successful. Once again Maggie Smith holds the stage with a wise gleam in her eye, benevolently feminine mischief in her heart, laughter in her spirit and an attractiveness that stems more from the whole composition of her qualities than from her physical person. In the cast, too, Laurence Olivier (artistic director to this company of fifty-one actors) plays a small part in a manner so absolutely right and original that it lingers emblematically as the obtuse, mendacious, boastful, good-natured, thoroughly self-satisfied (satisfied with the fun of cheating, fighting, guzzling, wenching) petty officer who is as much at ease in the army as a pig in a trough. This characterization, which should be set beside Olivier's unforgettable Shallow and his fop in Sheridan's *The Critic*, is a masterpiece.

The Recruiting Officer was followed on my schedule by Harold Brighouse's *Hobson's Choice*, a play first produced in 1916, though it mirrors the Salford (Lancashire) of 1880. The play foreshadows the breakdown of class snobbery in England; it also proves that a "corny" comedy can be art and that social reflection may be fun. The story is of a masterful lady of thirty, threatened with spinsterhood by her plainness and by her father's exploitation, who chooses a semiliterate cobbler as her husband and sets out to stiffen his backbone and give him the semblance of an education. In doing so, she shatters the paternal fortress. *Hobson's Choice* is an utterly charming stage piece—all smiles, sound sentiment and good sense.

Joan Plowright, with her spunk and dark, determined, glistening eyes, her speech that sounds sweetly of Midland streets (the accent is usually accounted ugly, but on Miss Plowright's lips it acquires a wonderful savor) makes Maggie Hobson a girl to treasure, the salt of womankind and of British moral will.

No less effective is Frank Finlay, an actor who plays bluff working-class characters with archetypal truthfulness and lends them a warmth one might not guess they possessed. He is the darling boob of whom Maggie makes a man. Michael Redgrave has been accused (partly because of the enormous beard which frames his face) of turning Hobson into a musty King Lear. It seems to me, however, that his performance was "saved" by that beard! There are actors who require a mask—a strong external characterization— to set their imagination free. Redgrave is such an actor. His Hobson, formidable in girth as well as in height, red-nosed, cunning and stupid, blustering and weak, embattled and pathetic, is both funny and forgivable. He provides the production with a strong anchor.

Chekhov's *Uncle Vanya,* with Redgrave in the name part, Olivier as Astrov, Plowright as Sonya and Rosemary Harris as the professor's wife, was given a thoroughly understanding production. The last two acts are especially moving. Redgrave is brilliant in the scene where he bursts out against his selfish pedant of a brother-in-law, and in his final grief, inconsolable by the brokenhearted encouragement of Plowright's Sonya, he reduces us to tears.

Still, for all its excellence, the production reveals something of the company's shortcomings. Mannerism often takes the place of mood. ("Mood" results from a confluence of the actor's being with the total environment or soul of the dramatist's creation.) In this production one recognizes a company of meticulous actors who have gone reverently to work. But for Chekhov, sound craftsmanship, even dramatic intelligence, are not enough. This *Uncle Vanya* lacks, not entirely, but enough to leave me a little dissatisfied, the true core of the play—that palpable *idealism* which is at the heart of Chekhov's writing and generally of the Russian character, even in some of its negative aspects.

Thus Rosemary Harris, exquisite as the beauty gone to waste, seems more like an affected bluestocking than a richly endowed woman in whom the sap of life is slowly evaporating. The effect is unintentionally comic, but not comic in Chekhov's way, which is never the least brittle or even faintly depreciatory.

Redgrave's Vanya, on the other hand, might assume more comic meaning in the correct sense if he were less the stifled intellectual at the outset (less "romantic" looking as well) and more the flustered, slightly disheveled, self-neglecting dreamer going to seed.

The visual sign of what I have indicated is the stylized plain wood setting, which is an abstraction of nothing. It suggests hardly any place either actual or symbolic—only a kind of literal dead end, wholly juiceless. The loneliness and ennui of Chekhov's world may be stultifying, but they are never dry.

The climax and sensation of the National Theatre's season is *Othello*. With *Macbeth, Othello* is the most closely knit, the most tightly constructed of Shakespeare's plays. Here poetry and action are perfectly wed.

As Othello, Olivier—and this production is all Olivier, though Maggie Smith is an appealing Desdemona—builds the part with crafty logic. But what is most remarkable about Olivier's performance is not the line of its dramatic evolution or the kind of commonsense realism he brings to the opening scenes, but the bravery, the tempestuous scenic courage with which he depicts the moments of Othello's agony. Here there is such an explosion of searing sound, of groans, of gasps, of wild and broken outcries such as few English-speaking actors would attempt. Such display of histrionic temperament—in this instance the savage orchestration of the emotion of jealousy—is, despite Hamlet's admonition against overacting, the proper style for the interpretation of Shakespearean tragedy.

The killing of Desdemona and Othello's suicide are staged with fierce imagination: Othello holds Desdemona in his arms all through the speech which precedes the moment when he stabs himself with a thin blade concealed in a leather band around his wrist. This, and the elaborate murder of Desdemona, exemplify the kind of red-blooded theatre which we long to see because, while it is supposed to be "traditional," it is rarely found on our "serious" stages today.

Audiences and critics, too, have been much impressed with Olivier's Othello as a *Negro* characterization: the special gait (a slight swagger on bare feet), the resonant low-keyed voice, the somewhat weighted tone and stress of speech, the sensuous mouth, the black man's particular smile and laugh. All this is notably well done, but my mind refused to acknowledge it because I could not help thinking that all this paraphernalia might be unnecessary if a Negro were acting the part.

Everything that consummate skill, splendid vocal and physical equipment, intelligence, observation, theatrical flair can accomplish, Olivier achieves. And yet—I am almost tempted to apologize for saying it—the substance of genuine feeling, which Olivier indicates magnificently, is not actually present. I am excited; I am not touched. I shake with the impact and daring of the performance. But I am not convinced of the authenticity of the play's emotion, nor am I entirely informed as to its meaning.

Olivier knows all about what happens to a man suffering the anguish of jealousy, but he can only imitate—not live it—on the stage. Something in this marvelous actor's nature is perpetually withdrawn. There is always a captivating mystery in Olivier's performances of tragic roles, but also a strange stoppage of personal feeling at their center. The inner sources of emotion—the "floodgates"—are unaccountably closed. Though he has a superb faculty for forcing their release, his secret and most intimate sentiments seldom emerge. That is why I am obliged to consider his acting in comedy or character roles more complete than his performances in tragedy.

Two more things must be said. The production is not especially euphonious. The reasonable realism of the approach makes most of the lines clear but rarely gratifying to the ear. This may also be due to Frank Finlay's utter unsuitability for the role of Iago. He was chosen on the ground that Othello would never be taken in by Iago if he were a "spectacular" character, one whose "honesty" was not of a blunt unvarnished nature. This is mere rationalization, a trick to heighten the effect of an effulgent Othello by a dun Iago. It has little to do with Shakespeare, whose realism is never commonplace but always heroic.

A far more important consideration is the fact that although Olivier is intuitively right in trying to make his "Negroid" characterization a means to reveal the crucial element of sensuality in *Othello*—the play is a "history of lust"—he brings to this aspect of the part a charm, a sort of subtle, leading-man sex appeal which is not precisely what the play demands. *Othello* is a tragedy of desire. There is more appetite than love in the "noble" Moor. Iago's machinations are, so to speak, only a function of Othello's concupiscence. His sensual passion is the cause of his torment, the true reason for his downfall. It should have a torrential force, a volcanic heat. When Olivier suffers the throes of jealousy he is human, all too human, which may endear him to us, but that very fact diminishes Othello's Shakespearean stature.

If I have seemed unduly crabbed about a week of playgoing, which at all times afforded me true pleasure and with a company

I hold in high esteem, it is because I have chosen to regard the work of the British National Theatre in the light of art, rather than as a series of "great shows" that may serve to give a kick to our spare time. One does not gush over art; one contemplates or ponders it as an event in one's life.

32

Brecht in Paris

[1960]

During my visit here, there were, as usual, several interesting plays written with that degree of sophistication which makes the French play, no matter what its real value, seem "superior" to most American and British plays. There was also (just about to close) Jean-Paul Sartre's three-and-a-half-hour brain buster *The Prisoners of Altona*, which, apart from Jean Genet's *The Blacks* (which had already closed), was the most impressive play of the year.

The great event of my latest theatrical expedition was the four productions of Bertolt Brecht's plays given at the Théâtre des Nations in its international theatre season—a splendid annual spring feature in Paris. The Brecht works were presented by his own Berliner Ensemble, which most critics today regard as the finest theatre company on the Continent, perhaps the finest in the world.

Much—too much—has already been written on Brecht's theories. In Europe, at least, they have already exercised noticeable influence and stimulated almost as much talk as the Method has with us. What struck me most sharply on seeing the Berliner Ensemble this time was the pointlessness of most of this talk in view of the actual performances.

The didactic element, the stylization, the detachment—all these have been repeatedly emphasized almost to the exclusion of the sheer facts of the production in their effect and meaning. In this respect the earnest thinkers in the theatre are almost as misleading as the ordinary folk of show business. Both stress what is most superficially striking: the "knockout" aspects of cleverness, laughs, excitement; and, in the case of Brecht, the scenic novelty.

The first thing we recognize in the Brecht productions is their *reality:* an utterly engrossing reality. We feel we are looking directly at the core and substance of what the plays are about. We do not sense any element of staginess, arty ornament or eye-deceiving illusion. At the same time, we are not only at ease—the ordinary naturalistic production always seems a little strenuous by comparison—but thoroughly absorbed. We are at once in the theatre—with all its sense of festival and fun—and soberly in the midst of life. We do not sweat with anxiety or often split our sides with laughter; yet we are stirred by what is serious and refreshed by what is humorous.

The didacticism of a Brecht play is always telling—unless one is intent on resistance—because the message seems to radiate from every element of the performance. The very props seem to tell a tale, convey some fundamental significance. Everything in these productions is so integrated that when an actor stops what might pass for an intensely dramatic scene (there is hardly any screaming and shouting except for purposes of caricature) to speak a bit of verse or to sing-recite a song, one hardly notices the break. The prose dialogue and the lyric interval are both phases of the same essence.

The Berliner Ensemble represents the truest theatre of our day in a very special sense. I do not yet know exactly in what esteem I hold the Brecht plays as literature, though as sheer writing they are superb. I am not at all sure that the company contains any great actors—a number are clearly mediocre—and I cannot say whether any other company in the same sets and costumes might not make the stage design appear dull. I do know that we perceive all as a single phenomenon. We are confronted with a living thing which is full of meaning and has immeasurably greater impact than anything I have witnessed in years. And *this* is theatre.

When one reads a play by Brecht—before or even after having seen it—one is astonished to find that for all the purity, simplicity and, with the plainness, the subtle elevation of its style, one thinks of it not so much as a complete play, but rather as a libretto for the opera of which it is a part, or as a film script in respect to the picture which is to be made of it. That is one reason why Brecht's plays may prove disappointing in productions not created by the Brecht company under the conditions which the Berliner Ensemble has been enabled to foster for itself.

The secret of the total power these plays impart in the productions which the playwright or his colleagues have directed is that everything in them emanates from a sense of life, a conviction, a will, a seed-sentiment transmitted in every moment, movement, color, gesture and thought, shared by everyone concerned in the performance. Not only one consciousness, but a single breath, seems to have given it life. The productions are not so much a collective triumph as they are the body of one spirit. Brecht's word has become flesh; his ideas have taken on visible form. The productions are literally a revelation; that is why—antinaturalistic, anti-"emotional" and (save the mark!) anti-"Method"—they are so unmistakably forceful, so wholly real, so inescapably immediate, so compelling and—for all the infinite care and craftsmanship involved in their making—so unaffected.

But what do Brecht's plays reveal? What, apart from their too easily captioned propaganda, do they express?

The Brecht plays I saw here were *The Resistible Rise of Arturo Ui,* written in exile in 1941 and first presented in Berlin (after Brecht's death) in 1959; *The Mother,* an adaptation of Maxim Gorky's novel, written in 1932; *Galileo Galilei,* written in exile in 1939 and presented posthumously in Berlin in 1957; and finally, *Mother Courage and Her Children* (pages 130–133), also written in exile and first presented by the Berliner Ensemble in 1949.

Arturo Ui is an epic caricature of the rise of Adolf Hitler and his gang. The word is used advisedly: Brecht has set his play in a mythical American city and Ui is the head of a band of petty crooks in the cauliflower racket. All the events and personalities connected with Hitler's rise to power—Hindenburg, Göring, Goebbels, Roehm, Dollfuss, the Reichstag fire and trial, the occupation of Austria—have their absurd counterparts in this panoramic farce.

Though the parallels between the episodes of the play and their historical sources are quite obvious, Brecht has the factual political items which he wishes us to recall projected on a screen at the beginning of each scene. Since the play was revived after the war, Brecht's last commentary is appended after the final curtain: "You are learning to see instead of merely watching stupidly. Act instead of gossiping. See what almost dominated the world. The people finally won. But none should proclaim victory too readily. The womb from which the vile monster issued is still fertile."

The "lesson" of the play is made explosively graphic and vastly comic in Brecht's treatment, and more particularly in the brilliant production directed by two of Brecht's disciples. Of incalculable value is the virtuoso performance by one of the company's younger actors, Ekkehard Schall, who plays Ui-Hitler as a maniacal neurotic, a trembling hysteric obsessed by fear of his own inferiority and an even more violent revulsion against this fear. From a spastic stammer to mad eloquence, the creature Schall projects with an energy which at times mounts to sheer acrobatics is unforgettably convulsive. One scene, especially, in which Hitler is coached by a ham actor on how to pose and speak, is deliciously funny.

I shocked my critic friends here by saying that in a certain sense the production of *The Mother* was even a more remarkable feat than that of *Arturo Ui*. They were shocked because *Arturo Ui* is, if nothing else, tremendous entertainment, full of invention and scenic ingenuity. What I meant was that *The Mother*, which is rather primitive Communist propaganda telling the simple tale of the transformation of an illiterate Russian woman of the working class to a heroic figure of the revolutionary movement from 1905 to 1917, is presented with such muted power, such quiet humor, such fine songs rendered inspiringly brave by Hanns Eisler's music and such grave conviction, communicated not only in the acting of Helene Weigel (Brecht's widow and the head of the Ensemble), but also in the stark staging. The staging, for all its bareness, manages to attain a sculptural and pictorial distinction which conveys in its very shape, color and composition something of the earthy strength of which the play is a poem of praise and an example.

I need not dwell on *Mother Courage*—I wrote about it when I first saw it in Berlin in 1957 and elsewhere (pages 130–133)—except to say that it impressed me even more this time. It is probably the finest of Brecht's achievements, a masterpiece of modern stagecraft in all its aspects.

The play and production which most strongly stamped on my mind a sense of Brecht's great stature as an artist of the theatre was *Galileo,* for which Erich Engel is credited with the direction. I believe, however, the first steps were undertaken by Brecht himself, who died in 1956 while the play was still in the early stage of study.

I had seen *Galileo* in the 1947 Hollywood–New York production with Charles Laughton in the leading role and, though Brecht had supervised it (Joe Losey was the director), that production gave only the faintest notion of its possibilities as a stage piece. Whether due to lack of means or to a misunderstanding of Brechtian aesthetics, which recommend a certain asceticism, it looked almost shabby. But a careful reading of the play (which takes place in Florence, Venice and Rome in the seventeenth century) shows that its physical presentation calls for opulence within that asceticism. This is fully realized in Casper Neher's all-bronze setting—a stroke of genius by this master designer—where scenes of poverty and of pomp, interiors and exteriors are all equally at home.

Galileo is the story of the struggle of reason against superstition and the forces which maintain superstition in order to hold the reins of social power. On the surface, both the thesis and the play's points appear too simple. But Brecht's simplicity is artful. He presents the case for the hierarchy, cannily aware of the dangers of Galileo's proof of the Copernican "heresy"—that the earth moves around the sun and not vice versa—with skill and something like sympathy. Indeed, when the court philosopher asks Galileo, "Are such stars that Galileo has just discovered really necessary?" the audience here seemed to turn against Brecht, for many laughed and applauded, thinking, no doubt, of our recent lunar expeditions and the fear they somehow inspire in many of us.

Galileo is entirely contemporary in view of the events of our atomic age and in relation to certain problems of conscience. When Galileo, in fear of torture by the Inquisition, retracts his theories, his most devoted pupil in an admirable scene cries out, "Unhappy the country which has no heroes!" to which Galileo retorts, "No. Unhappy is the country which needs a hero!"

But this is not Brecht's last word. At another point, Galileo admits that he ought not be forgiven his betrayal; his fear of pain is no excuse. Is the search for the truth, then, everything? Science, he says, must be concerned not only with its own findings, but with their consequences. There are thus two battles or fields of struggle. The play ends with the admonition "Protect the flame of knowledge, use but do not abuse it lest one day a whirlwind of fire consume us all."

This was not Brecht's first ending and there is evidence throughout the play that Brecht kept revising it to keep abreast of the various mutations of his thought and conscience (in one version, Galileo's defection was more or less rationalized). Here then is a play by an intellectual which is subtle, lucid, full of meat yet easily digested by a wide audience, a play which eschews "excitement" and yet remains dramatic.

There are two supreme moments of staging in this production which exemplify what I have previously written about the Berliner Ensemble. One is a scene, largely pantomimic, in which the rabble in the square and passing priests around a street procession reveal the popular effect of Galileo's inquiries. It is a comic scene—pure theatre—but its message of how the ferment of ideas manifests itself in ordinary social behavior is made indelibly picturesque. Another is the scene in which the Inquisitor attempts to persuade the Pope to put Galileo on the rack. The Pope is being dressed. When the scene begins, he is in his underwear: he is the "naked" man—honest and forbearing. But as the talk proceeds and ever more of his ecclesiastical robes are dropped on the Pope's body, he becomes increasingly "institutional" until, at the final moment, he stands in princely glory and orders that Galileo be "shown the instruments."

The quiet familiarity of Ernst Busch's Galileo typifies Brecht's manner and content, as does Helene Weigel's two "Mothers." Brecht is a poet of classic character. He wished his work to have the authority of an objective statement which needs no stress beyond a simple grace of speech, no "art" beyond the most engaging directness, no "passion" greater than that which the truth will elicit. His technique is a reasonableness which arises when a smiling skepticism sets out in quest of a small area of certainty. This, he hopes, will prove charmingly self-evident. Not wholly in vain did Brecht claim the Chinese and Japanese among his artistic ancestors.

What does Brecht ultimately say? Trust what your senses experience, what your mind has weighed and what your most fundamental human instincts dictate. Act with your fellowmen in the name of what you have all tested and found to be needful to your life in common. Seek always, do not allow yourself to grow rigid at any point and let your goal be the peaceful enjoyment of the goods of life.

From all the contradictions of Brecht's nature, his irony and his radicalism, his homely earthiness and his "peasant" cunning, his culture and folksy common sense, there emerges something that may very well be that ineffable quality: manly virtue.

33

Musicals: A Survey

[1962]

MUSICAL COMEDY is nothing to argue about: it is to be enjoyed. Yet
if you should stop to think about it, you may discover some fascinating and perhaps fruitful opportunities for dispute. It is said, for example, that the American theatre has become a musical-comedy
theatre. Some say it mournfully, others with pride and glee. And
there are those who deny it fiercely.

The facts favor the ayes. Recent statistics inform us that eleven
musicals were produced during the 1960–61 season, fourteen last season, and fourteen musicals, in addition to four revues, have been announced for 1962–63. There are ten musicals occupying the boards
at the moment, and only seven plays without musical benefit. As the
number of theatrical productions each year diminishes, the near
dominance of musical comedy on our stage becomes increasingly evident. As an astonishing corroboration of what one might call the
automatic popularity of musical comedy, there is the news item (not
mere publicity) that the Lindsay–Crouse–Berlin show *Mr. President*
boasts an advance sale before its New York opening of over two
million dollars.

Facts, however, are dumb things: they do not reveal the whole
truth. The theatre is a place where art, social pattern and economics
are inextricably commingled. So if musical comedy is to be discussed
apart from its fun, it must be examined in all these lights.

The hastiest and most superficial consideration makes the reason for the box-office potency of the musical quite obvious. Musicals are designed to please practically everyone with the minimum of effort on anyone's part. All possibility of offense is avoided. Every ingredient is scrupulously aimed at ease, comfort, titillation—as with a holiday resort. The musical is a large-scale entertainment package. Won't the man who invites his out-of-town client-friend on a business and pleasure jaunt to New York feel safer in reserving tickets for a splendid musical jamboree rather than for *Heartbreak House* or *Long Day's Journey into Night?*

Even the weakest musical promises at least two or three good jokes, a talented performer, a bit of rhythm, one or two pretty ladies, a tune one might hum and several nice dresses—or undresses. Musicals are show business' best bet because everyone nowadays seeks relief from real or pretended pressures. A drama might require some strain of nerve or brain muscle. The most resolute theatregoer will vow, in moments of exasperated impatience, that he would rather see a good musical several times than many supposedly earnest plays once.

Though scholarly gentlemen often point out that musical comedy has its antecendents in such European models as operetta and *opéra bouffe,* as well as in certain indigenous entertainments like the minstrel show and burlesque, the bare statement that musical comedy today is the one theatrical form in which America excels seems incontrovertible.

Enthusiasts learnedly explain, furthermore, that musical comedy as we now practice it, is a special and virtually new kind of show, of which Rodgers' and Hammerstein's *Oklahoma!* is often cited as a prime example. This claim of originality for the new musical smacks of hysterical complacency. Whatever fine distinctions are made between the musicals after the great Rodgers and Hammerstein hit and those of Irving Berlin, Jerome Kern, George Gershwin, Cole Porter and Vincent Youmans, as well as those of Rodgers himself (in collaboration with Larry Hart) in the twenties and thirties, it is certain that the work of those early days was of the same nature as, and of equal (if not superior) value to, that of our more "integrated" musicals today.

To be impressive, one might refer even further back to George M. Cohan, Victor Herbert and Ivan Caryll's *Pink Lady* (1911). The point is that there always seems to have been a vital and flourishing theatre of light comic character in America. If there is any fixed tradition in our theatre, this is it. The reason is social and historical. The story of America, by and large, has been one of energy, invention, adaptability, youthfulness, buoyancy, optimism, physical well-being and prosperity. No matter what troubles beset us, we try to remain sanguine. ("Pack up your troubles in your old kit bag—and smile, smile, smile!") Despite another strain of American creativity from Hawthorne and Melville to Faulkner and O'Neill, tragedy has been rather alien to us.

Still, there is a correspondence between our so-called serious drama and our lighter musical stage. For all theatre is one: It always reflects—in comedy as well as in tragedy—various aspects of the human landscape. Just as there was almost no important native drama at the time of *The Black Crook* (1866) and precious little during the Floradora days (1900), the sophistication of our musical shows increases as we approach the late teens and early twenties.

It is surely not a matter of chance that our musical theatre burst into effulgent bloom just as our more sober theatre produced its first crop of notable playwrights: Eugene O'Neill, George Kelly, Elmer Rice, Maxwell Anderson, Sidney Howard, S. N. Behrman, Robert Sherwood, Philip Barry. And just before the launching of the Group Theatre we had *Of Thee I Sing*. When we come to observe what is happening to our present musicals, we shall have to judge the situation in the broader context of our theatre as a whole.

There are those who maintain that while our musical-comedy theatre constitutes a masterpiece in the aggregate, very few—if any —of our musicals have achieved the artistic integrity or the staying power of the best in Gilbert and Sullivan, Offenbach or the Weill and Brecht of *The Threepenny Opera*. (Of course, none of these is, strictly speaking, musical comedy, any more than is Gershwin's *Porgy and Bess*.) Yet, despite such demurs, our attachment to the musical-comedy form is not only understandable but aesthetically justified. For musical comedy is that "mythical" phenomenon—true theatre.

What is true theatre? When still a young man, Bernard Shaw wrote: "The theatre was born of old from the union of two tendencies: the desire to have a dance and the desire to hear a story. The dance became a rout, the story became a situation."

True theatre is the telling of a story or the presentation of a situation through every physical means by which men and women, together in the presence of their community, are capable of rousing its interest and pleasure. Theatre bespeaks human action—movement and speech—raised to an intense degree of eloquence through dance, song, color, spectacle. From ghost stories and tall tales told around a campfire to the austere magnificence of Greek drama, this impulse has always shaped the theatre's essence. It is there in the performance of the Japanese Noh plays, as well as in Shakespeare. We find it in Brecht (at the Berliner Ensemble) as well as in *Pal Joey*. It was what O'Neill always dreamed of achieving.

Where on our stage today is there so much of this true theatre as in our musical comedies? Ballet, which has heightened its appeal for us enormously since the thirties, lacks speech; drama lacks song and (too often) color; opera usually misses acting. The straight play (what a terrible term) often contains ideas. But musicals may possess these as well. At times musicals would appear to be almost the only place in the theatre where ideas may take final refuge!

As we hark back to the past of our musical and nonmusical stages, we fondly recall the personalities which graced both. In the twenties our theatre—the two kinds—was illuminated by splendid constellations of players whose very presence cast a halo of magic over every occasion. In the thirties the stars began to move westward. Now they are mainly to be found on the musical horizon. How many shining bodies have we on the dramatic stage today compared with those we admire in the musicals?

The comparison may be invidious and unfair, but can you, reader, make a list of "legitimate" actors and actresses to set down beside Ethel Merman, Ray Bolger, Mary Martin, Judy Holliday, Julie Andrews, Gwen Verdon, Zero Mostel, Nancy Walker and Phil Silvers—and perhaps Tammy Grimes, Robert Morse, Barbra Streisand and Barbara Harris tomorrow? (And, oh, if she were only in the theatre —Judy Garland!) What brilliant additions to our stagecraft—not to speak of our satisfaction—have been made by such choreographers as George Balanchine, Agnes de Mille, Jerome Robbins, Michael Kidd, Bob Fosse, Herbert Ross and Gower Champion.

But halt! Some of those named have transferred or will transfer from the nonmusical to the musical theatre as others may take the opposite direction. Everything in our theatre today is in a process of flux and change—some warn of dissolution—and the musicals mirror the alteration perhaps even more strikingly than our drama.

Long ago—for convenience' sake, let us say before 1930—what was most important to the musical-comedy audience was beautiful girls (hail Ziegfeld!), comedians (those dear old Ed Wynn days) and, crucially, *music*—real tunes suggesting all the wonderful things the often paltry books of the time could not say. (Think of the *Show Boat* score—one which is most likely to survive.) It did not matter much if you interrupted the story to bring on the girls or to vamp into a bright, consoling melody.

The new musical strives toward "legitimacy." The book, or, more properly, the show's subject matter, must possess a little substance, relate somehow to our normal concerns, edge closer to the contemporaneous and the topical. Due in large measure to the refinement of our taste through the influence of our ballet companies, dancing has developed into a cardinal factor.

Above all, there is now an insistence on "integration"—of which *Guys and Dolls, My Fair Lady, West Side Story* and *Gypsy* supply outstanding examples. Integration demands that all the elements in a musical be thoroughly "cemented." The story, lyrics, music, acting and dancing must not only fit together, but extend or complete each other. The line or fabric of the whole must never appear to break: one part must carry on where the other leaves off so as to compose a closely woven continuity.

This explains, incidentally, why the girls in musicals today are seldom as dazzlingly attractive as they formerly were. All the advantages and talents—the ability to sing, dance, act and to look beautiful—do not often dwell in one person.

The new musical is designed to create a unified impression, a coherent tone, an all-pervasive atmosphere. At times this aim appears to be attained at the expense of melody. The scores of our recent musicals seem to have more utility than inspiration. They have become a means rather than an end. There are signal exceptions to this, as for example the score—which seems to improve with age—of *Kiss Me, Kate*. Still, one might point out that such a stylistic relic as *Kismet* was successful mainly because it was sustained by delightful—albeit borrowed—music.

What strikes many listeners as musical anemia in many recent shows may be explained in another way. It has been widely agreed that our theatre, in general, has become markedly less animated since 1956–57. Certainly there have been good things of various sorts since then, but there has been a definite shrinkage, not only in the volume of productions (and profits) but in every sense in which the word *abundance* may be construed. Our dramatic theatre has thinned out —foreign plays of quality, for example, preponderated last season— and something peculiar has happened to our musical theatre as well.

Serious drama has always encountered a certain resistance in our theatre—more particularly since theatre tickets have become so expensive. Such drama can exist and thrive only when it is fired by sufficient passion and conviction to make it thoroughly arresting. For the past decade, at least, we have been living in a state of spiritual confusion. Issues are not clear-cut: there has been inner, but hardly articulated, disquiet. Boldness is not feared so much as it is baffled by lack of social support and subjective assurance. We have grown publicly mute on serious matters, for we do not know exactly what there is to be said. We cover up and are not even sure what we are suppressing. Hence the repeated, but rather vague, outcry against conformism.

Yet we do want to express *something* about what lurks in our minds. We do not like to say anything which might be deemed heavy, humorless or offensive—we do not want to rock the boat—so we kid and joke. We mask our misgivings in gags.

The social themes of the thirties and early forties begin to emerge anew as grins and grimaces in the musicals of the late fifties and early sixties. After the war, we appeased our jarred souls with sweet, smiling images of the past (or of remote places): *Oklahoma! Bloomer Girl, Carousel, Up in Central Park* and *Brigadoon.* With *Finian's Rainbow* we began pushing the present, while *South Pacific,* despite its touch of exoticism, hovered around a controversial subject. Then our present begins to engage us pleasantly with *The Pajama Game,* a "labor" musical without contention, to be followed later by *Fiorello!,* a "political" show without rancor.

The contemporary keynote is struck in *How to Succeed in Business Without Really Trying,* which indicates by its very title the point we have reached. (To begin with, think of the number of musicals which are basically success stories, such as *The Unsinkable Molly Brown.*) We are unsure of our values—at least for purposes of theatrical presentation—so we are both obsessed by the idea of success (and by status or money, which is its goal), and a little ashamed of the obsession. It is no accident that *Do Re Mi, Bye Bye Birdie, I Can Get It for You Wholesale* and even, to some extent, *No Strings,* are variations on the themes of success, status push and money fixation. These are now what might be called our "social plays." They all deplore our addiction to the success–status–money fetish—but not too emphatically.

Love creeps into these shows, as it were, by the back door. They are only half-heartedly romantic. They suggest that love must ride a rough road in our competitive mechanized world. As a result, the embodiment of glamour, warmth, carefreeness and a poised enjoyment of wealth becomes strained. For shows deficient in these ingredients, it is no easy matter to write free-flowing tunes—melodies with a lift. One might as well try to put double-entry bookkeeping to music.

In *Musical Comedy in America,* one of the best books on the subject, Cecil Smith, clearly a devotee, ends by asserting that while musicals have moved "into an increasingly high plane of craftsmanship and literacy," they are still only entertainments, "and if they are art at all, they are only incidentally so." Though the distinction may be useful, one should be wary of it; it insinuates that art is that which does not entertain!

One might correct a misunderstanding here by remarking that present-day musicals are too often founded on a sort of industrial calculation, sales gimmicks barely related to true individual or personal impulse. The musical, in other words, far too frequently nowadays is conceived on a mass-production basis as a corporate effort by canny and capable showmen with an eye to profitable enterprise on the Main Stem supermarket. Art rarely springs from such sources. A musical play like the Offenbach and Halévy *La Vie Parisienne,* for instance, was a collaboration of two men who were as much imbued with a feeling—both satiric and gay—about the Second Empire as any artist of their time.

Whatever one's estimate of their separate merits, our musicals at present are as typical of the extraordinary accomplishment and the grave defects as are all the other manifestations of our native theatre. They, too—and perhaps even more at the moment than most other "attractions" our playhouses have to offer—are "the brief chronicles of the time." Indeed, certain knowledgeable folk tell us that the hope of the *Midtown* theatres lies in our musicals. It may well be so, since they, up to very recently, have proved commercially the most advantageous as well as the most popular of our productions.

Still, the high cost of producing and operating our super-lavish musicals forces them to court disaster. During the past two seasons there have been many more well-liked and lauded musicals which have lost money than we suspect. The relatively small cast and scenic modesty of *A Funny Thing Happened on the Way to the Forum* may be a portent. Should the fate of musicals be threatened by the economic hazards that menace the life of our dramatic theatre, the institution or concept known as Broadway may collapse. This, however, does not mean that the theatre in our country would die.

One good way to keep musicals lively, at any rate, is to avoid making too sharp a distinction between merit in one category of the theatre and another. A musical must be appreciated according to standards of freshness, imaginativeness and emotional authenticity similar to those we apply to other stage forms. Such criteria may, in fact, serve as a leaven for our theatre generally.

34

Fiddler on the Roof

[1964]

AFTER SEEING *Fiddler on the Roof* (based on some Yiddish short stories; book by Joseph Stein, music by Jerry Bock, lyrics by Sheldon Harnick) numerous members of the audience confessed (or proclaimed) that they shed tears of compassion and gratitude; others have asserted that their hearts swelled in elation, while still others were convulsed with laughter. My own reception of the show was cool.

I too found it endearing—worthy of the affection the enthusiasts had manifested. Yet thinking of it in its detail, the text lacked the full savor of its sources; the music simply followed a pattern of suitable folk melodies without adding, or being equal, to them; Jerome Robbins' choreography, though correct in its method, was not—except for two instances—as brilliant as I had expected it to be. Boris Aronson's sets did not "overwhelm" me; even Zero Mostel's performance, which cements the diverse elements and gives them a core and a shape, was open to objections. Then, too, were not those critics right, in the press and the public, who maintained there was a Broadway taint in the mixture?

Yet the longer I reflected, the greater grew my regard for the show! The steadier my effort to arrive at a true appraisal of my feelings, the more clearly I realized that the general audience was justified. By a too meticulous weighing and sifting of each of the performance's components one loses sight of the whole.

The production is actually *discreet.* For a popular ($350,000) musical there is a certain modesty in its effect. The vast machinery of production—I do not refer to the physical aspects alone—which must perforce go into the making of an entertainment of this sort has by an exercise of taste been reduced to a degree of intimacy that is almost surprising.

The choreography, for example, does not attempt to electrify; though it is rather more muscular, broader and certainly less "cosy" than Jewish folk dancing tends to be, Robbins has, on the whole, successfully combined the homeliness of such dancing with cossack energy. And though Aronson's sets may remind one of Chagall, they do not really attempt to achieve Chagall-like results. (Chagall's art is always more emphatically Russian or French than anything else. Whatever their subject, his paintings possess a certain opulent flamboyance that is hardly Jewish.) Aronson, faced with the need to move his sets rapidly, as well as to give them the atmosphere of impoverishment required by the play's environment without robbing them of a certain quiet charm, has made his contribution to the proceedings relatively unobtrusive—which a Chagall stage design never is. (There is also in Aronson's pictorial scheme a nice contrast between the ramshackle drabness of the places in which the play's characters are housed and the profuse yet delicate greenery of the natural surroundings.) Considering, too, the dizzying extravagance of Mostel's histrionic quality, his performance is remarkably reserved.

None of this, however, goes to the heart of the show's significance, which must be sought in its effect on the audience. That effect comes close, within the facile laughter, the snug appreciation of an anticipated showmanship, to something religious. To understand this one must turn to the play's original material: stories by Sholom Aleichem. Sholom Aleichem (pen name for Sholom Rabinowitz, born in Russia in 1859, died in New York in 1916) was the great folk artist of Yiddish literature—an altogether unique figure who might without exaggeration be compared to Gogol. The essence of Sholom Aleichem's work is in a very special sense *moral.* It is the distillation of a humane sweetness from a context of sorrow. It represents the unforced emergence of a real joy and a true sanctification from the soil of life's workaday worries and pleasures. Although this blessed acceptance of the most commonplace facts of living—generally uncomfortable and graceless, to say the least—appears casual and unconscious in Sholom Aleichem, it is based on what, in the first and indeed the best of the play's numbers, is called "Tradition."

This tradition, which might superficially be taken to comprise little more than a set of obsolete habits, customs and pietistic prescriptions, is in fact the embodiment of profound culture. A people is not cultured primarily through the acquisition or even the making of works of art; it is cultured when values rooted in biologically and spiritually sound human impulses, having been codified, become the apparently instinctive and inevitable mode of its daily and hourly conduct. Sholom Aleichem's characters are a concentrate of man's belief in living which does not exclude his inevitable bewilderment and questioning of life's hardship and brutal confusion.

In the stories this is expressed as a kindness which does not recognize itself, as pity without self-congratulation, as familiar humor and irony without coarseness. This is beauty of content, if not of form. For the Eastern (Russian, Polish, Rumanian, Galician) Jews of yesteryear "would have been deeply puzzled," Irving Howe and Eleazer Greenberg have said in their admirable introduction to a collection of Yiddish stories, "by the idea that the aesthetic and the moral are distinct realms, for they saw beauty above all in behavior."

More of this meaning than we had a right to expect is contained in *Fiddler on the Roof.* Is it any wonder, then, that an audience, living in one of the most heartless cities of the world at a time of conformity to the mechanics of production, an audience without much relation to any tradition beyond that expressed through lip service to epithets divested of living experience, an audience progressively more deprived of the warmth of personal contact and the example of dignified companionship, should weep thankfully and laugh in acclamation at these images of a good life lived by good people? In *Fiddler on the Roof* this audience finds a sense of what "togetherness" might signify. Without the cold breath of any dogma or didactics, it gets a whiff of fellow feeling for the unfortunate and the persecuted. It is a sentiment that acts as a kind of purification.

Is there too much "show biz" in *Fiddler on the Roof?* Undoubtedly. But apart from the fact that dramaturgic and musical equivalents of Sholom Aleichem's genius are not to be had for the asking, is it conceivable that a truly organic equivalent of the original stories could be produced in our time? The makers and players of *Fiddler on the Roof* are not of Kiev, 1905 (except for Boris Aronson, who was born in Kiev in 1900), nor do they live (even in memory) a life remotely akin to that of Tevye the Dairyman, his family and his friends, or of the author who begat them. The producers of *Fiddler on the Roof* are Broadway—as is the audience—and, in this instance, perhaps the best of it. Those who have attended some of the latter-day productions of the Yiddish stage itself will know that they too are as alien to the spirit of Sholom Aleichem as anything we see at the Imperial Theatre.

The name of Chagall has almost unavoidably come up. The nearest thing to that artist's type of imagination dwells within *Fiddler on the Roof*'s leading actor. Zero Mostel has "Chagall" in his head. Mostel's clown inspiration is unpredictably fantastic—altogether beyond the known or rational. One wishes this fantasy were allowed fuller scope in the show, even as compliments for its control are in order. For Mostel too, being part of Broadway, will fleetingly lapse into adulterations inhospitable to his fabulous talent.

35

Defense of the Artist
as "Neurotic"

[1958]

WHEN, DURING THE DEPRESSION, we read headlines of businessmen who flung themselves from the windows of their office buildings, we were shocked but not utterly surprised. One thing is certain: very few people felt impelled to comment that the nature of business produced madmen.

Many of us have been made uneasy of late to read statements or to hear television interviews in which an artist announced that he was undergoing psychoanalytic treatment. The fact itself is by no means objectionable; we are prepared to believe that such treatment for the artist, as for anyone else, may prove helpful. But this is a private matter. What disturbs us is that such public confessions are presumed to reveal something about the nature of artists and their work. This, I, for one, hold to be entirely false.

Two things are assumed: that art is itself the outcome of some maladjustment or neurosis and that, if the artist were to correct this, he might either function more efficiently or, a more ambiguous conclusion, he might beneficially cease being an artist altogether. In either interpretation, a supposedly normal person might emerge— the prototype of that person probably being the one who reads the confession or hears it on the air.

The reason this view is fairly popular may be set down to our secret envy of the artist who, despite all possible disabilities, is somehow regarded as a special being. The "bohemian"—usually a defective artist—often fosters the myth both as a boast and as an excuse for misconduct, which the community usually believes to be characteristic of him. It has been said that "no man is a hero to his valet," on which Goethe commented, "That is because the valet is a valet."

There may be a more cogent reason why the notion that an artist must be a basically "sick" person is developing into a local cliché. The idea began to gain ever greater acceptance with the spread of the romantic movement in the early nineteenth century. When the artist was no longer ready to celebrate the dogmas of religious institutions or the official policies of the governing classes, his position became more and more precarious. He was regarded with increasing suspicion. He felt himself estranged from the majority—the source of social approval. This was a hard time for him not only materially but spiritually. No man naturally prefers to live an alien among his fellows.

The artist's defense was, "I am in revolt against the centers of established opinion. They have turned me into a kind of pariah. Very well, I shall be a pariah, cultivate my differences, dwell in an attic, dress and behave in a manner distinct from that of the respectable folk who scorn me and whom I shall now scorn, starve if need be. But I shall persist. If this be madness, I shall nurture my madness and glory in it."

That this summary of a long cultural process is more than a surmise is exemplified in the work of such a master as Thomas Mann, whose *Death in Venice* and other early stories dramatize the artist's inability to cope with society, his morbid sensitivity, his anomalous psychology and behavior. All of which is supposed to explain why a person becomes an artist. Whether this was Mann's last word on the subject I doubt, but, as a description of how many people see the artist, it is not only accurate but by now commonplace.

My criticism of this is first a historical one: the artists in the sturdiest periods of artistic creativity—Greece in the fifth century B.C., the Renaissance, France under Louis XIV—did not think of the artist in this way at all. (Then, and later, the artist who was a general, a senator, a diplomat, a physician, a scientist was not uncommon.) Much more crucial than this, however, is my belief that the whole concept of art as a consequence of some inner disturbance is a distortion of the creative act.

"The nature of man is to know," Aristotle said. Art is a knowing. It arises from our contact with the world outside and within. Life is a challenge from the day of our birth. It is a challenge we accept through every hazard, or we should soon give it up. We face the challenge by a constant effort to understand it, to become, so to speak, intimate with it—to bridge the gap between our individual isolation and everything outside ourselves. The sense of connection we establish through this effort is a source of deep pleasure even if what we discover and the search itself are fraught with anxiety. The most rabid pessimism in art is still an affirmation of life. If it were not, the artist would not trouble to commit his blasphemies to paper, canvas, song or stage.

It is the nature of man, then, to develop and practice the artistic faculty. In this sense, all men are born to be artists. (We observe this in children whose health is judged in the perspective of their play.) The man who is not to some degree endowed with the artistic impulse is a dull, if not a positively maimed one. It is part of the imbalance of our times that we so often view art as an extracurricular activity, marginal to the serious concerns of living, an escape from reality.

"I'm very happy that I had writing as an outlet to my reactions to experience," a playwright recently said in an interview. "Otherwise I would really have gone off my trolley." Hard-pressed in the crisscross of confusions, the modern artist says the right thing. Not to express one's self—the expression need not be professional—not to articulate in some humane fashion what one has witnessed, felt, dreamed happily or apprehensively—that, in the last count, is to be truly unhealthy.

Many artists, in defiance of the indifference or condescension that often surrounds them, may overstate their case, but I am inclined to applaud when Stanislaus Joyce reports that his brother James believed "poets are the repositories of the genuine spiritual life of their race." And if the English critic Cyril Connolly says too much when he writes, "It is the quality of an artist to be more imaginative than his fellow men," it is nonetheless true that we seek this quality in the artist to echo, enhance and extend our sense of life.

If, as I say, art is life-affirming, how does one explain this to the person who listens, worried or smug, to the artist as he apologizes for his sickness, and who seems thereby to take it for a fact that artists, being artists, must necessarily be sick or, at least, neurotic people?

Before entering a discussion on this phase of the subject, I must begin by voicing serious misgivings about all the terms employed when we speak of "sick" artists as a class. Though there can be no question that many artists are at least as sick as the waiter who is too distracted to remember the dishes we order or the hackie who constantly mistakes the address he is about to drive us to, none of these artists is any more mentally disturbed than the butcher, the baker, the candlestick maker whose irascibility and ineptitude are becoming increasingly evident to the most superficial observer.

Another thing to be noted before we go on to the heart of our discussion is that, with the average neurotic whose inefficiency, rudeness or misdemeanor perturbs us, there is no compensating factor. The sick artist may be a trial to his friends and family but, at worst, his occupation leads to a result which interests or instructs even when it does not produce positive pleasure.

Let us now turn to the "modern" artist, about whom a Viennese doctor, Max Nordau, wrote a book, circa 1890, called *Degeneration,* in which he tried to adduce marks of insanity in such men as the Impressionist painters, Wagner and Ibsen (this book, by the way, was brilliantly refuted in a little-known essay by Bernard Shaw called *The Sanity of Art*).

We may take an indisputably half-psychotic artist like Strindberg as an example. In the sixty-three years of his life, he wrote more than fifty plays, sixteen novels, seven autobiographies and nine other works. He conducted semiscientific experiments, founded a theatre and helped foster dramatic expressionism. Many of his plays—which exercised a considerable influence on Eugene O'Neill—are still produced and read in many parts of Europe. Though this work—all of it beautifully written—veers from the idyllic to the hysterical, from religious exaltation to intellectual rage, the amount of concentrated effort, thought, study expended in producing this work indicates an energy and a creative force far greater than those employed by all the critics who dismissed him as "sick."

Art is the *health* of the artist. Insofar as the artist engages in his art—I do not refer to those who merely hang on to the fringes of the "art world"—the artist is always healthy. Art being a central function of man's life and a prime manifestation of his humanity, the artist is sane as long as he works as an artist. Apart from this work, he shares in the lesions to which all of us are subject. If he is made to appear more damaged than the rest of us, it is because he gets more publicity; the importance of his job makes him an object of greater social concern.

There still remains the problem of those awful, torpid, sordid, morbid plays, novels, etc. These adjectives rarely mean much more than that we do not like what they describe, but to the extent that our dislike is justified, we must remind ourselves that the artist has not created the world into which he is born.

The artist "imitates" nature in a double sense: he reflects society and, through his response to it, helps create a new world—one which may in some way be affected by what he has created. Much so-called negative (pessimistic, destructive) art has a positive purpose and a salutary effect. Can anyone maintain with equanimity that the world we live in today is an entirely smiling or stable one? Show me the person who answers with an unqualified "yes," and I will show you a fool.

Where does the idea come from that a play or any other work of art to justify itself must necessarily be "happy" or "encouraging"? The province of art is the whole range of human experience. Ecclesiastes is as sound Scripture as the Song of Songs. What miserable product of our contemporary dramatists (sometimes referred to as "decadent") matches the horror of the plots of Aeschylus, Sophocles or Euripides? *King Lear,* a black play if ever there was one, is as much a part of Shakespeare's greatness as are any of his comedies.

Our revulsion at certain "morbid" plays is often an unknowing plea for antidotes and narcotics. When the appetite grows for such dramatic sleeping pills—with a generous admixture of sugar—we ourselves become denatured. A quality of sanity is the capacity to endure what is difficult. Hope and faith which shrink from the recognition of evil are merely evasion.

We have heard it whispered, in tones which range from sniggering to indignant, that many of the new actors are "nuts." For that matter, one is often asked, aren't many of the people who are attracted to the theatre crackpots—in some way or other queer? My first impulse in answer to this is "Yes, these people are crazy if they suppose there is enough work to satisfy the needs of all those who would enter the theatre's ranks."

There are two curses in the theatrical (particularly the acting) profession—enough to drive anyone off the deep end: unemployment and the lack of continuity even after merit has been demonstrated. But insofar as acting is an art—and I believe it can be—it, too, shares in art's sanity.

It is true that certain neophytes gravitate toward the stage as a relief from inner pressures, in the expectation of indulging their troubled souls in the theatre's benign masquerade. We cannot blame them for this but, if they succeed in forging a career for themselves, they will learn that the stage, being full of constraints and duties, demands not only real training but arduous discipline. If what finally happens is that they have "sublimated" their personal dilemmas through their craft, we can only agree that they are to be congratulated and the stage blessed for it.

The amateur whose main objective in going into the theatre is self-therapy may arrive but will not long remain there. For every actor who "cures" himself through psychoanalysis in order to be able to function on the stage (I repeat there is nothing wrong in this), I can show you five whose distemper has become controlled or modified because they have made themselves true professionals. One does not enduringly act, write or compose out of mental illness.

The very fact that many of us are inclined to associate the arts with disease is either a sign we know little of the history of the arts or that we live in an environment which is itself tainted. The clamor for "healthy" art in the face of some of the most creative work of our theatre and other arts is frequently a clamor for conformity of the most stuffy sort. Quite apart from the question of dignity and self-respect, the last thing the artist today need do is to apologize either for his vocation or his mental condition. The artist able to work as one is indeed fortunate to be engaged in so wholesome an occupation. Whether he is sick or not, we should all cherish him—as long as he remains an artist, that is, a creator in our society, which wobbles halfway between prayer and destruction.

36

Plays and Politics

[1965]

To THE QUESTION "What has the American theatre to say at the
present time about the state of American politics?" the answer is
"very little." The question which might then more pointedly be put
is "Why?" Those who ask either of these questions are usually more
interested in politics than in the theatre. Still, they are good questions for people devoted to the theatre to ask themselves. The effort
to answer will momentarily make them ponder politics and also induce them to think a little less superficially about the theatre itself.

In any discussion of the theatre, one of the first things to inquire
about is the nature of the audience. On Broadway, where most new
plays originate in America, the audience never pays less than $2.50
for the poorest seat, and often more than $6.90 for the best. One can
hardly call this a representative audience, even in the era of affluence. It excludes most teachers and students, many people in the
professions but not in the high-income brackets, and what used to
be called the "working class." It is an audience of the business community: manufacturers, buyers and moguls of the plushier trades.
It demands titillation. Hence musicals and light comedies are almost
the only shows which sell out. The economic setup of the New York
theatre makes it extremely difficult for plays which do not sell out to
return a profit. And what does not make money soon disappears.
What is believed likely to disappear does not get produced.

This facile explanation tells less than half the story. To proceed
beyond it leads to perilous ground. I have no statistics, but I ven-

ture to say that in the main Americans are not genuinely concerned with politics.

The ordinary American might define politics as something to do with elections and graft. He is convinced that China is a menace, that Communism is evil, that taxes are too high, that juvenile delinquency is outrageous, that while the atom bomb is dangerous it is necessary, that our way of life, being the best, must be defended. Politics is something to which one lends one's self for a few minutes a day on TV, or that can be disposed of by a cursory glance at the headlines and by gossip about "personalities." Politics is a sort of sport, and no one except a politician devotes himself to it.

This view is understandable, given our history. There have been very few deeply disturbing political events since 1865. Compared to its effects on Europe, the First World War was for us a mere scratch. Such scandals as those of the Harding administration or of the Jimmy Walker regime were jokes. A mere handful of people were aware of the implications of Franco's assault on democratic Spain. To judge by the aspect of our big cities at the time, the Second World War was a happy occasion. We disapproved of fascism because of its bluster, and we heartily disliked the Nazis because they produced sickening sensations in our stomachs. The causes of the war, our own or our Allies' responsibility in its outbreak, were obscure to us.

The Depression of 1929–39 shook us up. For a time we responded politically, although when the crisis passed many of us grew impatient with Roosevelt and his reforms. But the Depression was a condition no one could overlook, and our theatre gave striking evidence of the fact.

Came Eisenhower, the new normalcy and Joseph McCarthy. The Senator scared the wits out of us before he destroyed himself, but we have not yet recovered from the infection he spread. For years now, not only political discussion but all discussion of vital issues has been timorous or feeble. Such discussion may lead to dissent. Nowadays we hardly know what to dissent from except such enormities as totalitarianism, the insults of inimical powers, narcotics and teen-age killers. Dissent usually involves criticism of our country, than which there is none better on earth. Dissent, moreover, smacks suspiciously of softness in regard to foreign ideologies. We had enough of that in the thirties.

Today the civil-rights struggle—especially in its painless forms—stirs a great many people. But when prejudice of this stamp is dealt with on the stage it is in a musical like *West Side Story* or in a sentimental play like *A Raisin in the Sun*. Nearly everybody, and especially those who are peculiarly touchy about aesthetics, shudders at the hate in LeRoi Jones' plays. I myself am frightened and mortified by it, but we occasionally need to realize its presence and to see it dramatized in full terror.

We hear that there is a new radicalism in the colleges and among the young who are exasperated by the flatness, the inexpressiveness of our lives. Though the manifestations of this trend are sometimes raw and foolish, it should be viewed as a hopeful sign if it leads to the discipline of study, thought and firmness of conviction. Nerviness is not enough.

The fighting in Vietnam troubles us and we are becoming increasingly vocal about it. The majority of our countrymen react automatically, either approving the government's policy as a matter of simple patriotism, or denouncing it without facing the central issue: whether or not the possible victory of Communism in Asia is something that non-Communists are prepared to accept.

If I am only partly right in these assertions, politics as such can hardly be expected to prove a proper subject for American theatrical entertainment. But should I be thought mistaken there are still other phases of the question which the liberal mind often overlooks.

Granted that plays dealing with politics on our stage usually are reduced to such convivial dramatizations of columnist chatter as *The Best Man* or to empty melodrama like the play made from Allen Drury's *Advise and Consent,* one must also recognize that very few political plays of more than momentary value exist in dramatic literature generally. What we sometimes name political plays are plays of social significance or historical plays of broad political application.

Shaw wrote several political plays—*The Apple Cart, Geneva, On the Rocks*—but they are hardly among his best. Shakespeare's histories possess general political meaning, but they are political only by extension and analogy, as is the case with Miller's *The Crucible,* Sherwood's *Abe Lincoln in Illinois,* Kingsley's *The Patriots.* There are also social–political "allegories," written in various veins, like most of Sartre's plays or Genet's *The Balcony* and *The Screens* (pages 304–308).

Not long ago a play about the Hiss case was produced on Broadway but, like most such accounts of recent events, it was an inconsiderable piece. Only the Germans and French have thus far accepted a stage version of the Oppenheimer case. Even Kingsley's dramatization of Koestler's *Darkness at Noon,* cited as the Best Play of the Year 1950–51 by the New York Drama Critics' Circle, remained largely inoperative. I could name several other similar plays, such as Maxwell Anderson and Harold Hickerson's *Gods of the Lightning* (about the Sacco–Vanzetti case) or John Wexley's *They Shall Not Die* (about the Scottsboro boys), which flashed by without attracting anything but the most limited attention.

Far more effective than any of these were the documentaries presented by the Federal Theatre Project at low prices—*Triple a Plowed Under* and *One-Third of a Nation*—which produced audience impact through their novel staging and immediacy. But for the popular treatment of topical subjects, the movies and television are more appropriate media. Even Odets' *Waiting for Lefty* (about the taxi drivers' strike in the thirties) proved forceful not because of its political message but because of its colorful idiom and youthful fervor. For the rest, with the exception of his anti-Nazi *Till the Day I Die,* Odets' plays are not political at all but social, akin in this respect to O'Casey's early work.

A social play stems from a particular environment which to a degree is a reflection of a political condition. Chekhov's plays and Shaw's *Heartbreak House* are examples. Osborne's *Look Back in Anger* has English social connotations though its political direction is by no means clear. Gorky's dramatic work, rightly held to be inflammatory in Czarist Russia, was not at all propaganda for a particular party or a guide to an unequivocal political solution.

Since all plays are the products of mores and attitudes common to particular sectors of society and are addressed to a public presumed to be attuned to the dramatists' state of mind, one might maintain that all plays are social. (Even Ziegfeld's *Follies,* I have often said, could be regarded as a mirror of its times.) The reason why the social basis of drama is not more often pointed out is that audiences and reviewers prefer to think of plays wholly in terms of entertainment or, betimes, of art. In this way they avoid the discomfort of dealing with troublesome matters. They want to divorce entertainment (or art) from their daily concerns. The wish is justifiable, since their concerns are often trivial, but by this amputation they frequently rob both entertainment and art of their primary value.

There is a sense in which the theatregoer who seeks relief from his workaday cares is right. The domain of the theatre is universal, nothing human is alien to it; but the most durable and hence most profoundly influential plays are those which transcend their immediate "journalistic" material. What we seek finally in the theatre is an escape—into reality.

Our ordinary activities are dross of transitory interest even to ourselves. What we truly long for is to be transported to some realm of truth, the purest consciousness. This super-reality which lifts us above the ordinary traffic of existence is what the theatre (along with the other arts and, some may add, religion) aspires to, and in its greatest and blessedly rare occasions achieves.

What makes Chekhov's plays so touching is not their depiction of the unhappy middle class of Russia at a certain period, but the use he makes of this subject matter. From it he wrings the "music" of idealistic yearning, the aspiration which both torments and elevates the hearts of not particularly bright folk everywhere. What lends stature to Ibsen's *Hedda Gabler* is not so much the psychology of a lady caught between two social classes, but our recognition that we are all a little like her—unable to find any sphere which completely satisfies our innermost needs.

Plays of so-called classic breadth, from Aeschylus to Racine, attain such heights. The better realistic plays of modern times move willynilly toward the same goals. Patently social plays, like those of Shaw and Brecht, Büchner's *Danton's Death* or Hauptmann's *The Weavers*, are sustained by a similar afflatus. Political plays, when they are intelligent and honest, are to be welcomed even when they do not qualify as art. How many plays of any sort do? Still, the annals of drama teach us that specifically political plays seldom reach the loftiest peaks—unless one calls Euripides' *Trojan Women* or Shakespeare's *Julius Caesar* "political."

Nearly all social plays of merit exercise political effect, although the degree or exact orientation of such effects are not always determinable. We may cite such old examples as Beaumarchais' *Marriage of Figaro* as relevant to the French Revolution and Gogol's *The Inspector General* as relevant to all bureaucracies. There is no doubt that the naturalistic plays of the middle and late nineteenth century exerted liberalizing persuasion, first in Germany and Russia, and later in England and France. On the other hand, a sizable portion of the Paris audience just before the Second World War applauded Shakespeare's *Coriolanus* as a reactionary play which others (Brecht, for instance) have interpreted in another sense.

We come now to what for our present purpose is the crucial problem: "How is one to account for the fact," a friend writes me, "that the more dramatic the general political situation becomes, the more intensely private and ingrown are the preoccupations of our more talented playwrights?"

The answer is that the plays referred to in this query, though hardly political, constitute our social drama! There *is* a connection between the theatre and politics. It is sometimes direct and positive, at other times indirect and negative. Today it is mostly negative. The Theatre of the Absurd, seen as a generic phenomenon without judgment as to individual talents, is, whether the writers themselves agree or not, a direct consequence of the social–political climate in most of the "free world." It represents despair and sometimes an oblique protest in regard to the societies from which the plays emerge. They are mockingly bitter outcries signifying a sense of impotence. They present our world as a frightful mess, a ridiculous fraud, a tragic farce. There is nothing left for us to do, they tell us, except to suffer and wait (for what?), jeer and try to avoid hurting anyone, or, in extreme instances, burst the bonds of decorum and reason (which have been of no avail) to find some sado-masochistic "mystical" release. America, they intimate, is smug and hypocritical. Britain's stiff upper lip has gone slack with indecision, France poses in a caricature of grandeur. The Soviet Union abides in a straitjacket; China is a threatening tyranny. According to some of these playwrights it is entirely possible that life itself is no damned good and probably never has been. So they turn their backs on all this and now and then seek repose within some no-man's-land of bleak contemplation or lunacy.

I do not speak in contempt. Today many artist–intellectuals (not to mention others) feel spiritually homeless. They believe themselves deprived of any reliable political, social, religious base. For them all the old faiths are meaningless. That is why in America they appear to take special satisfaction in patronizing the credulous thirties. Their political posture consists of their refusal to assume any. And, one should add, no wonder. The moral and political atmosphere of the world is confusing everywhere. It is easier to assail these new and personally benign nihilists by argument than to reassure them with concrete proposals. The most "advanced" among them are trying to formulate an aesthetics of nonart.

Insofar as these impulses represent protestations against all that is bogus in our society, and if in the process of protest new means of expression are discovered, this anarchic tendency performs a positive function. But a persistent turning away from the world ultimately leads to a conformism as dull and debilitating as complete accommodation.

Very few of the new plays have any action. Indeed, hardly any of them require it, because they deal with states of being in which will power has become superfluous. Since most such plays are based on the assumption that nothing is changeable, they present characters who never bother to change anything. We approach the dead end of drama.

To extricate himself from this dilemma the future playwright must consent to dwell in "error." He must take a walk into the awful world, get to know it ever more intimately and widely. What is chiefly wrong with Soviet realism is that it is not sufficiently realistic. It is usually little more than publicity. Still, the aims of that realism, liberated from officious supervision and Philistine dogma, are healthy. They bid the dramatist make contact with society, explore the hardships and triumphs of labor, probe the souls of men and women in the travail of the new civilization as it is being formed or of the old as it destroys itself. This tradition gave Russia and the rest of us such writers as Gogol, Turgenev, Tolstoy, Dostoevsky, Chekhov and Gorky—none of them literalists—and has still much to offer.

As soon as they have attracted notice through early success, American playwrights now tend to become encrusted in professional circles and thus rapidly to detach themselves from their creative sources. They deteriorate into provincials in the sterile ground of fashionable Broadway intellectual coteries.

When we learn to see ourselves and our neighbors truthfully against the broadest horizons of human concern, we shall perhaps not need to clamor for *political* plays; good ones will do.

37

One Hundred Years
in the American Theatre

[1965]

WRITING IN 1869, Walt Whitman in his *Democratic Vistas* complains, "Of what is called drama, or dramatic presentation in the United States, as now put forth at the theatres, I should say it deserves to be treated with the same gravity and on a par with the questions of ornamental confectionary and public dinners, or the arrangements of curtains and hangings in a ballroom—no more no less."

Seven months after the assassination of Lincoln in April, 1865, the "hit shows" were *Rip Van Winkle*, with the delightful actor Joseph Jefferson, and *The Black Crook*, the first of our big musicals in which "one hundred beautiful girls in short diaphanous skirts and flesh-colored tights" provided an unprecedented sensation.

This came at a time when our literature had already bequeathed to us *Moby Dick, The Scarlet Letter, Leaves of Grass*, not to speak of Emerson and Thoreau. We can sympathize with Whitman's reaction. But we are less astonished. The theatre is almost always a laggard art.

A single reader may be said to constitute an "audience" for a poem or a novel, one viewer may be sufficient to encourage the solitary artist who shows his painting. Theatre requires a larger number of people to convene at the same set time. The theatre is both a public and a composite art, *social* in the nature of its creation as well as in the circumstances of its manifestation. A history of the theatre must comprise not only a study of dramatic texts but an examination of acting, the mechanics and economics of production and, inseparable from all these, the audiences to whom the art is addressed and from whom it derives.

After they had passed through the primitive state of tribal rites the great theatres of the Western world emerged as forms of civic and religious celebrations. State and church—in effect the entire community—supported them. Later, when the theatre was no longer an organic part of governing bodies, when indeed it was frowned upon and its suppression was urged by those who held it to be immoral, the theatre still managed to survive through various devices of aristocratic or royal protection. Despite all the vicissitudes of its history, the theatre was recognized as a social benefit meriting special privilege. In a word, a *tradition* developed in Europe which bestowed care for the theatre.

This tradition was lost in the settlement of America. The Puritans thought the theatre sinful. With a civilization to be built there was no time for such frivolity. By the time the educated minority was able to provide for them, a few playhouses were put up in the main cities of the eastern seaboard. Plays and actors were usually foreign. The best fare consisted of mutilated Shakespeare. There was practically no native drama and hardly any native actors.

When preoccupations beyond those of material needs could be entertained, schools and universities were established, important writers and a few signs of original theatrical creation appeared. One of these was Anna Cora Mowatt's *Fashion* (1845), a satire on the American parvenu, which in our present estimation is hardly more than a chromo. Yet Edgar Allan Poe found it praiseworthy.

That Poe should have welcomed so slight a piece, though he probably would not have deigned to notice its literary equivalent, may appear paradoxical. But this paradox repeats itself constantly. (William Dean Howells in 1891 referred to James Hearne's *Margaret Fleming,* a crude and creaky bit of claptrap, as "epoch-making" because it was the first of our realistic plays.) We may discover a clue in this to the peculiarity of our theatre's progress.

"Hardly anybody listens in the theatre," the Irish dramatist Denis Johnston has said, "to anything he doesn't know already." For a play to prosper it must unite its audience—which to begin with must be homogeneous. A minority attitude, a heterodox premise are divisive, and the theatre's life depends on popularly recognizable interpretations of a common experience. The cultivated handful who were able to appreciate the Brahmans of our literature could not have filled the tiniest theatres of their times.

It has been said—and it is perhaps true—that the liveliest and most representative "theatre" of the period immediately following the Civil War was to be found in the riverboats, in the saloons, in the minstrel shows on the Mississippi and westward. These frolics possessed the rough vigor of their audiences, the hardy folk who were opening the country.

The situation in the East, as we have seen, was that which made Whitman exclaim, "Do you call that perpetual, pistareen, paste-pot work . . . American drama?" Still clinging to his faith in the American dream he was dismayed by a society ever more dominated by money values. Capitalism was set on its roaring course of empire building. Fortunes were being made by and for a most fortunate people. It was the Gilded Age. Theatres attracted folk eager to ease themselves with entertainment inducing the minimum of mental strain. The really poor never went to ordinary playhouses and thus poverty was never made the subject of any but the cheapest tear-jerkers. A large part of the audience was beginning to free itself from some of its Puritan inhibitions, though the "upper crust" in press and pulpit hypocritically persisted in upholding the Puritan code. Only the smiling aspects of American life or titillating melodrama were suitable material for such audiences. So rage as intellectuals might, the theatre between 1865 and 1890 was, in its own distorted way, a mirror of the times.

Even the intelligentsia does not go to the theatre for literature alone. Native acting during this period improved steadily. If America did not see any good plays (Shakespeare, remember, was bowdlerized), it had the opportunity of catching glimpses of such luminaries as Edmund Kean and Rachel, and later Salvini and Duse. Edwin Booth refined the red-necked robustiousness of Edwin Forrest, America's first tragedian (1806–72).

The actor–manager Lester Wallack, who beginning in 1861 ran a stock company for twenty years, was patronized by New York's gentry. His theatre was something like a London theatre in Manhattan. He never produced an American play because he found none that was good enough. After Wallack the big "name" producer from 1879 to 1899 was Augustin Daly, who had a sound sense of integral play production. Though he produced Shakespeare with excellent actors, the fare at his theatre was more frequently trash. Daly's "discovery," Bronson Howard, the first writer for our stage to become rich from his work, was the author of *Shenandoah* (1889), a Civil War saga which one cannot read today without indulgent laughter.

The theatre prospered, but because of the advent of realism the playhouses were built smaller. Playgoing became respectable; the social elite or "carriage trade" made it customary. Shows toured the hinterland. The theatre became industrialized. Henry James, writing in 1885, found that "scenery and decoration have been brought to the highest perfection while elocution and acting, the interpretation of meanings, the representation of human feelings have not long been the subjects of serious study."

To appreciate the frame of mind of theatrical leaders at this time one may cite the fact that in 1893 the dignified manager Daniel Frohman rejected Pinero's *The Second Mrs. Tanqueray* (about a woman who had been kept by four men before marriage) because it was "too frank." When it was produced, the reviewer of the New York *Herald* spoke of the play as being "for audacity surely without parallel in dramatic literature." Even as late as 1905, when Shaw's *Mrs. Warren's Profession* was produced (and suppressed), it was said by the New York *Sun* "to glorify debauchery."

Clyde Fitch, the most highly regarded dramatist between 1889 and 1909, was entirely sincere when he wrote, "I feel myself strongly the particular value of reflecting absolutely and truthfully the life and environment about us." He had the impulse to confess himself as much as to reveal the environment, but his play *The Truth* (1906), about a compulsive liar, and *The City* (1909), about the corrupting effects of the Big Town, are rather rickety contraptions. After all, plays, like most of the novels of the day, had to please the Ladies or they would incur the censure of the Gentlemen.

While Edward Sheldon may be credited with bringing social themes to the stage—the destitute in *Salvation Nell* (1908), the "race problem" in *The Nigger* (1909) and politics in *The Boss* (1911)—the plays themselves are sophomorically inept and timid.

(Stephen Crane, Frank Norris, Theodore Dreiser had already written most of their stories and novels.) Sheldon's true vein was that of *Romance* (1913), about the love of an Episcopalian minister for an Italian opera star. A play which harks back to New York in its Age of Innocence, it is chiefly memorable as a vehicle for the glamorous Doris Keane, rapturously admired by Stark Young. There *was* artistic substance in the American theatre of the day—not in the plays but in the players. Otis Skinner, Laurette Taylor, Maude Adams, the Barrymores, and later, Pauline Lord, Alfred Lunt and numerous others brought life to the boards.

One notes other progressive signs. The actor Arnold Daly champions Shaw, the intrepid actress Mrs. Fisk and the exotic Alla Nazimova do much to convince the retarded, including the shocked William Winter, the New York *Tribune*'s drama critic from 1865 to 1909, of Ibsen's worth.

Most indicative of the community's steadily growing sophistication is the effort sponsored in 1909 by J. P. Morgan, John Jacob Astor, the Vanderbilts, Thomas Paine Whitney and Otto Kahn to establish a "permanent national art theatre." A sumptuous house was built on Central Park West between 62nd and 63rd Streets, at this time an exclusive residential section for the well-to-do, and a remote suburb to citizens of more modest means.

Chosen to direct the ambitious New Theatre was the Harvard-educated Bostonian Winthrop Ames, a man of ability and taste. He enlisted an admirable company and produced Galsworthy's *Strife* (capital and labor), several plays by Maeterlinck (among them *The Blue Bird*) and Shakespeare. It was difficult to find American plays of corresponding caliber (only three, including Sheldon's *The Nigger,* were offered) because few American plays, with only such possible exceptions as Langdon Mitchell's brightly written comedy *The New York Idea* about divorce among the rich (1906) and Percy MacKaye's imaginative *The Scarecrow* (1910), were anything better than hack work.

The New Theatre collapsed after two seasons. Apart from the auditorium's unsuitability for the presentation of modern drama, its poor acoustics, its high prices and its inconvenient location, the reason for the New Theatre's failure was the absence of an audience great enough to sustain a serious repertory theatre.

Yet forces were at work to bring about a distinct change. Contact with Europe began to exercise a marked influence. The culturally alert became acquainted with stimulating and still unfamiliar dramatists (Tolstoy, Hauptmann, Gorky, Andreyev) on New York's Lower East Side—in both Yiddish and German. Little theatres were spreading all over the country so that by 1915 there were nineteen hundred. In 1916 the attractive comedian John Barrymore proved himself an actor of immense emotional power in Galsworthy's *Justice*. New manager–directors like Arthur Hopkins, inspired by overseas example, ventured into new fields which yielded fresh ideas, unusual plays employing the talent of that fine artist Robert Edmond Jones. A number of discriminating critics—their columns full of intriguing foreign references—began to clamor for a theatre in touch with art, literature and life. Chief among them was George Jean Nathan.

Most important, though little noticed at first, were the activities centered in the vicinity of Greenwich Village. The year 1915 witnessed the formation of the Neighborhood Playhouse on Grand Street, The Washington Square Players (transformed into The Theatre Guild in 1919), the Provincetown Players, who were to reappear in the early twenties as a triumvirate of the critic MacGowan, the designer–director Jones and the dramatist O'Neill. These new groups planted seeds from which a proud harvest was soon reaped.

In 1920 we became conscious of the flowering with the production—cautiously introduced at special matinees—of O'Neill's first full-length play, *Beyond the Horizon*. That event marks the *birth* of American theatre as a conscious art intended to contribute to our inner life what we expect of the best literature.

This "birth" in the theatre corresponded to a rebirth in American letters generally. For while the years between 1835 and 1850 gave evidence of our native genius in poem, essay, short story and novel, the fortune-hunting years between 1865 and 1913 had very nearly destroyed vital literary expression. During this interval Dreiser, on the one hand, and Henry James, on the other, dwelled in limbo. This is also true of Whitman, Melville and Thoreau, whose work was known to a rare few only. They came into their own just before and immediately after the First World War.

What made the twenties a feverish and wonderful time was our coming of age in prosperity, in power, in self-confidence, as well as in self-consciousness. This made it possible for us to recognize our character and to acknowledge our shortcomings. Our desire to learn and accomplish things as a great nation lent a tremendous impetus to all endeavors. We became cocky and at the same time self-critical. We were prepared to look at ourselves with unrelenting realism. We were rediscovering ourselves as Americans.

Many thought us fooled by the holiday of our success. Others declared our iconoclasm adolescent. The superficial traits of our Puritanism were raucously shed. Freud began to be read by the literati. We rejoiced in our afflatus and jeered at our rejoicing. Some said that America had become a jungle of competition; others read that Western Civilization was doomed. But whether the diagnoses and prognoses were rosy or black, everything took on a jubilant air.

New York playhouses doubled in number. One hundred ninety-six productions opened in 1920–21; two hundred seventy in 1927–28. The Theatre Guild assembled a loyal body of subscribers which assured its productions a minimum run of five to six weeks. The Guild did many unusual and stimulating plays by foreign authors, as well as by some Americans. After a while it clasped O'Neill to its bosom. Eva Le Gallienne at the Civic Repertory Theatre produced Ibsen, Chekhov and other "standard" European dramatists at popular prices.

Musical comedy, the one theatrical form in which we undoubtedly excel, with truly gifted tunes by Kern, Porter, Gershwin, Rodgers and others, sweetened the surrounding clamor. Ziegfeld's *Follies*, glorifying the American girl in gorgeous dress and suave undress, served as emblems of our high spirits. Among the lovely faces and the lush furnishings a parade of comedians close to genius cavorted.

The shadowy side of the picture was painted by the uncouth master figure of Eugene O'Neill himself. Apart from his concern with the complexities of personal psychology, O'Neill brooded on the drama of man's soul in America. Something had gone astray. The poet who yearns to explore realms beyond the narrow confines of his job fails to follow his bent and as a result wastes his being. The simple laborer proud of the strength which turns the wheels of our magnificent civilization finds himself scorned and adrift in a mechanism in which he is merely a cog. The artist wishes to attain the effectiveness of the man of affairs; the businessman envies the artist's imagination. Both suffer a sense of incompleteness. The would-be aristocrat from the Old World with his dream of grandeur is rendered absurd in the factory of a materialistic democracy. But without that strain of grandeur the dignity of a true manhood is somehow damaged. The son has little of his pioneering father's grit; the father in his struggle to master the soil of his farm (America?) impairs his capacity to love.

O'Neill dramatizes himself and us as people cut off from but still seeking some principle of coherence. For want of it everyone feels isolated and frustrated. O'Neill's strength lies in the persistence of his quest for a wholeness which has been shattered in the New World. We sicken in detachment from some age-old secret of sanctity. O'Neill is committed to its recovery. He told friends that his never-completed cycle of nine plays would be an epic of America's failure to realize its promise.

The Depression of the thirties exposed the moral as well as the social lesion in the national body. Having been wounded where we believed ourselves invulnerable, we began questioning ourselves in new ways. The plays of the Depression were not depressed. (Depressed plays appeared in the fifties in a time of prosperity.) The Depression was a time of hope. Youth would not accept defeat, would not take "no" for an answer. It condemned the illusions of the previous decade, which had exulted in the fun principle. The thirties sought and found a solution to our dilemma in collective action for social betterment.

The theatre was struck a bitter, though not fatal, blow. The number of productions shrank; playhouses were sold for use as grind-movie emporia and for burlesque shows. Actors left for Hollywood, which prospered because the disconsolate wished to flee the gloom of impoverished homes and streets. The disease wrought its own healing. As Roosevelt aroused the country with his New Deal, so groups, collectives, unions of the theatre were formed. What characterized most of them was the attempt to present plays confronting the times: the condition of the unemployed, the dispossessed, the unprotected worker, the dispirited middle class, the desperate farmer, the threat of fascism. All this was to be done in a new fashion: through organizations which would commit themselves on a *permanent collective basis* to a disciplined practice of theatrical craft.

The theatre of the thirties was thought to be political—a mistaken opinion. Its impulse was moral—even moralistic. That is the essence of Odets' work. He was the era's representative playwright just as the Group Theatre, of which Odets had been an actor–member, was the representative theatrical organization. That is why after the Group Theatre's dissolution in 1941, it still remained an influence in the ensuing years through its former actors, directors, designers, teachers.

One particular contribution to theatre technique made by the Group was a way of work which was the heritage of the Moscow Art Theatre's New York visit in 1923. This was the Stanislavsky System, which in time—through the Actors Studio founded in the forties—came to be known as the Method. While the Method is presumed to have narrowed the scope of American acting, though this is not at all its aim or necessary effect, it added a certain vibrancy and density of feeling to our actors' endowments.

With the scattering of forces during the Second World War and its immediate aftermath, in which not only the Group Theatre but the inestimably valuable Federal Theatre Project (the government's first entrance into the domain of the arts) disappeared, a subtle change took place. As business as usual resumed, there followed a cooling of social fervor which soon turned into a freeze.

This was hardly noticed at first since Arthur Miller's early plays and even those of Tennessee Williams sounded a more subdued and introverted variation on the mode of the thirties.

Social reform had failed to "save" us. Many suggested panaceas had proved delusive (or so it was thought) and some were considered positively treasonable. The source of our ailments, it would appear, lay in our unsatisfactory relations with parents, wives, children. Our traumas—our traumas were to blame! Though Tennessee Williams' work always had discernible social connotations, what public and press chiefly responded to was its private and especially sexual aspects.

The age of conformity and of McCarthy terror drove men of sensibility into themselves. Young folk exiled themselves in the ghetto of their egos. The faceless world, all perpetual motion without any core of meaning, was to be shut out. "Contact," as someone has said about the new dancing, "went out in the fifties."

Connection with the outside world, now threatened with annihilation, became attenuated. Some solace (or drug) which might alleviate the pain of aloneness or sink us more deeply into forgetfulness was craved. To be "beat" became an ideal by default. This laid the groundwork for the dramaturgy of the maimed.

The plays of Beckett, Genet, Ionesco, Pinter—usually presented at some distance from the theatre's supermarket—which were expressions of not altogether similar but of equally disabling stresses, became models for American writers. Edward Albee's "permanent vagrant" disturbing the complacent gent on the park bench is a youth who prefers contact through his own violent death at the hand of his neighbor to total neglect. At this moment Albee seems as representative of the early sixties as William Saroyan and Thornton Wilder were, in embodying the spirit of benevolent reconciliation (or "national unity"), in the early forties. Albee testifies to the agony of a society no longer real in which we try to live on debris of exploded faiths, a state which renders us savage.

Though, retrospectively, we may realize that since O'Neill our theatre has turned in earnest to the contemplation of our existence in a manner unthinkable a hundred or even sixty years ago, we remain dissatisfied. Broadway, as the hub of theatrical activity, has become an electrified desert. We still go there though its game is crooked because it is the only game in town! Seventy-five productions a season constitute the norm. At the moment of this writing only musicals and skimpy comedies are produced with much chance of public support.

Movies and television are not the cause of the downfall. It is show business itself which is destroying the theatre. Its arrangements are anarchic; the costs of production are too high, the price of tickets prohibitive. The greedy exactions of the stagehand unions are not the sole cause for this. They do what all the others do: treat the theatre as a business, which means every craft for itself, every man for himself. This inevitably becomes destructive to an art, the very nature of which depends on the planned and enthusiastic integration of its entire personnel. We have lost the tradition—indeed have never established one—of the theatre as a service, a social need. When business ceases to be profitable it has lost its reason for existence. There is "no foundation all the way down the line," in Saroyan's words, and it will take more than the Foundations to supply one.

Are we to end with a whimper? On the contrary, we may yet see a new beginning. Observation during my travels convinces me that the country is full of talent and appetite for theatre. Young folk are trying to rediscover a true theatre tradition.

The decentralization of the theatre is not the result of any special "idealism" but the response to a need for using all our unused gifts. In San Francisco, in Seattle, in Minneapolis, in Houston, in Washington, in Philadelphia and elsewhere new professional theatres have been, or are about to be, established. This trend is bound to grow.

These theatres aspire to be more than show shops. We are becoming aware that there are other "classics" beside Shakespeare. Many world-famous plays—ancient and modern, in foreign tongues and in our own—are still unknown to our stages because they do not sit well in the maw of commerce. One hears of productions in university and community theatres, as well as in cafés, of plays so "advanced" and "experimental" that even off-Broadway (now being assimilated into the stream of running rats) dares not undertake them. We are also beginning to get free theatre in the parks and on the very streets of certain cities—both in the South and in the North.

New York itself is now endowed with ambitious new theatre organizations. A heavy load of disdain has been hurled at the first two seasons of the Repertory Theater of Lincoln Center—some of it merited but most of it misguided. To found a theatre is not the same as setting up a series of productions. A considerable time of preparation and at least three years of performance are required as a preliminary test. The demand that these new organizations immediately satisfy our hunger for genuine innovation and artistic achievement is a way of applying the old hit-and-flop criteria of Broadway to enterprises with very different objectives and entirely different problems. The sheer fact of the Repertory Theater of Lincoln Center's having come into existence is a step forward. We must hope that the prolongation of its life, no matter under what auspices, will fulfill its serious artistic function.

If it is correct to speak of our theatre as having been "born" only forty-five years ago, we must agree that compared to the long years which went into the making of the Elizabethan, the French neoclassic stages, the recently founded British National Theatre, our theatre is in its infancy. It is part of our immaturity to expect immediate consummation. The misfortune of our theatre history—due to the absence of a tradition—is its fragmentation. We always seem to be starting from scratch. But perhaps this after all is not the case; there may be a continuity which we do not readily perceive because in our juvenile impatience we are forever grumbling, "Yes, but what have you done for me recently?"

38

The Homecoming

[January 23, 1967]

HAROLD PINTER's *The Homecoming* is a masterful play. I do not speak of its content but of its construction. When a play is praised in this respect what is generally meant is that the play conforms to a past model in the tradition of that subtly logical coherence Ibsen brought to the realistic form of the nineteenth century. Pinter's construction is of a different sort. Not to perceive this is to misconstrue the play.

To the unaware theatregoer *The Homecoming* may seem to have an ordinary continuity. But if he regards it in this way he will find it bewildering, unfathomable, unreal, to use adjectives which have been applied to it in most of the recent reviews. The play is none of these things. In fact it may be too simple.

It is superficially a family comedy. There is a seventy-year-old widower, resident of north London, a retired butcher, father of three sons. The youngest son is a construction worker training to become a prize fighter. The second son, whose occupation goes unmentioned at the outset, conveys unspoken menace in tight-lipped irony. He is an adept at the "game"—pimping. The third and oldest son, absent for years, brings home a pretty wife for a brief visit. He is the intellectual of the family, a Ph.D. in philosophy with a chair at a (perhaps Western) American university. There is also the butcher's brother, a correctly efficient, mild mannered, unambitious and generally impotent chauffeur.

The plot of the play, although it is misleading to call it that, shows the men gradually converting the philosopher's wife into a consenting whore. She must engage in the occupation to put her weight into the family budget while her father- and brothers-in-law look forward to enjoying her favors. She accepts the terms after driving a hard bargain, for she—a mother of three, by the way—is as unyieldingly calculating as any of them. Her philosophical husband leaves without further ado to return to his campus.

The scene in which the deal is made is not the climax of the story or the point of the play. It is only the finishing touch. Every scene and verbal exchange is as indicative of the play's meaning as every other. They are all facets of one theme. The play is a parable of insensibility, the death of values, a world in which little remains but primitive appetite.

It is significant that the characters—particularly the butcher father who is central to the composition—talk with orthodox unctuousness of family loyalty, of the sacredness of blood ties, reverence for mother, of all the hallowed virtues. But we see immediately that the old man despised his wife, is savage with his sons, cruelly contemptuous of his brother. What is genuine in him is his animal voraciousness, a brute clinging to existence. Since he is the fountainhead of all, the strongest too, each of the play's characters shares the same traits—except for the chauffeur brother who collapses when he announces that Jessie, his brother's wife, the family mother, had an affair at the back of his car with the butcher's much admired assistant.

What of the Ph.D.? When the family spiv asks him: "Do you detect a certain logical incoherence in the central affirmations of Christian theism?," the Ph.D. answers: "That question doesn't fall within my province." Like all the others, he's a "professional"; he refuses to extend his thinking beyond the bounds of his own interest. There is no connection with anything else.

The question and answer, funny as is so much else in the play, is as crucial to the whole picture as any of its more active or shocking moments. When, to take another instance, the youngest brother moves his sister-in-law to the couch and lies on top of her, while her husband and the others stand by and watch without a tremor, we are not confronted with a situation in a realistic story progression but an episode in a panel, an image which tells us more strikingly than some of the others what the total picture and meaning of the play are. The meaning is to be sought in the lack of feeling, absence of any moral or ideological foundation, the heartlessness which encompasses all.

This explains the attitude of the apparently wholly enigmatic character of the play: the soft-spoken philosopher's wife. There was a lack of living substance in the life she led with her husband on the immaculate campus, a place as barren of spirit and pulse as the home into which they have come. Being well taken care of as a whore will prove no worse and perhaps more honest.

How does Pinter make so absolute and damaging a statement theatrically fascinating and lucid? By constructing his play not on the basis of a simple narrative line, in which case it would indeed be incredible, but through a series of fragmented passages joined by brief but unmistakable breaks. The device renders the play abstract. There is a continuity of idea from one fragment to another, a unity of atmosphere. For example, after the bit in which the family watches the symbolic cohabitation of brother with sister-in-law, there is a sharp pause; she then gets up and says peremptorily: "I'd like something to eat," and an entirely new sequence commences in which another aspect of the general situation is played out.

Peter Hall's direction realizes the quality and scheme of the play to perfection. The production is one of the most complete I have seen on the English or American stage in some years, less striking but more organic than that of Peter Brook's *Marat/Sade*. What is script and what staging is almost indistinguishable. The pauses or breaks are not elements of character portrayal; they are "freezes" of action to indicate that we are passing from one phase of the material to another, that the play is not continuing in naturalistic order but shifting to a new "angle."

Adding to the overall unity of impression is John Bury's setting, which bears the same relation to reality as does every other element of the play. It appears to be a real place with fatigued furniture, murky walls in mist gray and muck brown corroded as if by dirt and fog. Yet its design is almost classically imposing, like that of an imperial mansion gone to seed and turned hollow.

The actors follow the direction with utmost fidelity. It is not psychological acting. In a vein of apparent realism consonant with the play's environment, it is chiseled and polished acting, with each line and speech sculpted to convey the incisive and mordant intention of the dramatist's thought. Paul Rogers' gross and yet towering monster of a father, sensual, hypocritical, vicious, grasping, and Ian Holm's acidly witty ponce, with the sterile power of a low-grade dictator are perhaps the best, but Vivien Merchant, Michael Craig, John Normington, Terence Rigby, in more limited roles, are nearly as good.

What is the sum of all this? Pinter's manner is icy: he does not declare himself. He leaves interpretation to the audience. (This is most brave.) He has a keen ear for dramatic speech, he writes with superb control: there is hardly a wasted word. At first one is inclined to think that he must be either wickedly unfeeling or perhaps that he has no convictions. But no! Only a prophet or a fanatic, fiercely moral, can be so damning. But Pinter is wholly of our moment: we refuse to be hortatory, to cry out, plead, condemn or call to account. Since we do not permit ourselves to "take sides" overtly, we grin or keep our jaws so tightly clamped that it becomes hard to tell whether we are kidding or repressing pain. The mask is one of horror subdued in glacial irony.

I do not see life as Pinter does. But it is imperative that he reveal his view of it: it is part of the truth. He is an artist, one of the most astute to have entered upon the world stage in the past ten years. Those who do not respect and appreciate his talent understand little of our times or its theatre.

39

Kabuki

[September 29, 1969]

THE GRAND KABUKI company of Tokyo, on a short tour through New York, Chicago, San Francisco and Los Angeles, provides a particular pleasure. No one truly interested in the theatre should miss it.

The sounds emitted by Kabuki actors, musicians, narrators, are frequently weird, startling or laughable to the Occidental ear. The movements, deliberate, pigeon-toed—the men playing women's parts walk with a slight break at the knees—are also peculiar. Colors are extreme, variegated, often clashing. The masculine costumes are elaborate, heavy with "trousers" which encase the feet so that one wonders how the actors manage to walk without tripping.

Yet all these elements evoke a passionate decorum, a special grace. Nothing is realistic; everything is right. There is a certain gaiety even in the tragedy; the differentiation between the serious and the comic can barely be discerned. Violence is made beautiful, bloodshed noble. Aesthetics are equated with morality. We who behold the wonderful figures before us gaze upon them as if we were gods bemused by the apparitions we have created.

Voices are not projected—one hardly sees lips move; sounds seem to proceed from the speaker's bowels. Forthright speech would be almost vulgar to these creatures. Anger is denoted by a sort of animal growl or an undirected hiss. Eyebrows twitch or rise sharply. The "ladies" coo like birds or sigh ineffably, while their hands flutter on wrists as delicate as stems. Benign persons are marked by chalk-white countenances: the faces of the less favored are earth brown with black stripes to lend ferocity to their expressions. Heavy breathing is meant to signify strong feeling.

When the hero of *Chushingura* (*The Treasury of Loyal Retainers*) strikes his antagonist, the flashing sword does not touch him (the stroke is indicated by the blade describing a swift arc), and his fury is shown by his companions gathering around him while he sways in their midst as if he were blown by the wind. The agony of hara-kiri is conveyed by the spasms of the actor's body and the distortion of his features. There is no "blood."

Apart from the perfection of the spare gestures, eyes are the most significant feature of this histrionic communication. They are clearly visible even at some distance because of the actors' masklike makeup. In *Chushingura*, the hero who has been humiliated by the governor reveals his resentment by glances as penetrating as a thrust dagger. The victim's attempts to show deference to his superior and his sorrow at what he knows to be his fate are the contraction of his brow and the lowering of his eyelids.

Much of this would be set down as mugging on the Western stage, but it is not so here. There is feeling behind the signs, which are economical, concentrated and, above all, hieratically formalized. All is style. Nothing is casual or accidental. The hauteur in these manifestations might be called grandeur if they were even a bit more ostentatious, but there is a modesty here which eschews the stress of personal emphasis. The acting seems to be an obeisance to a supreme law.

It is difficult to distinguish the precise degree of excellence among the individual players. Baiko, however, appears to possess the stuff and the finesse of craftsmanship of which great actors are made. There is enormous power in his bearing, in the keenness of his regard, and with it all, profound reserve.

In the second piece of the first program, Baiko first impersonates a lady-in-waiting called upon to dance with a lion's mask to ward off evil spirits. Frightened at first, she shies away from the task. Urged back she performs the rite in which butterflies (made of tin, held on long wires manipulated by visible "prop" men) come to tease the king of beasts, who at the beginning is only a wooden mask the lady holds in her hand while making its jaws snap. Soon the excitement of the frolic causes her to be transformed into the lion itself.

Baiko now returns as the lion, dazzling white of visage, blood-red around the eyes and lips. The previously soft, lilting lady has become cruelly menacing, except that the lion's mane is a flaxen blond longer than its body. It tosses in a way that suggests both awesome strength and a massive playfulness. Terror has become charm.

But what does it all mean? Is there any "content" to this colorful spectacle? Sustaining the entire event is a sense of honor: not alone the honor of man but that of the universe, the glory in the life of all things. Good and evil are equally celebrated. In his confrontation with all these the individual may be proud because he is part of the whole. He must be obedient to it with solemn splendor (and even with lightness of heart), so that in some way he may match it. This is pagan and feudal. Kabuki was the fruit of the rising merchant class of the seventeenth century, but it had not lost the desire to reproduce the magnificence of its forebears.

Why does Kabuki today still fascinate the Japanese? To begin with, because it is a gorgeous show and then because, despite its hectic plunge into modern industrialism, Japan is still a country where pride of manner, posture, self-discipline, tension directed toward balance, gracious ease born of strong will and practiced refinement are in themselves the deportment of wisdom. A savant asymmetry becomes loveliness in which the anarchy of existence is reconciled through cultivated care.

We talk a great deal about "total theatre." It is an ancient thing: Kabuki is one of its most brilliant forms.

40

Meyerhold

[December 1, 1969]

Meyerhold on Theatre * is an important, many-faceted book. Meyerhold was a great director—the greatest in my experience as a playgoer. His theories and work anticipate many of the catchwords associated with avant-garde practices today. "If the theatre is finally to rediscover its dynamic essence, it must cease to be 'theatre' in the sense of mere 'spectacle.' We intend not merely to observe, but to participate in a *corporate* creative act." This call for what we would now deem "total theatre" was written in 1907.

When I saw some ten or eleven Meyerhold productions in Moscow and Leningrad (1934–35) his career was approaching its end. He had begun as an actor in 1898 in the role of Treplev in the Moscow Art Theatre production of *The Sea Gull* and was also the first Tusenbach in *The Three Sisters*. Because of his campaign against naturalism, Meyerhold came to be regarded as an aesthete and even a "decadent" in the years before the First World War. But in 1918 he joined the Communist Party. He was then assigned Chief of the Theatrical Department for the entire Soviet Union.

On all occasions he spoke as a dedicated champion of the workers' revolution, even to the point of echoing on occasion the shibboleth of "Socialist realism" when that doctrine was introduced as integral to Soviet ideology in 1936. But his productions had very little to

* Braun, Edward, ed. and trans., *Meyerhold on Theatre* (New York: Hill and Wang, 1969).

217

do with "Socialist realism." In 1937 *Pravda* published an article denouncing Meyerhold's theatre as "stylized, mystical, formalist." At a conference during that year Meyerhold was expected to admit that "his false political and artistic policies had led his theatre to total disaster." Instead he reaffirmed his theatrical credo. His theatre was liquidated in 1938.

Stanislavsky attempted to save him by appointing Meyerhold assistant at his opera studio. But with Stanislavsky's death in 1938 Meyerhold was arrested. It is commonly believed that he was shot in a Moscow prison in 1940. During the Khrushchev "thaw" Meyerhold was "rehabilitated" and it was possible for Soviet theatre people again to speak of him with respect.

In *Meyerhold on Theatre*, Edward Braun has collected the various essays, lectures, notes which Meyerhold had published from 1902 on. These papers have not been previously anthologized (in English). Braun, who has devoted five years to the study of Meyerhold's life and work, has so edited the Meyerhold papers that one can follow the course of his career in the context of the social scene before and after the Revolution. Braun has thus rendered the field of theatre knowledge an invaluable service.

It might be said of Meyerhold, what Picasso said of himself, that he did not seek but discovered. Meyerhold's work was nearly always fresh and new. It was not "experimental" for he was a master. Like Picasso, Meyerhold always struck out on new tracks, in apparent contradiction to his previous "manner."

Constant from the outset in Meyerhold's productions was the refusal to adhere to the "slavish portrayal of real life." He regarded the actor as the principal element in the theatre. The spectator was always to be aware that the actor was *performing* before an audience. Hence Meyerhold's defense of the *cabotin*, the mummer, the mime, the stage virtuoso, the divine "clown." He was opposed to the theatre as the "servant of literature." "In order to make a dramatist out of a storyteller," Meyerhold suggested, "it would be a good idea to make him write a few pantomimes. . . . The writer will be allowed to put words into the actors' mouths, but first he must produce a *scenario of movement*." At a later time he wrote, "The role of movement is more important than that of any other theatrical element."

As with Craig, Brecht, Artaud and Grotowski, Meyerhold's pronouncements are to a considerable degree hyperbole. He finally admitted as much in quasi-retraction of his boldest statements. Innovators in the arts often indulge in polemics, paradox and metaphors which say more (or less) than they mean. Such is the strategy of the vanguard. Thus Meyerhold, always an admirer of Stanislavsky whose productions were at the opposite pole from his own, ended by affirming that Stanislavsky was not the realist he had always been held to be. Still Meyerhold's initial championship of a decisively stylized theatre is typical of him. His theories planted the seeds of what has inaccurately come to be known as the nonverbal theatre.

He proceeded by way of Maeterlinck to symbolism. He then went on to productions of Lermontov and Molière—exquisite, dynamically decorative and either sardonically romantic or obliquely distorted in the direction of a conjuror's criticism of the societies which produced them. These tendencies—brilliantly original and captivating—gave way to the constructivism of the early years after the Bolshevik Revolution. Except for his masterpieces in the mounting of Ostrovsky's *The Forest* and Gogol's *The Inspector General* (the latter largely rearranged and somewhat altered in the writing) Meyerhold in his later period had little to work with in the way of sound dramatic literature. Yet he made some mighty fine plays out of exceedingly skimpy texts.

Some of these were propaganda pieces, but they were propaganda with a difference—I particularly remember one with a scene which gave me a greater sense of what it is to be caught in the midst of a battle than anything I've ever seen in the most elaborate of war films. There was such consummate skill and imagination in them that one felt one's self in the presence of epic drama.

Most of what I have described concerns only surface style, not content. The great director doesn't simply "do" plays supremely well; he has, like all true artists, a face of his own. No parallel between Meyerhold and the other notable men of his day or our own quite defines his quality.

It is not enough to say that it was compact with dash, irony, physical prowess, grace and a perpetually compelling vivacity. (Meyerhold fashioned a form of body training for the actors which he called "biomechanics.") Beyond and above all there was in his productions an aura of mystery and magic very nearly demonic. It gave everything he did a special glamour.

In his early articles Meyerhold repeatedly refers to the pre-eminence of Fate, that sense of life from which he believed the greatest art forms of the past emerged. In all his productions, light-hearted or grave, there was always something weird, menacing, which made all the dazzling display of the play's actions appear at once splendidly brave and tragic. He himself called this note of strangeness the grotesque.

He loved the nightmare world of E. T. A. Hoffmann, and chose "Doctor Dapertutto" (literally Doctor Everywhere), a character from one of Hoffmann's tales, as a pseudonym. Meyerhold was a masked man who with crafty artifices lured us to hellish realms which seemed to promise glory. He leaped from one enticingly dangerous peak to another. No wonder the proletariat on whose behalf he believed himself to be striving were suspicious of him; no wonder bureaucracy feared him and decided to destroy him. There was a Mephistophelean mockery in him, a challenge to complacency, to the doctrinaire, the academic, the momentarily fashionable.

This arch-sorcerer also rebelled against his apprentices saying that they were suffering from "Meyerholditis." At every crossroad he left them lagging in the dust behind. The Soviet establishment called his theatre "alien" and indeed it was, as every truly original art must for a time appear to be. It was therefore entirely characteristic of him when bid, in the Bolshevik mode, to devote a speech to self-criticism to begin by saying: "My entire career, all my productions, have been nothing but self-criticism. I never approach a new production without first shaking myself from the previous one."

41

Jerzy Grotowski

[December 8, 1969]

IN ONE of his occasional writings Jean Cocteau cites a Chinese proverb: "Genius creates hospitals." Whenever a towering personality appears, a host of lesser men become warped in imitation of the greater one.

Jerzy Grotowski is a genius, but I shudder to think how many misbegotten "Grotowskis" his Polish Laboratory Theatre will spawn. Peter Brook, being a highly gifted craftsman, knew how to popularize certain aspects of Grotowski's art in his production of *Marat/Sade*. Other such adaptations—most of them inept—are already in use and more are sure to follow. To be influenced by a master is natural, but for the most part the result is dilettantism or disaster.

The reason for all such unfortunate developments is that the superficial characteristics of the original model are mistaken for their meaning and value. The artist's inner history, his basic sources, the social and emotional circumstances of his growth, are very rarely operative in his disciples. Thus a new "manner" is contrived, a fashion sold by the insensitive to the ignorant.

I am sure that Grotowski's methods of training, chiefly designed as preparation for his productions, may prove stimulating and constructive for student actors and other professionals, but they do not constitute the essence of his art. For its better understanding one must turn from the theories and formal techniques (a collection of Grotowski's writings and speeches is called *Toward a Poor Theatre* (New York: Simon & Schuster, Inc., 1968) to the works themselves. Three of Grotowski's productions (none of them more than an hour long) were staged at the Washington Square Methodist Church in New York from October 16 to November 26, for limited audiences: one hundred at most; in one case, only forty.

The first one of these was based on a Grotowski scenario which he made from a romantically baroque adaptation of Calderón's *The Constant Prince.* The second was *Acropolis,* no more than an extract from a play by the nineteenth-century Polish dramatist Wyspianski; the locale and stress were entirely altered. *Apocalypsis cum Figuris,* the third production, was "evolved by its performers under the guidance of the director by means of acting exercises and sketches." The spoken text was culled from brief passages of the Bible, *The Brothers Karamazov,* one of T. S. Eliot's poems, and from something by Simone Weil.

Grotowski is all paroxysm. Thus his is the most contemporary of all theatres, for it can no longer be denied that we live in a time of cataclysm. Our very entertainments mask the face of agony. In the internal and outer upheaval, forms disintegrate, language decays, communication is conducted in jerks. Electric circuses serve as temples. Flesh is macerated. What is left of the soul goes into hiding or cries out in howls in which the difference between mirth and sorrow can hardly be distinguished. Even the gayest expressions contain the infernal.

These tendencies were already discernible in the expressionist theatre after the First World War. But at that time there was an element of journalism and propaganda (especially in Germany) in the outcries of horror. With the end of the Second World War—in the work of Beckett, Pinter, Genet and others—an element of private anguish became apparent, of withdrawal into secret chambers of consciousness where mainly grotesque (sometimes muted) signs of agony were displayed as if more overt declarations were somehow indecently sentimental.

As we ordinarily understand the terms, story or plot does not exist in Grotowski's plays. There is only a design of fantastically contorted bodies and symbolically violent relationships hardly congruous with realistically purposive action. The figures move in space which with one exception (*Acropolis*) does not resemble any identifiable environment. We are in a fearsomely imagined Gehenna where laws of time, gravity and natural logic have been suspended.

Grotowski's theatre (I speak of it as a unit because he does not consider himself to be its sole creator) is distinct from its predecessors in the vein of modern martyrdom. The tone and inspiration of his theatre derive from the extermination camp. His productions bring us into the realm of the Last Judgment. *Acropolis* takes place on the threshold of mass extinction. The figures are last seen descending into a hole beneath the floor and when they have disappeared under its stovelike cover there flows back a final murmur, "Now we die."

Acropolis may not be the "best" of Grotowski's productions, but it is the most representative. Here the prisoners reenact moments of the mythical past—Hebrew and Greek—distorting them by the use of the props at hand—metal pipes, rags—so that a wedding ceremony is made hideous and the cohabitation of Paris and Helen is performed by two men. The lines spoken at incredible speed are not dialogue; they are tortured exclamations projected in the direction of another being, but with no shape as personal address. (It has been said that a knowledge of Polish does not make the lines readily intelligible, but it is evident in *Apocalypsis cum Figuris* that they are not meant to be taken as are the lines of an ordinary play; solemn and poetic passages are delivered in a mode which brutally contradicts and virtually obliterates their initial intent.)

In *Acropolis* the executioners and their victims become nearly identical: they are kin. The rhythm of the meaningless tasks assigned them is set by one of the prisoners who plays a violin while their labors are accented by the drumlike tread of their rough boots. This vision has nothing in common with the factual exposé of the Nazi crimes in Peter Weiss' *The Investigation*. There is no redemption here and except for the closing moment—the march to the holocaust—very little pathos.

What we have seen is the tragic farce of civilization's values utterly despoiled. The prisoners themselves have been reduced to savage blasphemy. They are no longer individuals but the debris of humanity. If pity and terror are evoked in the spectator, if his moral sensibility is affected, it is through a kind of impersonal revulsion, from which he recovers as if from an anxiety dream he remembers as something intolerably spectral. One cannot normally sustain or assimilate such experiences.

Still, there is nothing chaotic in the spectacle. The names of Breughel, Bosch, Grünewald are frequently invoked for purposes of comparison; but that is misleading, for there was a sumptuousness in those artists. Grotowski's stage, architecture, costuming are bare. Everything has been stripped to the bone. (It is in this regard that his is a "poor theatre.") The structure of the playing area changes with each new play, so that the spectators are always in a different relation to the actors. Sometimes they look down as into an enclosed pit, sometimes they surround the action at stage level, sometimes they are ranged in a tierlike elevation slightly above. The actors are always very close, but they never move into or mingle with the audience.

Much has been made by various commentators of the company's extraordinary technical achievements in the use of voice and body. They are certainly striking and display training, prowess and command of a most remarkable sort. The voices unfalteringly emit sounds which remind one of the strange leaps of the twelve-tone system, with startling crescendos followed by crushed whisperings that do not resemble ordinary speech. They convey an other-worldly sphere *in extremis*. The lament of the constant prince (the play itself might be called the slaughter of innocence) is so desperate and prolonged as to exceed the bounds of human grief. We have arrived at the point of doomsday.

Yet all this has been given precise form. The exercises of Grotowski are intended to make the actor surmount his supposed breaking point, to stretch him vocally and bodily so that he can hold nothing back; to remove his restraints, those "blocks" imposed by his usual social comportment. He is wracked so that he becomes nothing but his id and thus releases what he primally is. Whether he actually succeeds in this, or whether it is altogether desirable that he do so, is another matter which I have no desire to question or capacity to determine at this juncture. One may say that in this respect the outstanding actor is Rizzard Crislak as the constant prince and as the "simpleton" in the *Apocalypsis.*

To understand Grotowski's form and content as a single process one must consider certain other elements which have gone into its creation. Grotowski is an intensely cultivated theatre artist. He has absorbed Stanislavsky's lessons in regard to acting; he has responded to the impulse in Artaud; he has learned from Meyerhold's precepts on movement, and has felt the impact of the apocalyptic artists already mentioned. In addition and not unlike Brecht, he seeks to establish a certain space between the spectator and the spectacle so that for all their ferocity his plays may be appreciated contemplatively.

Grotowski's art is imbued with strains from Catholic and other litanies and rituals. In *Acropolis,* especially, one hears echoes of Roman and Jewish services, as well as Slavic melodies. It is inescapable that while Grotowski is not a "believer," his is a ritualistic, indeed a religious art. (He has said that he wished his productions to be received in strict silence.) He seeks purification and salvation through their opposites, a return to the humane through the inhuman. We are to be redeemed through hellfire.

Goethe has said that no man can thoroughly capture the meaning of an art form who fails in some knowledge of the land and people of the art's provenance. Grotowski is a citizen of that Poland which was razed and decimated through the Nazi invasion and by the concentration camps which were its concomitants. Born in 1933 he is the witness and heir—as are most of his actors—of his country's devastation. The mark of that carnage is on their work. It is an abstract monument to the spiritual consequences of that horrendous event.

And that is why most productions done à la Grotowski must be largely fraudulent. His theatre has roots in a specific native experience. It is organic with a lived tradition which was shattered and defamed by unimaginable iniquity and boundless shame. Where an art lacks the foundation of corresponding realities it is ornament, entertainment or mere pretense.

Countless times I have been asked apropos these performances of the Polish Laboratory Theatre (in existence since 1959 and still engaged "in research") whether or not I *liked* them. My answer: It doesn't matter whether any of us "likes" them. This troupe is what I have repeatedly called true *theatre*. It may always remain a theatre for the few (I do not refer to snobs), even a cult. Its "message" is well-nigh intolerable and its fanaticism forbidding. But its dedication to its vision of life and art is unparalleled in any theatre of our day.

42

Tennessee Williams: Poet and Puritan

[March 29, 1970]

THOUGH OUR playwrights are frequently celebrated, few are truly known. It is twenty-five years now since Tennessee Williams made his Broadway debut with *The Glass Menagerie*, on March 31, 1945. Since then he has written more than fifteen full-length plays, a good number of shorter ones, a screenplay, a volume of poetry, three volumes of short stories, and a novel. Our most prolific playwright, Williams has received three Critics Circle awards and two Pulitzer Prizes. Drama students undoubtedly list him as one of the four or five most important playwrights our theatre has produced. Yet one may query whether he has been wholly understood.

We are in the habit of judging our playwrights piecemeal. As with cars, we think in seasonal models. Last year's issue was a triumph, this year's is a bust. When several flops follow one another, we pronounce the erstwhile wonder "finished," or "dead." We may even question whether the golden boy's "glitter" was really as bright as we had once believed it to be. Racine's tart reply to his contemporary detractors, "The critics have vanished, the plays remain," applies here.

Williams is a dramatist of lost souls. His work describes a long laceration. No American playwright is altogether a pessimist. The conclusion of *Camino Real*, "the violets in the mountains have

227

broken through the rocks," simply means that idealism will ultimately smash the battlements of villainy in which we are immured. But this thought only marks a pause along the road. Williams' path leads to no final statement. He has no doctrine, unless it be the need for compassion. He traces a chart of the fevers that he has experienced in looking at the world outside and within himself.

The picture is muted and tender in the fragmented memories of *The Glass Menagerie*. Because of its gentle qualities, many folk prefer this play to all the others. It is the seedbed of his future work. Amanda, the mother, establishes the tone of a life gone by. She is a fading personality, the idealist become foolish for want of a foundation in the present. She remains wistfully hopeful as she recalls a time of greater stability and grace. Here too we find her daughter Laura, an injured girl withdrawn from life because of the visible handicap of her lameness. She consoles herself with playthings which will not endure. The memorable Gentleman Caller is the first example of Williams' ability to depict the average uneducated "good guy" with both truthfulness and sympathy. And there is the son Tom, oppressed by the lack of vitality in the meager maternal nest. He is eager to escape it and explore long distances. "I seem dreamy," he says, "but inside—well, I'm boiling."

Amanda is a Puritan. She shies away from instinct. "It belongs to animals," she says. What people like herself want are "superior things! Things of the mind and the spirit." This note is struck again and again, developed at length and more eloquently by Blanche in *A Streetcar Named Desire* and by Alma in *Summer and Smoke*. The yearning to transcend the senses is sometimes viewed as comic or pathetic but is never extinguished. It finds its purest expression in Hannah Jelke, the poet's daughter in *The Night of the Iguana*.

The Puritan seeks God as do all good poets, Williams intimates in *Suddenly Last Summer*, and Williams is both poet and Puritan. The world he has entered on his long journey is grotesquely harsh, depleted of sacred values; where they *seem* to obtain, they exist only in travesty. Specifically, Williams' milieu is usually the tense and still unreconstructed South, but that is only a locale typical of an environment we all inhabit.

Blanche Du Bois, Williams' most representative character, has been exiled through the loss of the ancestral site into a society in which she can no longer be "a young *lady*," that is, a whole person. The world she now finds herself in is self-sufficiently and complacently brutal. It is a world in which "superior things of mind and spirit" are scorned. Innocently and achingly, she depends on the "kindness of strangers." But most of these strangers are the devil's surrogates. They spell death. Bearing flowers, death haunts Williams and terrifies him.

The opposite of death is desire—the will to live, the need for the most intimate contact with those outside us. It inspires us with a sense of beauty. Blanche gives herself to desire in ignorance, confusion, dismay. She does not know that desire and beauty, through their simulacra, frequently lead to an impasse, to destruction, to death.

With only a few exceptions, Williams' characters are lost souls because they are torn between the god-seeking impulse and the pull of desire. In the shambles of our civilization, desire has been debased into raw carnality. Sex without the blessedness of love is death-dealing corruption. In this corrupt atmosphere—always captivatingly colorful in Williams, even to the very names of the vicinities in which his dramas take place—his men and women are destroyed by the poisons which emanate from it. The lacerations they suffer are the result of their bodies and souls being at odds. The sharpness of this division is a characteristic of Puritan consciousness. Unity of spirit is achieved only by the chaste Hannah in *Iguana* and the impassioned and therefore utterly loyal Rosa in *The Rose Tattoo,* in which sex becomes glorified through its pure flame. But Rosa is a Sicilian—a foreigner to our way of life.

When we speak of the world and of society, we imply a realm beyond the strictly personal. Sex, it is commonly held, is Williams' major theme. This, I believe, is only partly true; when this preoccupation with sex in Williams is insisted upon as the determining ingredient, such insistence leads to a falsification. Williams is also very much a social playwright. Sex being a central factor in existence, it becomes the area in Williams' plays where the social battles as well as the battle of angels rage.

It is in a fatal incapacity to integrate the conflict of body and soul, or, to put it more concretely, the struggle between power and love, egotistical acquisitiveness and social generosity, that we find the thematic core of Williams' work. The tension in these forces creates a split in the social order as well as in the individual personality. It causes his people to grope, trembling and bewildered, between that light and shadow to which he repeatedly refers. It also gives rise to personal self-deception and public hypocrisy.

The duality in Williams assumes many guises. It is merely a sidelight on his character, but those who have worked with him (myself among them) have noted that he wavers even in the judgment of his own creations and more especially as to the manner in which they are to be performed. He may say, for instance, that Stanley Kowalski in *Streetcar* points to America's future. This may mean that he fears that the gorillas will inherit our earth or, on the contrary, that he prefers the primitive drive of such folk to the palsied sensibilities of the super-aesthetes.

He will praise totally diverse interpretations of his plays and tell various producing companies in turn that they alone have done his plays as he envisioned them. This is not merely professional politesse but a sign of an inner uncertainty.

The doppelgänger or second-self ascribed to Alma in *Summer and Smoke* is his own. The accusatory ferocity in regard to our society, which becomes a debilitating fixation in his later plays, alternates with a certain calm or balance in *The Night of the Iguana* or even takes the form of goodnatured comedy in his *Period of Adjustment*.

There is a salutary humor in all his work. It is quizzical and given to grassroots laughter. His violence too is softened by the colorfulness and musicality which bathe his plays in glamour. "A kind of lyricism," a stage direction in *Streetcar* reads, "gracefully attenuates the atmosphere of decay." There is magic in Williams' realism.

In the illusionist sense of theatricality, he has no match in American dramatic writing. The rhythms of his colloquial speech are seductive. His dialogue excels in euphony and ease. It has a fragrance like that of a tropical flower planted in a northern soil. The diction is at once limpid and elusive, achieving both mystery and suspense.

Williams writes rich roles for actors. They are gratifying because they represent people who mirror some of his own ambivalence, assertive and tremulously vulnerable, staunch and retreating. His particular nature has enabled him to fashion several of the most perceptive and touching portraits of women our drama has produced. He is one of the few dramatists among us who writes genuine love scenes.

He is no intellectual. Some of his views and sentiments—as in *Camino Real*—are couched in terms which betray an almost adolescent sentimentality. His weaknesses, however, should not dim for us his mastery of stage poetics, his immense gift for theatrical effect and, above all, his vital contribution to the understanding of formerly undisclosed phases of American life.

Through his fascination with sin and his affinity with sinners, Williams, even more than O'Neill, has opened our eyes and hearts to the victims of our savagely mechanized society, the company of the "somehow unfit," the fragile, the frightened, the different, the odd and the lonely, whose presence in our world we have so long sought to avoid thinking about and recognizing as our kin.

Williams is nothing if not honest. He has acknowledged the tension induced by the dichotomy of his spirit which has led him to the verge of permanent breakdown. He dramatized this state bewilderingly in his 1969 play *In the Bar of a Tokyo Hotel* and in the unjustly neglected "The Gnädiges Fräulein"—part of his 1966 *Slapstick Tragedy*—where the romantic dreamer in the entertainment business, the leeches of publicity, the callous public, the profiteer and exploiters of talent are symbolized with originality and wit.

Breakdown, as with Strindberg, is sometimes the springboard for rebirth. At fifty-eight, Williams is still capable of renewal and growth. I look forward to his further progress in a career which has brought distinction and honor to our stage.

43

Will They
Awake and Sing
in 1970?

[May 24, 1970]

READING THE announcement of the off-Broadway revival of Clifford Odets' *Awake and Sing* caused me to speculate on what the reaction to it today might be. Much, of course, depends on the quality of its staging. Still, I could anticipate that many might find it "dated"— always an easy out for the careless spectator. After all, the play was first presented in New York on February 19, 1935.

All plays are dated. They are products of their time. Do we complain of *The Importance of Being Earnest* because its idiom is not Osborne's? Even those dramatists who aim at timelessness—Samuel Beckett, for instance—are representative of a period. *Waiting for Godot* could not have been written in 1912 any more than we can imagine plays like those of Congreve being written in Shakespeare's day.

The dramatist's datedness applies chiefly to the historical circumstances of his writing: what was going on in the world at the time he set about doing his work. He employs the speech of his environment, uses the techniques which he has inherited from the past and adds something of the present which (at best) points to the future. What is permanent in his creation is that element which his fellow countrymen still find nourishing to their inner health and pleasure in later days.

The thirties, of which Odets' plays are the outstanding dramatic expression, are chiefly remembered as the time of the great Depression. We are now presumably living in a period of affluence. There was much talk in those "ancient" times of rescuing the suffering working class, supporting the rising trade unions, and some even espoused socialism of one kind or another. Today many are convinced that the unions are not only greedily monopolistic but often reactionary, the working class by no means underprivileged, and "socialism" a dirty word.

Still, Secretary of the Interior, Walter J. Hickel, in his letter to President Nixon was able to say "What is happening today is not unrelated to what happened in the thirties." Secretary Hickel was not simply referring to the rash of "confrontations" which now afflict the nation. There is a considerable difference in meaning between the call to strike which ends Odets' first flaming outcry, *Waiting for Lefty,* and the demands of organized labor today. But the references to unemployment, starvation, breadlines, evictions, and the need for workers to realize their power, which resound in lyric exuberance or melancholy plea in Odets' early plays, are not what is essential in his basic message or to his intrinsic value for us at present. The correspondence between the upheavals of the thirties and those of the present, suggested by Secretary Hickel, lies in a sense of something fundamentally wrong in our society that statements of benevolent intention or minor reforms will neither satisfy nor mend.

Odets was never a political playwright, nor even a "revolutionary" one in the limited sense attached to that epithet then or now. His was a rebellion against our materialism, our subservience to the idol of Success as the supreme good. Odets' denunciation of this blight was not that of a sociological preacher. He knew its corrosive properties because they dwelt within *him,* and he hated them because they were crippling him and, at last, literally killed him.

There was a tormenting duality in Odets, as there is in most important artists, a duality which makes them dramatic. It is from the conflict within themselves (of different kinds within different artists) that they create. Where the duality is resolved or kept in balance, the result is benign; where the duality is finally insuperable, the artist's career is fatally damaged.

The duality in Odets consists of his being an impassioned idealist and, at the same time, a creature constantly lured by the trappings of the bitch goddess (Success) whose seductions he knew were lethal. If we examine Odets' history (his twelve plays and his Hollywood activities) we perceive the drama of defeat issuing from a foundation of the noblest aspirations. This drama is an American tragedy. It is related to what O'Neill had in mind when planning his never completed nine-play cycle, the theme of which he declared was to be centered in the challenge of "What shall it profit a man if he gain the whole world and lose his own soul?"

There was in Odets an inextinguishable, characteristically native, optimism. All but one of his plays end on an "up-beat" even when the curtain rings down on a death. His plays point to that future which would unify all men in mutual understanding and reconstructive effort. Odets' favorite author in his youth was the Victor Hugo of *Les Miserables* with its compassion for the downtrodden; later he turned to Walt Whitman with his dream of a truly democratic America peopled by sound individuals. "Life should have some dignity" old Jacob says in *Awake and Sing,* and the play's prophetic title is indicative of Odets' mood in this, his purest play. And to attain that dignity, Jacob adds, we must "go out and fight so life shouldn't be printed on dollar bills." To which his grandson's ultimate response is "Let me die like a dog, if I can't get more from life [than that which the Depression has produced]. . . . I want the whole city to hear it, fresh blood, arms. We got 'em. We're glad we're living."

This is not only youthful high-heartedness but a declaration of the activism (the meaning of "Strike!" in *Lefty*) emblematic of Odets and the thirties in their early stages. Jacob, who constantly cites Marx but who has not read him, describes himself as a man "with good ideas, but only in the head. . . . That is why I tell you—*do!* Do what is in your heart and you carry in yourself a revolution." All of Odets' first "heroes" are determined to "change the world," to make America yield the fruits of its promise.

But Ralphie, the twenty-two-year-old grandson, also hankers for his "name in the papers" just as Joe Bonaparte in *Golden Boy* yearns for "fame and fortune," which leads him to give up his musical talent to battle for more visible benefits. For the poor boy (Bonaparte–Odets) the booty of the battle is expressed in the purchase of an expensive car. This is a naïvely romantic image which signifies that American materialism is not only a monetary matter but manifests itself in the impulse to parade the success with which one's efforts have been crowned. Odets was nothing if not a romantic.

Right after *Awake and Sing* opened to generally enthusiastic notices, Odets bought an elaborate record player. (He had a genuine love of music.) When, after *Golden Boy,* his greatest commercial success, he signed to write screenplays for Paramount Pictures, he bought a Cadillac. Later, after *The Flowering Peach,* he bought a Lincoln Continental. When he undertook to write a picture for Elvis Presley, he rationalized the act, as he did his contract to supervise an undistinguished television series. When hard times ensued for him again—after 1955, Odets always lived beyond his means—he shied from dining at prominent restaurants for fear of the pity or patronizing attitude with which he imagined his colleagues might greet him.

The golden boy destroys his talent. Odets understood the pattern of the confused idealist intuitively and objectively. When he came to write about Hollywood in *The Big Knife,* his knowledge had become unmistakably subjective but shamefaced. (When, on reading the script, I objected that the movie star Charles Castle's desire to escape Hollywood was not convincingly plotted, Odets exclaimed "But he really loves Hollywood!" which was a splendid insight but was suppressed in the actual telling of the play's story.) "I wanted to be two other guys," Castle says when he has just been told point blank by the play's only uncontaminated character, "You've sold out." And in *The Flowering Peach,* Odets' swan song, old Noah, wearied of his virtues, decides to settle down with his complacently rich son, rather than with the socially rebellious one, because it's "more comfortable" that way.

Nothing is more typical of the struggle within Odets' soul than his testimony at the hearing before the House Committee on Un-American Activities in 1952. He did not wish to present an abject figure; indeed he intended to be defiant. Though he had long since abandoned his association with the Communist Party, he did not want to disavow the humanistic impulse which had led him to join it. Yet he acquiesced in the Committee's bidding by inculpating his closest colleagues in the theatre, while he tried to suggest that he still believed that there were some good arguments for socialism. The Committee did not thank him for his cooperation and he, later, wept because he had not been more courageous.

Odets once declared that he experienced in his flesh and bones every desire and emotion that the ordinary man feels, even when he (Odets) found them reprehensible. This consanguinity with the small fry in the American ferment gives Odets' work an authenticity which is not present to the same degree in any other playwright. Through this closeness to his people there arises in his best writing a warm intimacy, a special tenderness—"tenement tenderness" I once called it—which makes his use of the word "love" more than the fatuous slogan it tends to become. His actual love scenes are among the best in our theatre.

Odets' plays are rich with vividly defined characters. They are brimful with the juices of life. The fever of his writing directly communicates the turbulence of his spirit. His dialogue pulsates with the beat and whirl of the city. While his language is a compound of New York dialects, one cannot say that it is "dated" because no one ever really spoke exactly as Odets' characters do any more than the Elizabethans spoke as Shakespeare wrote.

Odets had a wonderful ear. His language is a personal poetry wrought from phrases, jokes, popular word-coinage and songs heard in the street and in homes, things he read in newspaper captions as well as in the funnies, remarks picked up from desultory companions and relatives. These have all been recast in the fire of his imagination and transfigured into a beautifully original rhetoric. *Awake and Sing* was not understood when it was produced in Israel because it is much less Jewish than thoroughly "United States." His writing is full of salty humor and melody. It makes us aware that even his most impatient outbursts were part of his exultation in the hope for a better life, a saner world.

This brings us back to our point of departure. Odets *is* still pertinent. For though our present economic and social problems are not precisely what they were in the thirties (except for our intensified sense of possible annihilation) the basic disturbances in the whole fabric of our living are due to a lack of truly generative ideals—practical ideals—not mere alterations in nomenclature. We want something to transform the conduct of our lives day by day.

The alarming "wildness" of our youth is a symptom of our failure to make our deeds correspond to our professions of faith. We know that the negatives of "anti-Communism" will not help, nor will or should our young be content with the solace of comparison with other people who "don't have it as good" as we do. We know that we must act so that we radically affect our physical environment, our economic and political structures, our buildings, the aspect of our streets, our manners, our educational institutions, our arts, our entire comportment.

Even when they don't rightly understand it, know how to organize it, and are often corrupted by some of the diseases which afflict their elders, there is a revolution going on in the hearts of the young which must either lead to the "new world" invoked in *Awake and Sing* or to a veritable hell of destructiveness (to the self and to others) which is always the consequence of idealism betrayed.

This is the crux of Odets' dramatic statement and what in its totality it portends.

44

London

[September 21, 1970]

THERE ARE new plays of sense and sensibility to be seen on the London stage: more than I recently found in Paris, more than I saw in New York last season.

I designate the English plays in this mild fashion; London reviewers employ a more enthusiastic vocabulary, and they are probably right to do so. Very few superior (not to speak of "great") new plays are ever to be seen anywhere at any time. Anything above the trivial—anything that adds even a little to the sum of our pleasures—is to be cordially welcomed at the moment of its emergence. The higher criticism comes later.

The London plays I refer to are enhanced by admirably professional acting. To be "professional" is to possess proficiency in conveying a dramatic intention with the maximum clarity, intelligence and arresting effect. There is a level above such acting: it is inspired acting, a profoundly personal expression that flowers as though unmotivated by the actor's conscious will. Such acting transcends definition in technical terms or in the coin of commonplace critical encomia. It is the fourth dimension, the poetry, of acting.

The performances in London were at times so brilliant that they made me forget momentarily the possible existence of something more. That "something" is even more rarely attained nowadays than is the composition of important plays. American actors do not appear frequently enough in a diversity of parts and thus have less opportunity—even where there may be the capacity—to achieve the goal I have in mind; English life is more formalized than American, and while that is in some respects an asset, it is for acting a considerable impediment.

The old forms are now breaking down in England and that, to some extent, explains why the English stage for the past twenty years has been producing a greater number of interesting actors. The quality of English acting has greatly improved since the time (1901) when Max Beerbohm found it possible to say, "We have a few good English actors. Very few indeed. Most of the good actors in England have some strong taint of foreign blood in their veins. . . . As a general rule, Englishmen cannot act. . . ."

Of the new plays the two I found most absorbing were *The Philanthropist* by twenty-four-year-old Christopher Hampton, and *Home* by David Storey, who also wrote *The Contractor*. Both current plays were first produced at the nationally subsidized Royal Court Theatre. The first is still at that small house; the second has moved to the West End.

What is most noteworthy about *The Philanthropist* is not its smooth and witty writing, nor the unexpected turns Hampton uses when excessive wordiness threatens to strain our attention, but the creation of a character who is usually accounted undramatically flaccid and who Hampton has nevertheless made entirely worth concern.

He is called Philip, a professor of philology, but no fool. The author is at ease with such folk and does not treat the type as an oddball. He neither reveres nor condescends to the man. Theatrically speaking, what is special about Philip is his mild nature, awkward but gracious, kindly without gush, good without self-consciousness; but he has one marked flaw: benevolence to the point of indecisiveness.

He is therefore a loser. He goes to bed with a girl he does not desire, because she insists on his doing so and he does not know how to refuse her. He loses the girl he wishes to marry because she is rendered insecure by his lack of will. He wants everyone to like him, is indeed terrified by the prospect of loneliness. But his very amenability makes his acquaintances doubtful of his brain and/or good faith.

We are not urged to commiserate with him; we even laugh at him. Yet we do feel for him, seeing that he lives in the 1970 jungle in which his virtues are not apt to win even the most modest prizes of companionship or marriage.

Though constantly engaging, the play is yet immature in craftsmanship. It begins by way of a prologue with a funny but irrelevant *coup de théâtre,* and continues with reams of conversation, amusingly representative of smart talk in educated London circles. At first I thought that what I was to see was a sophisticated version of a Neil Simon comedy. But in the latter half of the play—particularly in the passages where Philip is confronted by the girl who has seduced him only to find him a dud—and then by the girl who gives him up because of his unassertiveness—the evening comes into happy focus. There is later some further overdiscursive wobbling but the final moments are perceptive and touching.

Alec McGowen as Philip gives what for me is his best performance to date. In *Hadrian VII* his mastery at making points was hailed as supreme artistry—everything was immaculately framed for our self-congratulatory appreciation; in *The Philanthropist* he creates a real person.

David Storey's *Home* extends this dramatist's dim view of "things as they are." In this play, however, the picture is more abstract and more "poetic" than in *The Contractor.* The atmosphere—well caught in the bare setting—is gentler and more muted.

I call the treatment "abstract" though the audience appears to accept it as realistic. For the "home" of the title, though we do not know it at first, is an institution for the mentally disturbed, people given to some more or less harmless but probably incurable aberration. At the same time this "home" may be construed as England or, quite baldly, the world today.

At the center of the play stand two elderly gentlemen, who seem to be meeting casually at a glum seaside resort. They exchange banalities, desolate and ludicrous; they hardly ever complete a thought and when they do, how lamentable, self-contradictory and laughable it is. They yearn for communication but each dwells in a realm of which only the periphery touches that of the other. They are of another time—the "older generation." They are in awe of their country's achievements; they marvel uncomprehendingly at the new strides in scientific and technological discovery; they recall the geniuses of the past—Darwin, Newton, et al.—but nothing within sustains them and all without is barren. Their lives are shadowy dreams, shattered memories. From time to time, without apparent cause, they quietly weep.

Pitifully, one laughs at them and ruminates, "Yes, this is typical of much that we too have seen, apart from the certifiably lunatic sphere." The horizon here is even less fleshed than are those with which Pinter has acquainted us. How pathetically bleak is the picture. But, I must confess, I do not fully believe in it: even the dullest beings have more substance, greater density of experience.

Near-farcical traits are drawn in the presentation of two women inmates of the asylum. They are less "symbolic." They may be likened to colorful cartoons of cockney characters. In these there are sudden intimations of violence and suicidal bitterness. Contemporary youth is limned in the image of a boy maimed by an operation which has removed part of his brain. He is nothing but brute muscle. His only address, to man and woman alike, is: "Do you want to fight?" spoken with no real hostility.

All this might become depressing, not to say monotonous, if it were not lightened by humor—saturnine, but still funny—and softened by an ambience of regret and restrained compassion. The acting, above all, saves the evening from oppressiveness. Ralph Richardson's natural dreaminess, his charmingly wan presence, which suggests a spirit that wanders far off to heaven knows what area of the unnameable, contribute immeasurably to the occasion. The music of his voice, the stress and rhythm of his speech, turn the most ordinary lines to magic and mystery. Thus the play as a whole comes to weave a spell which somehow consoles. Opposite him, John Gielgud is one of the "stately homes of England" in tears. The man appears heartbroken through a faint awareness of some unspecified fault. The two actors play together like masters of chamber art.

I have alluded to the overheated praise of meritorious new plays. On the other hand it strikes me that the National Theatre's *Hedda Gabler,* directed in part by Ingmar Bergman along the lines of his original Swedish production, has been underestimated.

Certainly Ibsen did not mean his Hedda to be as unmistakably neurotic as Bergman has made her. I myself once called her a "normal woman"—and perhaps, too, Ibsen's Lovberg would not have manifested his passion for Hedda in so directly physical a manner as Bergman has him do. Still, this interpretation of the play makes sense without abusing the fundamental import of the author's dramatic thought.

The action takes place on an almost empty stage, divided in two by screens. The screens are dun red, either to match the color of the theatre's walls or to establish an emotional tone. One-half of the stage is the inner room into which Hedda retires when she wishes to escape company, but it is also the locus of her inner self. At the very outset we see her in a convulsion of despair, already contemplating suicide. The other half of the stage, containing nothing but a sofa and two chairs, is the area of Hedda and her husband's social exchanges. While the stark setting diminishes the impact of the bourgeois burden which is part of Ibsen's meaning, it sharpens the play's formal structure and lends it a fierce tension.

Indeed intensity, almost melodramatic in its insistence, is the keynote of the production. Though I have seen the play countless times, I have never before been so thoroughly gripped by it.

The anguished dialectic of the characters' minds is envisioned as in the light of an X-ray. Elements which make Hedda part of her time and have much to do with her plight fade in this staging. Facets of her nineteenth-century romanticism—when she speaks of Lovberg with "vine leaves in his hair," for instance—are eliminated, as is almost everything which lessens the sense of the play's contemporaneity. Hedda here is a woman destroyed by her self-repressed libido as much as by the pressures of middle-class convention which Ibsen indicates plays a large part in her undoing.

Maggie Smith, a comedienne born, would not seem to be the right person for the role, but she is an exceptional actress. She does not possess the physical prowess for certain of the emotional climaxes; nevertheless, she makes almost the most vivid Hedda I can remember. It goes without saying that she brings a special wit to the personage—wit gleams in Maggie Smith—but she captures Hedda's frustration and pain as well. Her Hedda is an exposed nerve.

45

━━➤━━■>●<●━━━◄━━

The Body

[September 28, 1970]

BEFORE THE FIRST WORLD WAR and shortly thereafter, burlesque was family entertainment. But its best comics defected to vaudeville, the musical comedy stage, radio and finally to television. To save burlesque, the striptease was introduced during the Depression. At first this produced ladies skilled in semi-erotic titillation; some of them—Gypsy Rose Lee, for instance—were able to practice this trick with a kind of jovial malice. To hold the audiences in the last hangdog days of the Hoover administration, the girls no longer teased, they just stripped. It has occurred to me that the use of verbal obscenity and performances in the raw have come onto the stage, in some similar fashion, as a booster to the theatre.

There are certainly other and better explanations. There exists today not a rebellion against "puritanism"—we had that in the twenties—but against vacuity. The Body, in all its fun and functions, is *real,* and very little else is nowadays. We can *believe* in the Body. All that alludes to its basic drives, in the language which speaks most unmistakably of them, may now be celebrated in orgiastic rites. The spate of sexual play may induce a tonic effect. However, there is nothing Greek, Rabelaisian or Elizabethan in the impetus of the phenomenon. It is something like a rattling of chains.

What makes it suspect is that the bawdiness hardly ever becomes fresh, eloquent or passionate. It is rarely funny or hilariously dirty

243

as the burlesque shows occasionally were. The best of *Oh! Calcutta!* was not in its sketches but in six or seven minutes of naked cavorting that provided a certain merriment and innocence.

There is very little that is innocent but much that is foolishly pretentious—innovations in hypocrisy—in this vein of the "new theatre." The unclad bodies now prancing about with more energy than aptitude in *The Dirtiest Show in Town* (Astor Place Theatre) are pleasant to look at, but the words (there is no "book" or skits) are amusing only as exercises in complex patterns of smutty insults in camp style. I laughed once or twice.

I found especially intolerable the phony admixture of "social significance"—the silly charade is supposed to satirize our civilization. Tom Eyen, its author and director, proclaims: "We no longer live complete lives—stop—only parts—stop—and these parts are not our own—*stop!*" References to air pollution and to the hostilities of our lovemaking are supposed to provide the exhibit with its "ideas." To which my most polite response is—*crap!*

None of this however turned my annoyance into outrage. The publicized quotes from two *New York Times* critics and several others were what rendered me rabid. If they had said: "The young people in this show have attractive figures and their sexual tangle (enhanced by reflections in a mirror) is beguiling," I should have had no objection. But wit was found in the proceedings, *wit*, the element so desperately lacking throughout. This from the most influential reviewer in New York who finds little to admire in Shaw. And not only wit was found in this frenzied juvenilia but also emotion. Thus the mess has become an off-Broadway smash. To have puffed it up for what it is (Kenneth Tynan, for example, confessed in public print that he approves of pornography because it encourages masturbation), such admiration would hardly suffice. With certain reviewers it is imperative above all to prove that they are "with it," that they are not squares. Youth (and the avant-garde) must be served.

46

---◆▶●◀◆▶◆---

The New Theatre, Now

[January, 1971]

Two ATTITUDES PREVAIL in regard to what is referred to as the "new" or "avant-garde" theatre. There are the unqualified champions and those who are its entrenched detractors. Both are mistaken. In practice, the phenomenon is so diverse in aspect, so eclectic in methods, as to defy categorization.

It is, above all, a reaction against commonplace realism. There is nothing particularly new in this. The realistic theatre is itself a comparatively recent development—hardly much more than a hundred years old. The Japanese Noh, the Kabuki, and the classic Greek theatres were, and insofar as they still exist are, "total theatres." They have little in common with nineteenth- and twentieth-century realism.

In the main, new theatre eschews literature as its central factor. Drama as a text which has to be extended, illustrated, interpreted by stage action is not crucial in the new theatre. What we ordinarily call the "play," the work of a dramatist whose language is the core of the theatrical event, is no longer dominant. A respected text may be the springboard for what we see on the stage, but it is employed in a way which its original author might find hard to recognize or even acknowledge as his own. The words employed have been absorbed in a context of physical movement, sound, light, improvised episodes, and incidental "business" which, apprehended as a whole, constitute what amounts to a new play and possibly a different meaning.

All drama in the theatre goes through such translation from an initial seed or theme articulated in dialogue into the vocabulary of the stage: acting, setting, and direction. Shakespeare's *Hamlet* exists in print only; what we see in the theatre is this or that actor's *Hamlet* or this or that company's *Hamlet*. Still, in the normal theatre of our era everyone's point of reference is always the original text. Gesture and mime, costume, stage properties, light and sound, improvisations which may include audience participation, may supersede the importance of the spoken word or literary text. In new theatre the Play is the product of a collective "game."

The reduction of the dramatist's work to the function of a scenario within the larger scope of the company's total performance is the new theatre's first and most striking trait. Meyerhold, the great Russian director and to a certain extent the unacknowledged forerunner of much of what is now thought "modern" in the theatre, phrased the new *esthétique* by saying, "Words in the theatre are only embellishments on the design of movement." This was written in 1908 before Gordon Craig, in 1911, published corresponding views.

Most pioneers are rarely cited by American devotees of the new theatre, except for Antonin Artaud, a French actor and theatrical prophet. Two chapter titles in his book, *The Theatre and Its Double,* have become slogans for the epigones. They are "The Theatre of Cruelty" and "No More Masterpieces."

To make sense of Artaud's ideas, his essentially poetic pronouncements require translation into more sober language. "Cruelty" in Artaud means intensity. He wished theatre to achieve the force of natural phenomena, like lightning and thunder. "This cruelty," he wrote in a letter to a friend, "is a matter of neither sadism nor bloodshed. . . . I do not systematically cultivate horror. The word 'cruelty' must be taken in a broad sense. . . . From the point of view of the mind, cruelty signifies rigor, implacable intention and reason, irreversible and absolute determination."

In certain American new theatre manifestations, much is expected from elements of chance and accident, things which may happen in the free interplay of performers and public. In Artaud's example of a "faultless performance," that of the Balinese theatre, a theatre of the utmost refinement, he finds "everything . . . is established with an enchanting mathematical meticulousness. Nothing is left to chance or to personal initiative."

As to "no more masterpieces," it is a summons to replace the pre-eminence of the written word by spectacle, movement, music, shouts, cries, and other sound effects. Artaud's prescription approximates Gordon Craig's "When literary men shall be content enough to study the 'art of the theatre' as an art separate from the 'art of literature,' there will be nothing to prevent us from welcoming them into the house."

These quotations belong to the rhetoric of the movement, and such rhetoric, as in politics, is neither illustrative nor conclusive. Craig and Artaud were never fully permitted or able to embody their ideas in actual production. Instances of things actually performed are more illuminating than manifestos.

In "Motel," a segment of the triptych called *America, Hurrah!,* staged by Joseph Chaikin and devised in collaboration with the writer Jean-Claude van Itallie, we see a dummy which mouths the attractions of a motel. "Her" speech is a tape recording. While the spiel issues from the mechanism, a man and a woman enter, both grotesquely masked. They are perhaps newlyweds on their honeymoon. They write obscenities on the wall. They very nearly wreck everything in the room just before going to bed. As they proceed to this climax, blinding lights flash in the audience's faces, and a deafening din—the cacophony of our civilization—fills the auditorium. "Motel" is a theatrical metaphor typifying our environment. What is spoken is only significant in relation to what we experience through the aural and visual assault on our senses.

Dionysus in '69, freely adapted from Euripides' *The Bacchae* by Richard Schechner's Performance Group, employs many of the elements suggested in Artaud's program for a "theatre of cruelty." In his book *Up Against the Fourth Wall* (New York: Grove Press, 1970), John Lahr, an enthusiastic supporter of the new theatre, describes part of the evening's activities:

> [The] theme [is] the new self-consciousness toward the body and the unshackling of the sexual instinct. The actors in *Dionysus* are trained to a heightened, acrobatic concept of performance. The males stripped to a jockstrap; the females in brief body tunics (sometimes nude) move through a series of carefully disciplined images. . . . Men lie prone

on the floor while the women straddle them, fixing their legs tight between groins. Bodies pass under legs and bare backs squirm in a tortuous rebirth. . . . The audience, too, is conditioned to new emotions by an environmental stage, a series of three tiered constructions allowing the audience to watch the performance from a variety of perspectives. They can climb, or hide, or walk about. . . . By making the theatrical expression a physical adventure, Schechner's Performance Group wants to expand the audience's understanding of liberty.

Some of the actors play recorders, others strike drums. They invite the audience to dance with them and trace movements of loving embrace with individual spectators. At times the actors speak lines which relate to their personal lives; on occasion refer to persons in the audience. The night I attended the show there was an allusion to "the great god Harold Clurman." Euripides is not entirely omitted either in theme or verbiage. But Euripides' "message" has been reversed in the light of an ideology consonant with contemporary youth.

Euripides' *Bacchae* dramatizes the conflict between repressive and militant asceticism and Dionysiac license. The Greek dramatist as moderator demonstrates the hazards involved in both extremes. The ascetics tyrannize over the senses and are thus destructive; the passion of the Bacchic celebrants progresses toward murder. But Schechner's "bacchae," handsome boys and girls, win the day: they bathe in the blood of the censorious dictator and march triumphantly through the town. Theirs is "the politics of ecstasy."

The term "environmental stage" in Lahr's description of *Dionysus in '69* is one which will ever more frequently crop up in discussions of the new theatre and may therefore demand further elucidation. The stages long familiar to us are those we contemplate from a distance; we are separated from them. The environmental stage includes and surrounds us; we dwell within it.

The most striking example of this in theatre architecture (it has precedents in the Middle Ages) is the *Orlando Furioso* produced by the Teatro Libero di Roma recently in New York, an event of which I reserve description till later (page 255).

All these otherwise dissimilar examples have one thing in common: *abstraction,* or, to put it negatively, nonrealism. They do not "hold a mirror up to nature." The path toward abstraction, the departure from realism—to go no further back in time—was first set for us by the previous example of the dramatists lumped together under the tag imprinted on them by Martin Esslin of London: "Theatre of the Absurd." The tag is perhaps unfortunate because it designates such men as Beckett, Ionesco, Genet, Pinter, who are distinctly different from one another.

These playwrights are not to be confused with the new or avant-garde theatre. They are, for all the strangeness or novelty in their manner and meaning, entirely traditional, that is, literary dramatists. If I mention them in the present context, it is simply to indicate that their departure from the techniques of their immediate predecessors served to liberate a later generation of theatre folk from the confines of naturalism, the representation of life as we customarily view it. Their two mottoes might have been that of the French actor Coquelin, who said, "I am for *nature* and against naturalism," and Sartre's, "The Theatre is not concerned with reality. It's concerned with truth."

If any further generalization is to be made about the "absurdists," it is that the truth they perceive is the falsity of appearances, the folly of assuming that our "rational hypotheses" reveal life's essence. What they see is the grotesque paradox of being, which is comic as much as it is dismaying. In Saul Bellow's play *The Last Analysis,* the prevalent mood of the absurdist theatre generation is summed up by the line, "Things have gotten all mixed between laughter and insanity."

Another way in which the "rebel" playwrights of the fifties (at first, mostly Parisian) influenced the generation under consideration is in the depiction of *characters.* These are no longer individual persons but states of mind, ideas, types, symbols, masks. "Psychology" is virtually nonexistent. We cannot speak of Beckett's figures, for example, as we do of Ibsen's Hedda, Chekhov's Gaev, or Othello. What all the new dramaturgy tends toward in this respect is a reversion to the very oldest form of drama. (One might say that Oedipus *is* a "psychology," but has none!) The intention in such drama is to project basic patterns or structures of human existence. They are parables or "myths."

To a certain degree, this explains another characteristic of the new theatre. Actors often change roles from one performance to another and sometimes within the same play. They are used to perform set tasks. What they do physically and what they say (if anything) constitute their entire "characterization." Individual nuance or subtleties hardly matter: the figure's function in the general scheme of action is what counts. Thus there is usually very little distinction in the acting of new theatre productions. Energy and a willingness to carry out the assignment with fearless enthusiasm ordinarily suffice.

There are gifted craftsmen among the leaders of the new theatre groups, but thus far only one genius: Jerzy Grotowski (pages 221–226). He is the "ace" of the "school" not simply by virtue of his originality, but through the opportunity given him by his government to conduct a workshop where actors may be trained in his arduous system to form a permanent company guaranteed continuous work.

Grotowski forgoes "scenery" and naturalistically identifiable costumes. There is no sensuous appeal in his art. For close contact with the players, the number of spectators is limited to no more than a hundred. At times the audience is seated above the "stage"; the audience witnesses the drama which takes place, as it were, in a pit below. The restricted public surrounds the action.

The texts used are adaptations of famed works, but their words are more incantations or stabs of passion than normal dialogue. Tempos are so hectic that intelligibility becomes difficult, even for those who understand Polish. Vocal tones create the effect of howls, groans, sobs, and imprecations. We are reminded of the dodecaphonic scale. The actors seem to attack rather than to address one another. They grovel, fall or are thrust backward, are carried about and, in the furious course of the proceedings, are thrown into positions which one might consider acrobatic or balletic if their purpose were not entirely different from gymnastics or dance.

The strangeness of Grotowski's art is not dictated by purely formal choice. His theme is the slaughter of innocence. He was a boy of eight during the Nazi occupation of his country; he learned early enough of the world of concentration camps. What we behold in his work in "abstraction" is the torture of humanity. The tormentors and their victims are bound together in mutual horror; all appear equally cruel. Grotowski's inferno is one in which all are as guilty as they are innocent.

Without moralizing or preachment the spectacle suggests purification through martyrdom. Salvation is wrought from suffering. There is a religious strain imbedded in this concept and, though secular rather than denominational, the traces of a special Catholicism may be divined in it. Grotowski's is indeed a theatre of cruelty peculiar to him and to him alone.

In view of this we can understand why the Grotowski system presses the actor through bodily and vocal training of extreme strenuousness. The feats of virtuosity or what strike us as fantastic contortions are such as have hardly ever before been carried out in the theatre. They are calculated to free the actor of his "false face," all the inhibitions, the masquerades, the social reticences and evasions which prevent the actor from yielding the truth of his innermost being. When the actor is able to do this, so the theory goes, we may ourselves be transfigured.

Several of our new directors have been greatly influenced by Grotowski classes in which they have participated in Poland, in France, and in New York. But such influence, we must hasten to add, is more technical than substantive. The context of Grotowski's art is not transmissible, it allows of no duplication.

On this subject, the imitation of masters, passages from Grotowski's book *Toward a Poor Theatre* should be cited:

> Stanislavsky was compromised by his disciples. . . . When in numerous . . . theatres we watch performances inspired by the "Brecht theory," and are obliged to fight against utter boredom because of a lack of innovation of both actors and producers . . . [we] think back to Brecht's own productions. . . . They showed a deep professional knowledge. . . . The "theatre of cruelty" has been "canonised," i.e., made trivial, snapped for trinkets, tortured in various ways. . . . As for the wretched performances one can see in the theatrical avant-garde of many countries, these chaotic, aborted works, full of so-called cruelty . . . which only reveal a lack of professional skill, a sense of groping, and a love of easy solutions. . . . When we see these sub-products whose authors call Artaud their spiritual father, then we think perhaps there is cruelty indeed but only toward Artaud himself.

The Living Theatre (now defunct) is the best known or most notorious of the avant-garde groups in America. It had its beginnings in New York as an organization devoted to new playwrights. After a stay in Europe, impelled in part by the Grotowski model, it altered its artistic methods and objectives. Its performances impressed and scandalized many. On their return to the U.S.—in New Haven; Waltham, Massachusetts; New York—the Living Theatre stirred considerable controversy. It had fervent admirers and followers.

Certain elements in the Living Theatre's early productions of Jack Gelber's *The Connection* and Kenneth Brown's *The Brig* were extended in its European phase. Despite its post-Pirandello touches, *The Connection* was not essentially new theatre. Its form was naturalistic, though its effect was quasi-poetic. A play about drug addicts, it raised the curtain on the traumatic symptoms in the social complex of the fifties. The people in the play wait for the "connection," a person who will deliver the heroin which is their means of escape from the dismal reality of the day. What we were made to feel was their need to be connected with something other than our "normalcy." It was a quest for some sort of inner freedom.

While the most shocking scenes were those in which we saw these lost creatures in the process of injecting heroin into their systems, the most poignant moment was the one where they listen enraptured to the playing of a jazz band on an old phonograph record. There was something ritualistic in this. *The Connection* foreshadowed a rebellion, still amorphous, which the sixties were to make articulate, ardent, combative.

The Brig was very nearly a "documentary." In the depiction of the brutal treatment meted out to the inmates of a Marine Corps brig, one could discern a symbol of the deliberate smashing of human morale by an official arm of the feared and detested Establishment.

In *Frankenstein,* the most coherent of the Living Theatre's later productions, we see Man eviscerated and dismembered, then reshaped as a gigantic robot. The visualization of both these operations was brilliant. These scenic images embodied what the Living Theatre's various manifestations—sketches, songs, direct appeals to the public, incitations to riotous action—were protesting against.

Julian Beck and Judith Malina, the leaders of the Living Theatre, were self-declared anarchists. Their theatre was a forum from which the police, the army, the banking system, war were denounced. They summoned the audience to storm the bastions of power. As heralds of an anticipated revolt, they engaged in other acts of defiance. The actors lived communally, they dressed more or less strangely, they called on the audience to mount the stage, share their views in conversation or disrobe with them.

Now and then a satiric skit hit the mark, a song might prove touching, an image (the corpses of the war dead heaped on top of one another and dragged away) struck home. All this went with a kind of willful sloppiness: "professionalism" was taboo. While some of the externals of Brecht and Grotowski techniques were assayed, very little was done with true craftsmanship. The thinking was even more shapeless. While the company invoked a world in which man could be free and loving, the atmosphere of its performances was itself often hostile. There was hardly any pleasure, either in their execution or in the audience's reception of them.

Still, the sincerity evident in the fanaticism of the group—it lived as it preached—commanded a certain respect. Their most valid contribution was something beyond theatre. We may set this down to their credit at a time when our theatre is preponderantly banal and complacent. "What is essential in this time of moral poverty," Picasso has said, "is to create enthusiasm."

If the Open Theatre's *America, Hurrah!* in its first two episodes was closer to the expressionism of Elmer Rice's *The Adding Machine*—itself a derivative from such German playwrights as Georg Kaiser—and the final ("Motel") episode on the threshold of new theatre, the same organization's *The Serpent* may confidently be placed in that category. Indeed *The Serpent*, directed by Joseph Chaikin and Robert Sklar, with a "scenario" by Jean-Claude van Itallie, is perhaps the best single piece that the avant-garde theatre has as yet produced in the United States. Its aesthetic source is in Grotowski; its manner gently humorous, lyrically wistful.

The Serpent shows Eve's emergence from Adam's rib, her subsequent temptation by the reptile, and her seduction of Adam. Following this there is a modestly indicated mass copulation, to the accompaniment of the Biblical "begats" intoned by two female voices. At the conclusion of this the participants ("all humanity") emit agonized groans: sex isn't all fun! There is a remarkably effective pantomime of Abel's murder by Cain. The play closes with the company humming, "We were sailing along on moonlight bay," after which the actors sit down quietly among the spectators as if ruminating on the unfathomable mystery of it all.

There are no costumes, the actors are barefoot in simple workclothes. Percussive and flutelike sound is employed. There is the music of plant and animal life in their generative stages, to which the actors add their own little bleats, neighs, moos. At one point the serpent is seen in a swaying tree (formed by the actors' bodies), aglow with glistening red apples: an enchanting image.

One aspect of *The Serpent* merits special remark as representative of a particular tendency of the new theatre. It moves toward ritual. Ritual is born of a shared memory of the past or a widely, that is, "tribally" accepted practice. The choice of the Book of Genesis as a framework for *The Serpent* was a happy one: we all know the "story." But many of our latter-day theatre efforts to achieve ritualistic status are abortive because they are not based on a common ground in which multitudes of our fellow citizens feel themselves rooted. Indulgences in pot and other similar pastimes, no more than Macy's Thanksgiving parade, are adequate foundations even for a "youth culture."

Groups, more eruptive and virulent in their methods than the Open Theatre, make sporadic appearances. Their names—like the Guerrilla Theatre—furnish some inkling of their character. The Gut Theatre, directed by Enrique Vargas, addresses itself chiefly to the people of East Harlem and the ghetto (mostly Puerto Rican) neighborhoods. The aim of these theatres is more directly socio-political than that of the Open Theatre. They are usually short-lived because they are rarely sustained by money grants so that they might develop permanent companies. The street-theatre movement extends to the West Coast. When one is liquidated still another crops up. Sometimes they are forced underground.

There is the Manhattan Project (graduates of the theatre program, New York University). Its production of *Alice in Wonderland* reveals its director André Gregory as an earnest and able theatre artist whose study with Grotowski has helped him foster physical courage and agility in his company with occasionally bold results. Still, I found that the application of Grotowski "ferocity" to the pages of Lewis Carroll's masterpiece, apart from a few amusing passages, failed to culminate in a satisfying aesthetic "statement." But there was in the performance the promise that the company's exuberant energy may at some future date be rendered more meaningful with the use of more appropriate material.

We must now raise a basic question. Are my reservations about André Gregory's *Alice in Wonderland* relevant to his intention?

After all, he was not trying to "interpret" Lewis Carroll. He employed Carroll for new ends. Such transformations, it may reasonably be argued, are motivated by theatrical rather than literary considerations.

The answer, I believe, is that whatever the text used, it must be made part of a coherent whole which makes sense, communicates an idea. The play's text should not simply be an excuse for a formal experience; it must in some way be made organic with the entire theatre event. Text and stage both must be seen to be of the same substance. We must feel that each is the correct and inevitable correlative of the other.

This occurs in the brilliant embodiment of Ariosto's sixteenth-century *Orlando Furioso*. If one knows nothing about the text, this extraordinary spectacle may strike one as nothing but a sportive feat. The audience is required to stand in the middle of an arena (in a church at Spoleto, in an ice rink at Edinburgh, in a "bubble" theatre in New York) at both ends of which are platform stages with a rostrum at the center between the two. Action and speech go on on both stages at the same time and often in the central rostrum as well. Personages on horseback (the horses are metal constructions) come dashing out from various sides of the occupied space forcing the audience to scurry to safety. The acting is vociferously extravagant, deliberately hammy. Under these circumstances, it is hard to make out what is being said even if you know Italian.

The production nevertheless remains faithful to the spirit of Ariosto's epic poem. It is largely a comedy reflecting the Renaissance surge and quasi-mockery of the age of chivalry. The show is a species of "camp." It lends appropriate flesh to the powerful sensationalism in the poet's era as it expresses his fascination with medieval times. In doing this a sense of the colorful and bewildering modern turbulence of the present age in all its chaotic bluster is triumphantly conveyed. Form and content here are one.

The furthest limits to which the new theatre reaches are Happenings. They go so far that they stretch the meaning of "theatre" to the point of extinction. (Ionesco has occasionally spoken of his work as anti-theatre but that is a sort of gag to attract attention. His plays are "legitimate.") The Happening sets up conditions in street, playground, subway, anywhere at all, to which those in attendance may react in any way they please or are spontaneously moved to do. In his book *Public Domain,* Richard Schechner gives this description of part of a two-day Happening devised by Allan Kaprow, one of the leading exponents of such experiments:

> In the work, a girl hangs upside down from a tree. She is one of five persons dangling from ropes at various spots in the rural New Jersey woodland. From distant places in the damp glen, other persons—searchers—begin calling the names of the five who are hanging. When a name is called, the dangling person who is addressed answers, "Here." Homing in on the sounds, the searchers locate each upside-down caller and quickly cut or rip away his or her clothing.

The Happening is a game, an amusing or an irritating *folie,* rather than an artistic event. There are some who claim that the socially defiant eccentricities of Abbie Hoffman's public behavior are "theatre in life" or still another form of a Happening.

The various innovations in theatre practice referred to in the preceding account have stimulated the writing of a body of plays which have been produced not only off-Broadway but in the off-off-Broadway theatres. Many of them were first given in the tiny Café Chino in the West Village (the pioneer in the latter trend was the café's proprietor, Joseph Chino) and then in Ellen Stewart's ever-expanding "La Mama" enterprises.* The list and relative renown of these plays and playwrights have become impressive. The more prominent among these young playwrights are Sam Shepard, Paul Foster, John Guare, Megan Terry, Israel Horovitz, Leonard Melfi, Lanford Wilson, Terence McNally. I do not include LeRoi Jones, though his *Slave Ship* is more stage picture and pantomime than written drama and indirectly a new-theatre by-product. He is a genuinely gifted writer inspired by the upsurge of black race consciousness which is in the process of producing ever more significant plays. But these fall outside the range of our present subject. Nor is Edward Albee to be aligned with the people just mentioned. His work is marked by the imprint of Ionesco, Beckett, and Pinter. A few of the playwrights just listed reveal his effect upon them.

One of the traits La Mama's "children" share is a difficulty or an incapacity to write full-length plays. There is nothing inherently

---

* Ellen Stewart has informed me that some of their plays by their playwrights were *first* done at "La Mama."

inferior in the one-act play as contrasted with the more extended dramatic forms. Still, it is worth speculating on why these young new dramatists appear afflicted with short breath. Their work usually seems to be sprung on momentary insights, clever conceits, whims, gags, and fancies which are rarely susceptible of development. They are flashes in the pan rather than the seeds of pregnant ideas. They illustrate states of being; they do not build situations. (An invalid in bed is in a certain state of being or condition which becomes a dramatic situation only when he attempts to get out of it!)

The initial inspiration of such plays is often provocative, but their authors show little capacity for prolonged thought and the examination of consequences. Their plays, therefore, result in something like a bright slogan rather than a comprehensive argument. I am reminded of the man who thought of a joke and decided to build a musical comedy from it.

Still, utterly to dismiss these writers on the grounds of their immaturity would be wrong. What motivates them is important and the very crux of the entire new-theatre phenomenon. It is a protest against contemporary civilization, the rottenness of our corporate state, the lethal effects of the consumer society. They are the voices of a youth fed up to and beyond the point of maniacal disgust and violent derision at the hypocrisy, the fraudulence, the stupidity, the asphyxiation, the waste and horror of a world they did not create: the world of the Bomb, of atmospheric pollution, of racial injustice, of ghettos, of religion without substance, of patriotism without heart, of politics without human content, of overkill and oversell, of lovelessness.

Thus "Flout 'em and scout 'em—and scout 'em and flout 'em;/ Thought is free" is the tune to which the new dramatists dance. It is the song of Caliban's mates in *The Tempest*. It is barbaric. Barbarians are upsetting, they make a mess, but they have also been known to eradicate the decay of sick societies. Their depredations may clear the ground for creation. Order is sometimes bred from chaos.

Our barbarians are cursed with the sins of their fathers. They are frequently repellent; their yawps are, in the main, echoes of the vile clamor of which they complain. They have inherited many of the diseases which they wish cured. Their theatrical romps and frolics are symptomatic of the ills they denounce. Their thinking is simplistic, often adolescent. Still, our own health depends on our understanding them.

To the routine playgoer, new theatre evokes the shocking image of nude bodies and the blatant sound of four-letter obscenities. What this bespeaks, however, is something more than a commercial strategy. It is true that merchants of the "latest thing" are always eager to cash in on every device to attract the paying crowd. But at a time when all previously honored values have become hollow and nothing formerly sacred is credited as real, the Body is the one remaining, unmistakable truth. There is no shameful secret in nakedness. It is a symbol of freedom. To exult in sex is an act of liberation. To be stripped is to be honest!

"Dirty" words are employed both in defiance and in joyous confrontation with reality. They declare our courageous acceptance of the "low" as well as the "high" in existence. Nudity, obscenity, even pornography, are exultant battle cries against the false face of our society. Youth and its spokesmen in the theatre want "out," out of the wickedness of the rigidly mechanized status quo. They prefer non-sense to common sense.

There is an enormous amount of self-deception and sheer mindlessness in all this. The raucous hurrahs of deliverance are often little more than a rattling of chains. Despite all his enthusiasm for the new-theatre movement, Richard Schechner in his book *Public Domain* admits:

> When the lid comes off and we are given the opportunity to express ourselves, we find that we have very little to say. Or, more precisely, we do not know how to say what we want to say. We toy with nudity, sexuality, political organization, democratized artistic creativity. But we don't get very far. . . . Begin to remove . . . repression and we reveal not the "natural man" but groups of people who mill about in confusion. It is a desperate situation socially and a distressing one aesthetically.

Another threat to what is valid in the new theatre, particularly in its American component, is absorption by commerce and the "squares" who at all costs desire to prove themselves fashionably "with it." John Lahr recognizes this in *Up Against the Fourth Wall* when he writes:

The avant-garde, far from being the anathema which gives danger (and integrity) to its enterprises, has become an important cultural bric-a-brac. Its newest frustration is to become at once popular and curiously powerless. . . . The underground life-style, once intended to be a shocking fist in the face of the Establishment, is now predictable because of publicity.

The impetus which has propelled the new theatre will not abate even were it to provoke a backlash. What is more likely to happen, what indeed has already begun to happen, is the assimilation of some of the insurgent techniques by the popular theatre. What is *Hair* but the fabulous hit of the rock-and-roll theatre ritual?

. The man who has profited most by the upheaval in theatre thought and practice is Peter Brook. A cultured person, galvanized by Grotowski, with a sympathetic understanding of Beckett and Genet together with a lively devotion to Shakespeare, he has been receptive to the most penetrating injections of the avant-garde needle. In Peter Weiss's *Marat/Sade* and *Midsummer Night's Dream,* Brook has turned some of the "poisons" of the new pharmacopoeia into vitalizing medicine. He has enlivened the English stage, and his example will no doubt help others to further explorations.

The new theatre, in short, has in both its positive and negative phases immediate social implications. It is not, as some believe, an offensively bragging frivolity, a "send up" by aesthetic ruffians, but a mirror reflecting a disturbed world turning a dangerous corner. Aesthetically the new theatre has added a rich and vast vocabulary to the lexicon of stage expression at a time when many affirm that the film alone can hold sway.

"To be new is everything in America," said Ellen Terry in 1883. We have not changed. We are hung up on novelty. It is this drive toward the "different" which constitutes our conformity. Chekhov's aesthetic credo voiced in *The Seagull,* "I came more and more to the conviction that it is not a question of new and old forms, but that what matters is that a man should write without thinking of forms at all, write because it springs freely from the soul," is surely in need of qualification. But it is nevertheless a sound point of departure.

It is as true that there is nothing old in the world as that there is nothing altogether new. Every generation has its particular way of experiencing existence because the world is always in the process of change; and every individual of marked personality originates some special variation on the theme of his time—often in contradiction to it. Therefore art, the most universal form of human communicatión, changes. But as long as man remains man, his essential needs remain more or less unaltered: health of body and spirit, the hunger to feel and understand his connection with his fellowmen and beyond this his dependence on all else to which he owes his being. Judgment in artistic matters must perforce turn back to those sources in man's nature. The biologic and the moral are a continuum.

A true evaluation of the new theatre's products resolves itself to the same criteria we apply to all art, new and old. Otherwise we deal in mere fashion which has only a tenuous, accidental, commercial relation to art. The noisy nomenclature of new artistic movements is helpful to those eager to break through conventional ramparts; they do not in themselves establish values. In a letter to Flaubert, Zola, whose "naturalism" was the *dernier cri* of the mid-nineteenth century, showed how aware he was of the advantages of catchwords. "I consider the word *Naturalism* as ridiculous as you do, but I shall go on repeating it over and over again, because you have to give things new names for the public to think that they are new."

If I were challenged to identify the human core of the new-theatre movement I should mention that it is a reflection of our *estrangement* (or "alienation") from contemporary society and in some instances a defiant response to it. In the first case, it is disheartened; in the second, crudely lyric. Because we have become suspicious of so many words which are now employed to confuse and betray us, the "movement" tends to be anti-literary. For youth especially, action speaks louder than words. And theatre, it has been notably asserted, is to begin with and fundamentally performance, *action.*

Whatever we think of these general aesthetic or craft arguments, in the end we must assign worth to individual offerings within every artistic manifestation in relation to the degree of genuineness, power, breadth, and depth we find in them, that is, to the extent they satisfy our basic human appetites and hungers. All the rest is modishness, and the applied rationalizations, no matter how high-sounding or startling, are fraudulent.

47

A Midsummer Night's Dream

[February 8, 1971]

A Midsummer Night's Dream is Peter Brook's masterpiece. His gift
is greatest in stage frolic. Eminently conscientious, he is rarely profound. He is fanciful, colorful, full of merry pranks. He addresses
himself almost entirely to the eye. His production of this sweet comedy about the waywardness of love offers no literary satisfaction: it
is entirely theatrical. There is little romance in it but much wonderfully bright invention.

Watching it I recalled an anecdote I once heard Henry Kahnweiler, the art dealer who first sponsored Picasso, Braque and Juan
Gris, tell. Kahnweiler complimented Gris on his newest cubist painting. "But is it really a *picture?*" Gris worriedly queried. After the
passage of several scenes in this production, I asked myself if what
I was seeing was a brilliant studio exercise or truly a *play*. A reliable
answer could only be provided by someone who had never before
seen or read it. It is possible that such a person might not be able to
follow the play's argument.

I suppose what disturbed me in the opening scenes was that I
heard the lines faintly. The readings were not only dim but rather
flat. I noticed that throughout the evening the speeches I never
missed were the funny ones. Brook seemed not to be concerned with
the play's verbal beauties; dwelling on them might lessen an appreciation of the jest. The loveliness of such a familiar air as, let us say,
"I know a bank where the wild thyme blows . . ." etc., the tender

counterpoint to the play's sport, appears to be deliberately eschewed. It would not be in tune with the production scheme or, for that matter, with the temper of the time. Glamour is gone, fun is in.

Of the composition's jocose side, full advantage has been taken, and that with nimble and coruscating mastery. In this respect Shakespeare's text not only serves as an apt scenario but as a justification for some of the play's pleasantest devices. Brook is like Puck, "the goblin" who leads the characters "up and down, up and down." A "man is but an ass, if he go about to expound this dream."

On both sides of the stage narrow ladders rise to a platform high above the stage floor, a platform with a metal railing. On this upper stage we find a small band of musicians who punctuate the action with appropriate percussive sound. Here too the actors who are not engaged in the immediate scenes in progress look on and enjoy the antics of their fellow players. When we enter the theatre, we behold the play's sole scenic background—brightly lit white wooden walls on which an immense red feather is attached. This feather, later hoisted aloft, becomes Titania's couch as she lies asleep and falls victim to Oberon's stratagem.

The flower with which Oberon befuddles the various lovers is a silvery plate that can be made to rotate on a wand, a toy we occasionally have seen children play with. Coils of gleaming metal wire hanging from poles manipulated from above represent the underbrush of the woodland in which the love games take place. Oberon and Puck make their first appearance on flying trapezes which descend from the flies. Other characters—Hermia in a rage—also hang or swing hecticly on them.

Extravagant, gimmicky? Certainly, but does not Shakespeare say "All this derision shall seem a dream and fruitless vision"? The lovers' awakening is marked by the ringing of an alarm clock openly displayed by one of the "property men" on the upper stage. When an actor needs a "prop" (such as a calendar) it is thrown to him from the overhanging platform. Brook's motto here is Shakespeare's "And those things do best please me that befall preposterously."

On the nether level a guitarist supplies the sentimental strains which the actors avoid. The costumes are near-contemporary workclothes for the auxiliary players and for the rustics: Bottom and company. The highborn Athenians and the fairyland nobility wear costumes of satin, tulle or voile—their whiteness dappled with green or pink spots—making them look like pantomime Pierrots or circus clowns. Some of the scenic jokes would appear to appeal most directly to affluent "hippies" in their taste for high camp. But in general, there is a healthy exuberance.

This then is a director's rather than an actors' triumphal occasion, except to the extent that the actors are his enthusiastic coadjutors. A youngish, physically well-trained company is bold and agile in movement, sometimes performing acrobatic tricks to superb comic effect. There are dull spots only when laughs are not in order.

Standing out above the company's general competence and good will are David Waller as an authentically humorous and robust Bottom, and the lanky Frances De La Tour as the "painted maypole," Helena, whose every word is funny as well as distinct. Patrick Stewart is a charmingly simple-minded Snout, and little Hermia is well played by pretty Mary Rutherford in her tantrums, though not wholly audible at other times.

Many questions occurred to me as I followed the show, and after I had left I wanted to see it all over again—which I shall probably do in the coming weeks of its limited engagement. That is a tribute to Peter Brook whose *Marat/Sade* and *King Lear* also aroused the desire for renewed acquaintance. Thinking back on these earlier—always interesting—productions, my feeling is that while *King Lear* was most gravely committed to an interpretation of its text (though not altogether satisfactory to me as such) and *Marat/Sade* so devoted to directorial virtuosity that its substance became subservient to it, *A Midsummer Night's Dream* is archetypal of Brook's talent at its most gratifying.

But to return to the questions. It is a good thing that so much emphasis nowadays is put on the quality and originality of theatrical staging; yet one wonders if this is not due, in part, to the paucity of significant new scripts. This production will undoubtedly inspire ambitious theatre folk, but will it not also turn them to much frivolous imitation, more manner than matter? And why does the new stagecraft one hears so much about apply itself mainly to old texts and not evolve new ones? We are constantly required to determine how the classics have been "treated" rather than to judge an organically created work. The marriage of writing and stage work into a true unity has chiefly occurred in recent years only in such productions as Brecht's *Mother Courage* (pages 130–133). But consummations of this sort are likely to occur only when truly total theatres are established; where writers, directors, actors, designers are partners who speak together on subjects about which they harbor strong mutual feeling.

These afterthoughts are not for the moment at issue. The simple fact is that Brook's latest production is a signal piece of theatre work in the English-speaking theatre of our day. It will be hugely enjoyed by many, it may puzzle some, it will be condemned by very few—I think wrongly. But there is no doubt that it should be seen by everyone eager for fresh theatre experiences.

48

Hedda Gabler

[March 8, 1971]

THE PRODUCTION of Ibsen's *Hedda Gabler*, directed by Patrick Garland, with Claire Bloom in the title role (Playhouse Theatre), is a most careful one. All its points are in italics. And they are all thoroughly false.

Hedda Gabler may be said to be a Nora who didn't slam the door on the doll's house. Hedda hadn't the courage. She is a romantic, dreaming of Dionysiac vine leaves in her imagined hero's hair, eager for adventures of the mind and, if she dared, exploits of the body.

Gabler *père* was a general; the military aristocracy was a declining class. There were lively parties in her father's house, peopled by rakes of the "upper crust," none of whom offered to marry her. Eilert Lovborg was one of the guests, a gifted, attractive, passionate man, but being a bohemian, given to riot. Hedda was tempted to an affair with him, but she was too proud and rigorously correct, as such ladies had to be amid the concealed licentiousness of her time and environment. So she drifted into marriage with an adoring but mediocre middle-class "academic." Having been raised with a taste for high life, she found the humdrum routine of being a professor's wife unbearable.

Hedda suffers because there beats in her the blood and yearning for a freedom she dare not grasp. The creative urges of her spirit are repressed. That which should have led to positive action becomes destructive. Hedda's despair is aggravated by the sight of her former schoolmate Thea Rysling who, less intelligent and worldly than herself, does leave her crude husband and make something worth while of herself.

There is little significance in the play if Hedda is viewed as a neurotic without cause, or even as a victim of sexual repression, a *femme fatale,* a demon, a mental case (I have seen the part played in all these fashions). In *Hedda Gabler* Ibsen dramatized the crippling consequences, dangerous to the self and to others, of the modern woman whose energies are curbed by men who use her as an ornament, an object of personal gratification or a domestic convenience. Such women either become bored to death or turn malefic, or like Hedda, do both. Ibsen's play and Hedda's character are sharply diminished in interest if Hedda is not seen as a person of stature in imagination, desire, wit and breeding, as well as in beauty. The suppression of Hedda's nature has not sapped her passion: it has poisoned it.

Patrick Garland's direction turns Hedda into an icy bitch. Her glacial indifference makes her rude and vulgar. Ibsen makes it clear that Hedda's slight of her husband's aunt seizes her in a momentary spasm of spite. Claire Bloom's (or Garland's) Hedda is insulting to the old lady from the outset. When Hedda commits the crime of burning Lovborg's manuscript (his "child" by Thea), Garland has Hedda do it with catatonic coldness; it is in fact an impetuous burst of violence, the insane release of her smothered impulses. The one thing which would make Hedda utterly dull and insignificant as a dramatic figure is frigidity. And that, with an occasional bellow of hysterical laughter or anger, is what this new Hedda provides—a "dead" Hedda.

To make their states of being evident the actors pose as in photographic tableaux. They speak at the rapid pace considered to be what our nervous, impatient audiences demand—so that much vital information about Hedda's background is more or less lost, and the ensuing action turns into somewhat obvious melodrama. We are not confronted with characters who speak to one another, but with well-rehearsed players who hear nothing but their cues. Garland's *Hedda Gabler* is "theatrical," but lifeless. Even the stove in which Hedda burns Lovborg's book is without fire. The production is at best a bloodless demonstration, not an embodiment of Ibsen's play.

49

All Over

[April 12, 1971]

BECAUSE EDWARD ALBEE's latest play, *All Over*, is one which many
people may have trouble appreciating, I feel constrained to begin by
saying that it is the best American play of several seasons—a manner
of speaking of which I disapprove! The play comes to us, moreover,
in a remarkably fine production, one that is so much a part of the
total impression of the event that one is not sure in discussing it
whether one is referring to the text or to its stage embodiment. John
Gielgud as director has given Albee his most thoroughly realized
interpretation.

To quote one of the characters in *All Over*, Albee is shocked by
the "sad and shabby times we live in." Though wholly immersed in
the present, he appears to be withdrawn from it, to set himself apart.
He "alienates" himself. *All Over* seems written from a tomb, a world
on the other side of existence. Its people, though recognizably contemporary, produce the effect of wraiths recalled from a bygone life.
The play conveys an existential shudder which has its origins in the
soul's dark solitude.

The theme is man's relation to death. Americans tend to shy away
from the very thought. When death is dealt with on our stage it is
nearly always in a sentimental, pseudo-religious or sensational vein,
any of which betrays evasion. This indicates a spiritual error. Death
is a definition of life, and life is made precious by an acknowledg-
ment of its containment within the bounds of death. Maturity is

267

possible only when death is fearlessly confronted and freely accepted. Without such acceptance, life itself ceases to have dignity.

All Over is a view of American life (or certain salient aspects of it) in the perspective of death. A wealthy lawyer—many honors have been bestowed upon him—has been brought home to die. "Brought home" not only because he is said to prefer dying there than in a hospital but because for many years he has been living with a mistress and away from his home. The play takes place around the unseen deathbed. Gathered there are the man's wife, his mistress, his son and daughter, a lawyer who is his best friend and partner.

Little love is lost among them. The wife is contemptuous of her children. The son is a weak incompetent, rapidly going to seed; the daughter a venomous woman who is having an affair with a racketeer. She scorns her mother, who despises the daughter for her crude impatience and failure to understand the older generation's way of life. The daughter hates the mistress because, so she rationalizes, the mistress has robbed her of her father. The mistress, a sturdy counterpart of the more delicately fibered wife, is strong, realistic, unsentimentally humane. There is a bond of understanding and sympathy between the wife and mistress because they have shared a love for the same man. The best friend is an average intelligent citizen who tries to mediate in the family's contentions.

The play offers little of what is usually called "action." Instead, there is a constant revelation of character and idea through the interplay of motivations and the clash of temperaments. At first one tends to see the play's personages as heartless and loveless, hence unworthy of interest. There is a steady exchange of insults, with the daughter pitted against both mother and mistress. There is also some acid scoffing about the son: the rich boy spoiled by paternal indifference and a cushy job in his father's firm for which he has no particular aptitude. Only the old doctor and the attending nurse, both of whom have long lived with death, are entirely without rancor or despair. The characters reminisce (there is a passage about a garden that should be abbreviated); they joke, indulge in trivialities and engage in an exchange of barbed sentiments as if they had forgotten that they are in the presence of death.

Listening attentively, as one must to understand this largely verbal play, one comes to recognize that it contains not only feeling but pathos all the more poignant for its severe repression. Albee is saying that, despite all the hasty bickering, the fierce hostility and the mutual misunderstandings which separate us, we need one another. We cry out in agony when we are cut off.

On close examination, the bitterest dramatists today prove to be the most moral. Albee condemns the vulgarity of an age that refuses to perceive the sanctity of the human condition and the responsibility for mutual respect. Instead of struggling for balance amid the conflicting drives within us, we retreat to hypocritical subterfuges. Albee decries the younger generation not for its well advertised "sins" but because it refuses to comprehend the validity of tradition which the past has so valiantly fashioned to convert chaos to order. He also accuses the older generation of having depleted tradition of its content by neglecting to persevere in the arduous task of maintaining it. Tradition has been reduced to the mouthing of its nomenclature: loyalty, honor, home, country, etc.

So much may be agreed upon in the abstract. But what about the play itself? It is not important in this instance that, as some insist, the dying man be seen. His person is not the issue. All we need to know of him is the part he played in the history of the living: the two women who loved him, the children, his friends. The play is their drama, not his. Nor does Albee mean to "move" us in the sense of eliciting tears. (Art is not for crying.) He wants to show how these apparently cold and selfish people, the damage of their souls expressing itself in malice, sum up their experience in a confession of searing unhappiness and sense of loss when their connection with a fellow human being is severed.

It is a stylized play; its characters do not speak "naturally." The language is that of an artist who sees things through the peculiar spectrum of his brooding spirit. His is a frozen fire. No one else in our theatre writes in this particular way. That makes Albee truly original.

I must cavil, in passing, on a matter too often overlooked in the consideration of theatrical events. The choice may be no one's fault, but the Martin Beck Theatre is too large for so intimate a play. Unless one is sitting up front, one is likely to miss important points in the closely woven fabric of the dialogue.

John Gielgud has staged *All Over* as a "ritual." This treatment is not arbitrary; it is suggested by Albee's style and meaning. The setting, which might have been realistic (a paneled bed-sitting room, tapestried walls, family portraits, etc.), is admirably rendered by a sepulchrally diagramed space, bare of everything but indispensable furniture, in which the figures stand out in emblematic isolation.

The pace is deliberate rather than "slow," with every phrase carefully shaped in congruence with Albee's writing, a vernacular artificial as verse is artificial. It is the prose of a man who desires to restrain the too overt expression of the extremity of his passion and pain and yet purposes to be stringently honest. A strange wit flickers over the dark background.

The acting company is well chosen. There are no bad performances. Colleen Dewhurst as the wise and earthy mistress is seen here to better advantage than perhaps ever before. Betty Field as the nurse manifests a delicate and charming astringency of humor. As the wife, Jessica Tandy possesses the right air of intelligence and breeding, together with inner firmness. Madeleine Sherwood is somewhat more adept at conveying the daughter's resentments than her hurt. (Her voice carries best in the large house.) Neil Fitzgerald as the doctor, James Ray as the son, George Voskovec as the best friend bring to their assignments something more than skill.

Gielgud has not attempted to make his players "profound"; he has sought to present them in sharp outline. The play's transcendent message is thus projected in a memorable pattern or picture.

[May 3, 1971]

A reader, Frieda Arken, has written me a nice letter suggesting that Albee's *All Over,* which she "unhesitatingly labeled a meritricious bore," might be something to read but is not suitable to the stage. Her letter gives me an opportunity to comment further on the play to which the reactions, with a few exceptions, have ranged from boredom to sadistic hostility.

I find *All Over* every bit as *theatrical* as Pinter's *Landscape* and *Silence,* Marguerite Duras' *A Place Without Doors* (now being admirably played in French at the Barbizon-Plaza Theatre under its original title *L'Amante Anglaise*) or Beckett's *Play*—all of them pieces I have reviewed favorably. Indeed, what isn't "playable" nowadays!

Still that is not my point. The truth is that what I prefer is a "swinging" theatre, by which I mean—Shakespeare! I love movement, color, physical excitement, bravura as much as "thoughtfulness." Since Ibsen, drama has become ever more introverted: this tendency has now reached the static. The atmospheric or social oppression of our day has brought about an explosive reaction to this: a theatre that is chiefly movement, sound, hectic imagery, in which ideas, when they exist at all, may be inferred. We are bound to accept these opposing trends in the theatre—they both mirror realities—providing we find them in one way or another meaningful.

What I seek in art are personal statements or manifestations of human experience. I wish to be convinced that the artist has really felt something about the world in which he lives and has found his own way of expressing it. I have often written that what Beckett says is alien to my nature but that I respect him greatly because his is a real experience (akin to one we all share at times) and that he has found his own special mode of expression. Most of what is seen in the theatre—even when agreeable—has a "ready-made" quality of secondhand content and form.

My temperament is totally different from Albee's. I find that, having become increasingly dour, disheartened and withdrawn, he nevertheless expresses a genuine response to the aridity of much that we now sense about us. There is a terrible tension in his work, as if he were about to howl his distress but somehow does not dare to do so. It "screws" him up—his language gives evidence of this— but there is an emotional significance in his writing that I find moving.

The result, theatrically speaking, is a degree of abstraction which emaciates his characters and makes "patterns" of them. Still there is more body in *All Over* than in *Box-Mao-Box* which was a graph of Albee's discouragement. For this reason, while I approve of John Gielgud's attempt to visualize the structural element in *All Over* through a thoroughly nonrealistic setting as though a place in which corpses were to be dissected and through acting which may be too formally verbal, I conceive another sort of production. It would still be stylized, but a precise environment would be suggested and the play's characters, somewhat less obviously isolated from one another than they are now, might take on more body.

Most damaging to the play in its present "format"—I wager it will be seen elsewhere in the country and more especially in many cities throughout Europe—is the size of the Martin Beck Theatre. *All Over* demands intimacy of presentation, a small house.

Finally in reply to my correspondent I feel obliged to repeat a tenet basic to my and, I hope, to all criticism: what counts in criticism is not agreement in opinion—in terms of "yes" or "no." What is important is how and why a critic arrives at his opinion, whatever it may be.

50

Reflections on Movies

[May, 1971]

IT IS WIDELY HELD that movies nowadays are much more interesting than the theatre. Arithmetically speaking, it is a fact. It should be immediately admitted that a moderately entertaining film is much more attractive than an indifferent play.

The reason for this is simple enough: there are the *pictures*. Most films today are admirably photographed. The pictures' locales are diverse, often exotically fascinating, bold in the maneuvers of their execution. The faces and bodies we see are, with the cameraman's aid, more sensuously gratifying than those beheld at present on the stage. Physical beauty, which should be one of the theatre's lures, is now sadly lacking.

While the theatre for centuries has been taken as an adjunct of literature, its very name derives from the Greek "theatron," which connotes seeing. In our country at least, the theatre has become visually impoverished as well as verbally depleted.

Drama signifies action. In this respect also, the theatre has become poor. It is generally deficient in movement. By their very nature, films, even if we think of them only in regard to editing, are all movement. In pictures we are present at the accidents of daily living, the disasters of war, the upheaval and wreckage of nature. Movies act directly on our senses. Because of all this they "grab" us more readily than any other art.

Have I, who began my playgoing career at the age of seven and spent over forty-five years of my professional life in the theatre, then turned movie buff? Have I lost my appetite for stage spectacles? The debate over or contrast between the two media is specious . . . I have been going to the movies since the days of Bronco Billy Westerns. I did not give them much thought then, I just went. It never occurred to me, later on, to engage in any argument over the comparative merits of theatre and cinema. Such discussion is usually more a matter of pragmatic or commercial than of aesthetic concern. No art replaces another. My addiction to the theatre and my growing interest in the movies have never interfered with my reading of poetry and novels, my love of the dance, my attentiveness to painting and sculpture, my enjoyment of old and new music.

Films are a new and exciting mode of expression. They do not, I repeat, render any other medium, however ancient or neglected, obsolete. What we are called upon to enjoy and evaluate in all the arts is the weight and quality of what they express.

The film, I have always believed, is an essentially silent medium. I found myself disturbed at first by the third dimension of speech which intruded on the two dimensionality of the screen image. I held John Ford's *The Informer* in special esteem because he used so little dialogue. (I can remember only two or three lines of the spoken text.) But we have talkies and screenwriters now, and they have added a great deal to the scope of the cinematic form.

Another addition to film vocabulary is color. Its employment has become virtually mandatory not only because of the public's taste for it, but because of the TV companies' insistence upon it. Still, I cannot help but feel that in this way many pictures lose something of their truth. This is a paradox because we do perceive objects in a variety of shades. There are certain films the effects of which are thus enhanced. But the tints employed in most films are more pigment than true color. Faces are too often drenched in an intensity of hue which makes them look glazed in a bath of cosmetics, as if they were on sale.

Many scenes photographed on big-city locations (including the slums) become glamorized to the detriment of the film's artistic intention. Paris in René Clair's *Sous les Toits de Paris* or Agnès Varda's *Cleo from 5 to 7* appears more truly itself than do the usual film images of that town which look like ads for travel agencies.* One could hardly believe in the wretched garishness of the dance hall in *They Shoot Horses, Don't They?* because of the chromatic lushness of the photography.

It is possible that, in time, greater delicacy in this regard may be achieved. In any case, except for travelogue enchantment, we have more or less ceased to notice color in films: it is just there. The subliminal effect of its use is to make the world appear opulent, which is perhaps a solace for a fatigued population.

I am now chiefly concerned with the intrinsic content to be found in the films seen in the past two or three years. As I choose only those recommended by people I respect, I can honestly state that I have had a pleasant time at most of them. If I enjoy fifteen or twenty minutes of any film, because of a sequence made exhilarating through an actor's personality, interest in the subject matter or directorial ingenuity, I do not feel myself cheated.

Though it is entirely proper to speak of the art of films, I find very little art in films except when artists make them—and they are exceedingly rare. I view most films—especially the American—as *documentaries*. They tell us more of the time and place in which we dwell than any of the other media. As fiction, drama or art, they lie. They are primarily designed as diversions, games, toys; yet they are willy-nilly full of instruction. The response they elicit from their vast audiences is as much part of their message as their material—often more telling than volumes of statistics. Thus, no matter how frivolous they may be, I take them seriously.

Cultured folk, when I began seeing movies, held them in contempt. This was so for many years. Not only were movies primitive in technique, they were also paltry in content. They were kid stuff and as such may have done more harm than good. Even when they became more sophisticated, educated people rarely regarded them worth adult consideration. The big studios made them conform strictly to the myth of America as the land of the pure, the brave, the just, and above all, the happy. There was no ill that our benevolence could not remedy. Love conquered.

---

* *Sous les Toits de Paris* was photographed in a studio, *Cleo from 5 to 7* in the streets.

All this has changed in the past fifteen years. The increasing interest in foreign pictures plus the breakdown of the old Hollywood system—the dissolution of the monopoly by which producers controlled the industry through ownership of the movie houses—and the ensuing financial panic, forced the remaining film entrepreneurs to meet the challenge from Europe and that of the ever increasing number of independent filmmakers and theatre proprietors. At last freedom was attained. No holds are now barred. Everything may be shown or said. Should the new films be deemed too licentious, the release may be marked R (restricted) as a warning to parents and a caution to the squeamish.

This newfound freedom has, in my view, opened the way to a new sort of falsity, a fresh factitiousness, a special type of opportunism more dangerous, though more masked, than the old. There is no less distortion and sentimentality in today's daring films than there was when the heinous movie moguls reigned. While the sweet and soupy product of former days was debasing through its avoidance of real issues and facts, the recent spate of knock 'em dead or gut movies blows our brains and hearts through benumbing sensationalism. To expose vice and corruption as a spectacle for fun, no matter how well decked out in psychoanalytic hearsay and radical palaver, is just as corrosive of sensibility and intelligence as the indulgence in vacuous daydreams of well-being.

Stag films have become superfluous. Ever since *Hiroshima, Mon Amour,* scenes of nude bodies in tight embrace followed by explicit images of sexual activity have become almost obligatory as emblems of filmic emancipation. But this is a minor matter. The erotic has always occupied an important place in the world's treasury of the arts. There are masterpieces of pornography. I am always gratified by the sight of a beautiful nude body—though such sights are vouchsafed us under much more favorable conditions elsewhere. The issue now is what role such images play in the context of the complete picture.

I do not refer to films primarily intended to arouse desire or to shock or to serve as a come-on to the prurient, although such purposes are by no means overlooked by the film's purveyors. I speak of so-called socially significant films, often praised by film critics in good standing.

Take, for example, *Getting Straight.* It is a picture about the formal education of youth, in other words, about college life. Youth is represented in this movie by a great lummox (supposedly very bright) in the shape of a popular favorite, Elliott Gould, who is probably about thirty. He has great appeal because he is like "everybody": coarse in manner, somewhat thick-tongued in speech, generally crude and blunt. The fellow he plays—like presumably so many of the young—believes our educational institutions to be little more than factories for the production of degrees. (Some of them are just that.) He is, we are to assume, an advanced student, eager for knowledge. His problem is that the college doesn't provide it. What do we get to know of him?

Apparently he spends every night "sexualizing" with his girlfriend, a typical coed in the person of Candice Bergen. When he behaves boorishly, she forbids him her bed. This is too great a deprivation for him to bear. He immediately compensates for it by sleeping with a beauteous black girl who asks if he finds this novel experience especially pleasurable.

There are funny scenes—mostly caricatures—showing how dumb the academic doctors are, and there are others in which police brutality on an "epic" scale is photographed: half-measures never suffice in such pictures. Thus the film is not only topical but "revolutionary."

The principal characters in many of these films are shown to be "alienated" when they are not just morons. *Easy Rider,* made at a relatively low cost and so successful that it inspired a "trend" in the big studios, introduces us to several nonconformist youths: which of us is not sympathetic to their like? How do they use their liberty? To profit from their freedom they undertake to transport drugs from Mexico to California.

The best thing in the picture, apart from Jack Nicholson's performance as a drunken dude, is the sight of the landscape. Nicholson is beaten to death because he taunts some red-necks who resent the free life of the long-haired youths. Later the two boys are wantonly shot down by passing red-necks for no reason except that they are hippies. There is a moral to all this: one of the boys, before his death, murmurs "We blew it." In other words, he now realizes that he and his buddy muffed their chance at a good life. Nevertheless they are presented to us as folk heroes of a sort.

The filmmakers are always on the side of the angels. In the supposedly satiric *Bob & Carol & Ted & Alice,* four nitwits experiment in wife-swapping. But they can't make it after all. They are basically "beautiful people." Aside from a few hilarious bits (one of them in a psychoanalyst's office), the picture is a setup for jokes about permissiveness in promiscuity in which little else (children, work) comes into play. One might conclude, then, that this is a picture about sex, but it is really nothing of the sort. Sex is something more than a physical function. Emotions are taken as a matter of course, real sentiment is never suggested, except that the couples do not consummate their cross-copulation. Given the circumstances and the nature of these citizens, this is rather stupid of them.

One of the most engaging among recent films with some truly amusing scenes and several excellent performances is *Five Easy Pieces.* Its central figure is a man who might have been a musician (he was reared in a musical family) and, when we meet him, is a totally disoriented person. He is without any specific direction or impulse, except to drink, fornicate and run away. He is loyal to pals and is capable of momentary affection but has no regard for women, though he makes passes at all within his reach. At best, he is sorry about his state. He is to be accepted as the maimed hero of our subculture. To see him in this light is surely to indulge in wishy-washiness, a widespread trait in a society in which an understanding of human frailty means to exonerate ourselves from all moral judgment.

There is considerable validity in the theme posited in *Joe.* Racists and reactionaries, the film implies, well-heeled businessmen as well as uncouth hardhats, lacking the sustenance of sound values, are, when balked, impelled toward murderousness. But the plot has it that a "respectable" commercial executive who earns $60,000 a year will go back to the squalid quarters of a vicious drug addict to pick up his daughter's things—she being the fellow's girlfriend—things which consist of a few odd and soiled rags. Here, in his fury at being scoffed at by the derelict youth, he knocks the boy's brains out. Skeptical of the picture's initial steps, we are led from one lurid improbability to another in support of a thesis based on a loosely held ideology which demands proof. Everything finally is made subservient to the fabrication of a bloodcurdling movie replete with thievery, sexual "orgy," drunkenness, playing with pot.

Minute clues reveal the meretriciousness of the whole. Bonnie and Clyde in the picture of that name are played by two spectacularly good-looking actors who needn't have gone hungry even in the darkest days of the Depression. Hollywood was prosperous then; they could have gotten jobs in the movies. More folk heroes? A jolly ballad? Seeing this film and several others less craftily made reminded me of the old cowboy song: "There was blood on the saddle, blood on the ground . . . blood all around." Blood? No, ketchup and Technicolor, as unbelievably fake as the vitals which, along with all manner of high jinks, are supposed to provide a sharply satiric comment in *M*A*S*H*, a movie practically everyone acclaims because we are all against war and especially ashamed of the Korean and Vietnam adventures, aren't we?

Everything in these films is spelled out. There is, for example, Clyde's impotence and his recovery from it through his loyal and gorgeous mate Bonnie–Dunaway. What a thrill in the mowing down of the two hapless marauders: the girl's body riddled with bullets bounces voluptuously from their impact. When that presumptuous idiot and distinguished novelist in *Diary of a Mad Housewife* disrobes Carrie Snodgress, we observe each separate article of her clothing slowly drop from her body. Then, as a clincher, we are favored in an isolated shot with an ample view of the actress's glowing bottom. If it hadn't actually been shown, we might not have known that she had one. There is more decency in the filth of *Trash.*

Is it really possible to give credence to the extremely pretty and healthy Jane Fonda as the haggard, half-starved, hopelessly beat victim of the dance marathon in *They Shoot Horses, Don't They?* followed by her inviting death at the hands of her sweet partner? For all the degradation through which her miserable life has dragged her, she cannot bear the thought that even such as he may have "deceived" her. Because of this, her contempt for life and love expresses itself by the exercise of fellatio on the master of the sordid ceremonies whose normal approach she refuses in horror with the fierce command, "Don't touch me!"

Our behavioristic flicks tend to assault: they conspire to kick the stuffings out of us. They are unabashed in the use of four-letter words—the more the merrier—though this will soon prove ineffective as an instrument of titillation. The earth shakes, the heavens howl, the beasts yowl and clamor, walls crack and crumble, the world's chaos is magnified tenfold. Calm is unknown, contemplation impossible. For the quiet and calm we find in the films of Bresson, Ozu, Bergman, Satyajit Ray, Olmi, the early Antonioni, Renoir, or the Fellini of *I Vitelloni*—the repose essential to perception—our big audiences have little patience. Truffaut's unemphatically tender *The Wild Child* is a flop. Attention to the little pleasures and the unexplosive dramas of daily life is ignored. The tumult of our civilization has become our films' drug on the market.

Sentimentality may be defined as the disproportion between the reality of feeling and the means employed to convey it. To present reality as a charnel house and a bordello for the sake of arousing superficial shock is as sentimental and as poisonously misleading as to jerk at our tear ducts on behalf of motherhood or the Stars and Stripes. Ugliness, like beauty, is in the eyes of the beholder. The ferocious realism of our tough new pictures is as bogus as the sweetness and light of the old.

No matter how savage their imagery or high-minded their ostensible purpose, most of the new filmmakers treat us as though we were morbidly spoiled children who will heed nothing unless whipped. Their protagonists are themselves nearly always infantile or persons of low-grade mentality. With a slight insinuation from sub-Freudian social psychologists we are, for instance, called upon to understand and therefore to care for and forgive the sadistic hustler of *Midnight Cowboy*. It may be argued against Eric Rohmer's *My Night at Maud's,* or his latest picture, *Claire's Knee,* that they are too verbose and thus insufficiently cinematic. But they are remarkable in one thing at least: they deal with grown-ups whose preoccupations reach beyond the realm of thugs or fatuous slobs.

The rediscovery of sex in recent films—sex without affection, love or even joyous sensuality—is something more than mere exploitation; it is a sign that we are in doubt about everything else. These films possess one positive asset: they compel a realization that our values are not simply all in question, but that they have never previously been confirmed in us by profound experience or probing inner examination. We have ceased asking ourselves fundamental questions when we satisfy ourselves by predigested answers. These are supplied by "those who know," usually members of various

Establishments—right and left—whom at the same time we profess to scorn. Those who shout the loudest are the only ones heard. We will not take pains with anything which demands protracted study, concentrated effort, time.

The great mechanism of our society, in which we jiggle and are flung about, wearies us. We do not in consequence demand privacy and peace of mind or socially useful action, but even more of the brutal battering of body and spirit which is driving us senseless.

There is something to ponder on in *Gimme Shelter*, no matter how contrived it may be thought to be. The killers and the victim, lawyers, arrangers, impresarios, agents, publicity men, and crazed acolytes of the Rolling Stones *are* our neighbors and kindred. Little wonder, then, that we accept the roughhouse improvisations of *Husbands* as a huge joke or as a faithful picture of marriage and homelife in America today. Still, a little sober reflection should make us aware that even the stupid and stupefied, the crass and the cruel, the fools and the criminals, are something more than what such films represent them to be.

We shall never be any wiser if we seriously believe that all the new pictures to which we are now asked to pay tribute are truly examples of films coming of age in a new realism. They are the product of gifted, well-intentioned craftsmen in the service of the same old profit-oriented movie industry they and we imagined had been destroyed and abandoned. In the toils of this Moloch, it is all but impossible to preserve genuine thoughtfulness, insight, stout-hearted integrity. With the general acceptance of the platitudinous notion that the modern world is nothing but a stinking stew, an acceptance which has become a complaisance (often disguised as a denunciatory judgment), most filmmakers with the backing of the corporate powers have been sucked into the surrounding bedlam. Their pictures are not antidotes to our diseases; they are both the symptoms and among the most potent of their conveyers. Hence for me they are eloquent documents and documentaries of our time; they require scrupulous study. One should see them and see them again!

51

···>······◄▶●◄▶◄···◄···

Long Day's Journey into Night

[May 10, 1971]

IN THE LAST ACT father-and-son scene of O'Neill's *Long Day's Journey into Night* James Tyrone says, "The praise Edwin Booth gave my Othello! I made the manager put down his exact words in writing. I kept it in my wallet for years. . . . Where is it now, I wonder? Somewhere in this house. I remember I put it away carefully—." To which his son Edmund replies, "It might be in the old trunk, along with Mama's wedding dress."

In the play's final moments the mother, benumbed by morphine, enters dragging a wedding gown on the floor. She doesn't recognize it as hers. James, her husband, takes it from her, pointing out that she might get it dirty, and she murmurs, "I remember now. I found it in the attic hidden in a trunk. But I don't know what I wanted it for. I'm going to be a nun—that is, if I can only find . . ." She breaks off and then resumes, "What is it I'm looking for? I know it's something I lost."

The four Tyrones are bedeviled by a terrible unnamed loss. The loss inspires guilt in them; they thrash about in a vain effort to identify it, though they hardly realize the nature of their quest. They blame one another for the absence of what is essential to them, and immediately thereafter apologize, knowing that the accusations are misdirected. Each is isolated in his or her sorrowful guilt. Only one of them, Edmund, may emerge from the morass—as Eugene O'Neill did later, through his plays.

The long day's journey is a bitter self-examination into the darkness of the self. The journey for the dramatist constituted a process of self-discovery. But the play's characters, bound together by their dilemma, which makes for a kind of tortured love, are rarely able to touch one another. Each suspects the others of being the cause of his sufferings. An audience sufficiently attentive, and aided by a wholly sound production, should comprehend the source of the Tyrones' tragedy.

They have lost their faith. Loss of faith is the main theme almost throughout O'Neill's work. For him it was more than a personal tragedy, it was *the* American tragedy. As individuals and as a nation, we have lost that spiritual coherence which makes men and societies whole. O'Neill declared that his *magnum opus*—the nine plays, of which he completed only *A Touch of the Poet*—was the dramatization of the question, "What shall it profit a man if he gain the whole world and lose his own soul?"

What innocent and trusting Mary Tyrone has lost is her religious faith, a faith in God which sustained her in the genteel home and the convent in which she was raised. She fell in love with James Tyrone, a star actor of romantically heroic roles, "and was so happy for a time." But the actor in the crude theatre of that day (middle and late nineteenth century), with its long national tours in generally shoddy shows, stopping in every sort of hotel in numerous one-night stands, led a life that offered no haven for so delicate a being as Mary Tyrone. Her husband believed in the theatre, especially in Shakespeare; "I studied Shakespeare," he says, "as you'd study the Bible." Shakespeare was central to his religion, on whose account he rid himself of the brogue of his Irish birth.

But then he found a play which had an enormous success. His many years of immigrant struggle against poverty had made him acutely aware of "the value of a dollar." This turned him to a miserliness to which his sons ascribe all the family's misfortunes. His anxiety to avoid the specter of the poorhouse caused him to abandon his deepest desire to be a great Shakespearean actor and give himself to the exploitation of the box-office hit which he played for more than twenty years to the exclusion of everything else. He betrayed his religion. "What the hell was it I wanted to buy that was worth—" He falters as he asks the question.

The vagrant life of the road led to Mary's intense loneliness (James's boon companions, his fellow actors, were no fit company for such as she) and so unwittingly she became addicted to drugs. On this account, her older son, James, Jr., lost faith in his mother, becoming a cynical drunk and patron of brothels, a blasphemer against his mother's religion and his father's profession, always a little jealous of his younger brother whom he also loves. Edmund is a seeker after truth. He declares himself not so much a poet as a faithful realist. Still, he feels that he will forever be less than whole if he is unable to recapture that sense of belonging to something "greater than my own life, or the life of Man . . . to God, if you want to put it that way. . . ." He experienced such a state at moments in his year at sea. It is this ecstatic relation to existence which Edmund says he lost—"and you are alone, lost in a fog again, and stumble on toward nowhere. . . ."

If the desolateness of this condition in the Tyrone household and the agonized quest for a light beyond the dark are not present in the production, it becomes only the chronicle of an unhappy family—though, even as such, very moving. The triumph is that here a solidly constructed realistic drama is rendered integral with social meaning as well as the soulful poetry of despair and forgiveness. That is what makes *Long Day's Journey into Night* O'Neill's masterpiece.

The sympathetic production under Arvin Brown's direction should be seen. Its actors are intelligent and personally winning. What is missing is a grand design wrought of deep inner characterizations and understanding of the play's basic mood—its tragic essence. As it stands now, the production is only a good domestic drama, though it is impossible to overlook the elements of grandeur in the wonderful scenes preceding the play's end.

Robert Ryan looks right as Tyrone. He has a mildness of temperament that is appealing without actually being impressive. (But where on the American stage today is the heroic tragic actor?) Geraldine Fitzgerald, who properly enough stresses the childlike side of Mary Tyrone and is by nature a sweet and sensitive woman, does not sufficiently convey the unfathomable bewilderment in suffering which is at the heart of the role. A promising young actor, James Naughton is a straightforward Edmund. He reads the cardinal speech of his part well—only there should be much more to it than that. Stacy

Keach alone brings the searing torment of the play to the role of James, Jr. There is fire in him but perhaps not enough of a certain boyish candor, which also exists in the character's spoiled nature.

To achieve an "ideal" production for this play directors and actors must not shy from the painful, as Arvin Brown willy-nilly appears to be doing. There is a bit too much standing and walking about on Geraldine Fitzgerald's part—particularly in the third act—in order, I suppose, to avoid her having to sit quietly while speaking what amounts to a long sequence of monologues. (Morphine reduces energy in movement, but the character here, supposedly deep in her drugged musings, acts as if she were merely overtalkative.) To eschew the "heaviness" of serious drama everyone smiles too much, tries to keep things light, "natural," unemphatically simple. How afraid we are today of emotional power, of magnitude! We make everything "clear" and small. "The tragedy of America is its fear of tragedy."

52

Old Times
(London)

[June 28, 1971]

AT HAROLD PINTER's new play, *Old Times,* given by the Royal Shakespeare Company, I was reminded of a quip: one man asks another, "Have you seen *Last Year at Marienbad?*" The other answers, "Perhaps."

Meticulously written, with an odd lucidity in which every speech is shiningly clear and at the same time, in its context, bewilderingly ambiguous, *Old Times* suggests (it never says) that the past is a kind of palimpsest, so that one's memories overlay one another and one can't be sure which of them really happened and which are in fact dreams.

However, there is more to the play than that rather familiar proposition. The mind in which events are chiefly recalled is that of a man tortured by sexual apprehensions which he cannot resolve because his recollections as to what occurred or may have occurred twenty years ago are troubled by contradictory testimony from his wife and from her long absent friend, now living in Sicily and come to visit the couple in a quiet English village by the sea. At first he appears to know nothing of the visiting friend (she is called Anna), but later he says that he had stared at and presumably desired her when they sat opposite each other in a London pub in the bygone days. Anna does not refute this; indeed, she affirms that she knew him, remembers him well.

The foregoing is complicated by puzzling corroboration followed by contrary evidence. Husband and wife had met for the first time at an old movie, *Odd Man Out,* and he was immediately attracted by her. Anna professes to have met the man's wife at another showing of the same picture. (Were they all there together? It is possible but by no means certain.) What disturbs the man is that the friendship between Anna and his wife was so uniquely intimate that he somehow feels shut out, excluded, by their mutual reminiscences of the days and nights of their former companionship. He even suspects that their relationship may have been something more than girlhood camaraderie. They say nothing to allay his jealous fears. Perhaps his troubled state in this regard—hurt and anger—stems from a sense that he is or was sexually aroused by both women and thus in some way frustrated by both.

I am not positive I have all these twists right and, to a certain extent, it hardly matters. The main point is how difficult it is to recapture old times and how evanescent is the substance of reality. And since so much experience is centered in sexual longing, our lives tend to move toward a never fulfilled yearning for the satisfaction of some true knowledge, a confirmed consciousness of what life has been to us, an unequivocal grasp of its meaning. However, all that is left to us are imprecise but haunting "old time" melodies, songs that linger in the air.

Is it so? For Pinter it is. Subtle craftsman, shrewd dramatist, he builds his plays as metaphysical melodramas, their ambivalences fostering suspense. Nor does he omit the irony and surprising comedy of the situations he posits. With all this, Pinter remains a master of contemporary theatre writing with something more than a "manner"; he is no mere trickster or aesthetic tease.

Having acknowledged that much, I must extend my review with a few subjective notations or statements of personal prejudices. My tastes veer toward a less ascetic art. I favor fullness; I enjoy rich surfaces, greater body, broader canvases. Hence my attachment to Shakespeare, and among novelists my preferences are Dickens, Balzac, Tolstoy, Dostoevsky. These men lived in more spacious epochs. We have "conquered" space and have become dismally constricted. Each of the artists mentioned above was in one way or another also a moralist, but their creations were founded in flesh and the boundless miracles of action amid a world of color. Perhaps there is no help for it, but I am discomfited by the bleakness of so much of the "modern." Why, I ask myself, must our own art be so sedulously "minimal"?

There are too many things around us and we are overwhelmed. We move too rapidly, cover too much ground, rest very little. We find it difficult to cope with the environment. Serious artists experience a tendency to withdraw from the external tumult, to make ever more abstract graphs of reality, to dwell within themselves.

In drama, Ibsen occupies a middle point between the prodigality of the "old" and the narrowness of the "new." With Pirandello, we arrive at the desperate skepticism of our age. We can no longer be sure of anything—not even for the hell or the fun of it. Certainty eludes us. We are in a grotesque dreamland. Shakespeare, toward the end of his career, seems to have arrived at a similar state, but how much more ample, colorful, zestful the journey. Now the stage of our insights and perspectives has shrunk: we have become very small. This, as I say, may have been inevitable, but should we take pride in it?

To return to Pinter's *Old Times,* it is called his first "full-length play" since *The Homecoming,* though it runs only eighty minutes. Directed by Peter Hall, the production of the Royal Shakespeare Company is especially fine. Like the text itself John Bury's sets and lighting are spare and yet utterly telling of place, time and atmosphere. Their simplicity and neatness are somehow eerie, chilly in the sense they create of vacancy and isolation.

The acting is beautifully precise, with an edge of cruelty and pain. It seems perfect in its verbal and intellectual articulation: its form completely conveys Pinter's essence. Vivien Merchant as Anna, Dorothy Tutin as the wife, and Colin Blakely as the husband not only express the play but seem to contain it in its incisiveness, its own kind of elegance and its brilliant mystery.

For all my alienation from the Pinteresque "landscape," I nevertheless admire *Old Times* for the probity of its delineation, the authenticity in the projection of an individual vision—which is part of the truth of our day. The play will be produced in New York before long, where, I venture to say, its press reception will not be wholly enthusiastic as it has been here.

53

···>·—◆>●<◆—·◆··

London

[July 19, 1971]

ENGLAND is weary. So at least its clever new plays testify. The lassitude is expressed either in scorn of the past or in mockery of the present. Old folks indulge in nostalgia. Still there is patience (which may be a form of discipline) and acceptance or passivity in the face of the dismal. The inertia at the core of these plays is rouged with ribaldry or imprecations. But they are comedies: comedies of inaction.

The audience laughs, thinking it unseemly or futile to cry. It tolerates the sordid; as if resigned to a condition it does not possess the strength to change. It also laughs at its own patience and orderliness. Perhaps it finds safety in the thought, "This too shall pass." There is no genuine ardor in the rambunctiousness of the young.

In America we tend to blame personal hebetude on mothers; in England it is blamed on fathers. The dramatization of both these grudges soon becomes tiresome. *Forget-Me-Not Lane* by Peter Nichols, whose *Joe Egg* and *The National Health* are more original plays, pulls its punches in amiable humor, but is rather sick at heart. Frank, its reminiscing nonhero, can hardly bear his fool of a father, who also drives Frank's mother up the wall.

What's wrong with old da'? He's complacently immersed in the muck of lower-class country prejudices. He is defiantly ignorant; no fresh air or new light can be forced into his consciousness. Frank cannot actually rebel against his father, "consideration" being the impediment. He understands that the old duffer cannot help being what he is, a victim of the static society of bygone times which rendered him content to live in less than a mediocrity of means, aspiration, education.

So Frank becomes a listless teacher, a poor husband, an inadequate lover, a failure in everything that matters. He strikes one as being as hopeless as his father, with the additional burdens of realizing his condition and being unable to do anything but jeer at himself. It is all treated as a joke. These characters would be pitiful, if not somewhat boring, were they not so well written and well acted. The English impersonate such misfits—especially the elder ones— with comic relish.

More probing and much more acerbic in language is David Mercer's *After Haggerty*. It is more ambitious in intellectual scope though more ungainly in structure than the Nichols play. The central character, Bernard Link, is a mildly Marxist theatre critic. He has little respect for his profession and his radical proclivities are lamed rather than fortified by the chain of events in Budapest, Prague, China, Cuba and Chicago. Why does he so lack ideas and gumption? The fault, once again, is papa's. His old man is even more resolutely obtuse than his coeval in the Nichols comedy. He is very nearly a monster, and the son, though enraged, is merely sorry for his parent and rather ashamed that he bears him so much animosity.

An American woman is introduced as contrast to Bernard. She was formerly the mistress of a shadowy (never seen) Irishman, Haggerty, who was also a bookish leftist. She is forthright, brash, desirous of companionship with intelligent and determined men. She is noisily impatient for "redemption" through an active and courageous leader. Haggerty, we learn, in despair over his own strictly mental insurgency, committed suicide by standing between the fire of two contestant (presumably "Communist") forces, while Bernard to the very end remains a nice bloke with no real direction and therefore no positive energy.

The pivotal characters in the Nichols and the Mercer plays are fortyish; a younger group is on view in David Hare's *Slag* and in E. A. Whitehead's *The Foursome*. E. A. Whitehead describes himself in this perhaps significant manner: "I was born without benefit of clergy in Liverpool's Scotland Road, educated by the Jesuits, survived Cambridge, held back the Red Menace in Germany, did the usual rounds as a milkman, postman, busman, drug peddler, *and am still seeking revenge for it all.* [The italics are mine.]

I reviewed *Slag* briefly when it was produced at the Public Theatre in New York. The acting (especially that of Lynn Redgrave) is much more persuasive in London, so that a play that seemed a foulmouthed lark at home has more meaning here. It reveals three young females who are incompetent teachers in a failing girls' secondary school. The most literate of the three bursts with half-digested women's lib fervor. She is tortured by her antagonism to everything in today's social setup, while remaining a tempestuously outspoken virgin who faints at the very suggestion of a lesbian encounter between the two other girls. The role strikes a serious note amid all the guffaws which the license of its language excites, because we find that the girl reflects the anguish caused in her by the native environment without the knowledge or experience to cope with it by any means other than insult.

Another of the trio is simply an addlebrained pussycat, chiefly eager for sexual satisfaction. The third girl ("the head mistress") is a semi-efficient cog in the existing though badly running machine of the status quo, and probably a lesbian.

Though totally dissimilar in factual and technical content than the plays about the men, the pattern *Slag* traces comes to the same impasse. There is a whirl of occasionally brilliant talk—all these dramatists write with admirable fluency—which is largely invective peppered with gross epithets that serve only to increase the sense of general impotence.

The Foursome is a "slice of life," presenting two young fellows of the crudest working-class background and two chicks of like stripe, whom the boys have picked up in a pub of a Saturday night. All of them drunk, they have spent the night in the boys' van. When we meet them they are at a beach near Liverpool on a Sunday morning. The men's basic contempt for the girls is plain throughout the sexual byplay and afterplay. They are not "bad" men but uncouth, with elements of sensibility peeping through their habitual sadism. It can be seen in their semi-submerged disgust at the sordidness of the surroundings in which they live and seek their fun.

The merit of this play is that the situation is set forth with unrelenting honesty. I wish the audience were not so prone to think of it as if it were a comic turn, an English equivalent of *The Dirtiest Show in Town*, which is being presented with apparent success in a nearby theatre.

I have spoken of these exhibits in what may seem a crabbed manner. They trouble me, not because of their inadequacies as drama—on the contrary, though one cannot claim great distinction for them, they are respectable efforts by serious playwrights not yet in their prime—but because they are symptoms of a situation, a world at dead end. It may even be encouraging that more such plays are being written now in England—Edward Bond's *Saved* was perhaps the best of them—than in America, and that they are nearly always better done.

Generally the acting in London is technically proficient and responsive to the plays' social relevance. At the subsidized theatres—the National, the Royal Shakespeare, the Royal Court—the level of performance is often truly superior. *After Haggerty*, though now playing in a West End house, was originally done by the Royal Shakespeare Company. *Slag*, an experimental group production has been redone at the Royal Court, where *The Foursome* originated in its own tiny "rooftop" quarters. And Paul Scofield who is so heartwarmingly effective in Zuckmayer's *The Captain of Köpenick*—a true achievement in character acting—is at the National.

54

---✦---◈▸◉◂◈---✦---

Ne reveillez pas madame

[August 2, 1971]

JEAN ANOUILH's latest play, *Ne reveillez pas madame* (*Madame is Not to Be Disturbed*) is another of his successes. It has already run more than 250 performances, and the night I saw it the house was sold out. It has been awarded the Paris Critics' Prize as the best creation of the season.

It is ostensibly about the private lives of stage folk in relation to their profession or vice versa. "Don't wake mother," the little boy who is to become a director and the play's central character is told; being an actress, she works late at night and needs to rest mornings. She rehearses during the day. So, the boy sees only his neglected and intimidated father to whom his wife is indifferent because he is not of the theatre. Besides, mother has lovers as the boy's actress wives will have when he grows up.

The play repeats the usual Anouilh theme: the deception and despair of the decent person in a corrupt society; the fragility of human relations, especially the marital ones. Women are fickle but perhaps they have a right to be: they endure childbirth and sustain the race. On that account they are sturdier than men. Then again, the wholly earnest male is something of a bore, frequently puritanical and yet himself far from consistent in his morals. This situation is aggravated when the man and the woman belong to the notoriously unstable and disruptive world of the theatre, and perhaps more especially that of the French theatre.

This is another version of the same author's *Colombe*. But, whereas the earlier play (which I directed in 1954) possessed a certain emotional authenticity, probably because of personal circumstances, the attitude has now become a complaisant cynicism. There is a commercial taint in it. Anouilh's pessimism is how he makes his living. The Paris theatregoing public enjoys his witty denunciation of its vices. It somehow finds itself absolved by it. *C'est la vie, quoi!* I find the trick the more offensive because Anouilh manages it so skillfully.

The acting of the play is typical of the present-day Boulevard—professionalism gone rotten. It reeks of staginess. Some of the actors, genuine enough in films, carry on in the theatre with a facile and flagrant falsity of which they seem absolutely proud. One is very nearly persuaded to admire their confident effrontery.

There is something more to this than just overacting: it is shameless exhibitionism. Heavy "characterization" takes precedence over character. Every point is hammered out; stereotypes abound. One has the impression that each of the personages has put on many times more makeup than is needed for visibility or credibility. Scenes in which the players caricature the extravagances of a former stage generation (the old "Sarah Bernhardt" days) are hardly more absurd than what they do as pretended naturalism during the ordinary course of the evening's drama. (Sarah Bernhardt had a temperament that justified her giddy excesses.) Anouilh, in the person of his protagonist, says that audiences don't listen to or understand most of a play's lines: they care only about situations. So exposition is rattled at a dizzy pace, after which the actors pause to mark their "big moments," so that no one can fail to notice that that is what they are. The audience responds to these florid or hysterical declamations—the writing has a certain brilliance—with gratified rounds of applause. This is "theatre"!

I do not scorn artifice. It may convey grace, wit, elegance, polish, —bespeak refinement of manner and delicacy of sentiment. One finds this in such an actor as Pierre Fresnay and among a number of English and German actors. But, though the kind of acting we see in Anouilh's play has its origins in the French inclination toward flamboyance of the romantic age and the modified bombast of the neoclassic, both have become infected by a vulgar showmanship, a phony and clamorous "Frenchiness" which the best representatives of Gallic excellence from Copeau to Vilar abhorred. These men were purifiers of the theatre of their time, the last and finest example of which in acting was Gérard Philippe.

Acting too is rooted in the social environment. The bad acting I speak of is a sign of the decline of the French tradition through the grossest, most self-indulgent elements in the newly fattened French bourgeoisie with its greedy eye on the tourist trade. In the classless American world, with its vast variety of backgrounds ("high society" has vanished), the stage has developed an honest, truth-seeking actor —often blunt and insufficiently discriminating in matters of style and interpretation—impeded chiefly by lack of broad artistic training, wide repertory and continuity of practice. The English actor has gained something from the decorum imposed by the class breeding of former generations, and now with the liquidation of the Empire is being refreshed by the emergence of articulate forces from the working, regional or rural strata of the country.

I now find American and English acting of sounder and more vigorous fiber than present-day acting in France, once held to be the most dazzlingly admirable in the Western world.

55

London

[September 27, 1971]

MOST OF THE ENGLISH, as I noted in a July 19th report from London, have begun to look askance at their papas. John Mortimer, by contrast, has achieved success with his affectionate *Journey Around My Father*. The playwright's affability may be a purely individual matter without social connotations, but it happens that the father in this instance is a barrister (therefore "upper class") without strong convictions about the law or for that matter about anything except good manners, while the paternal parent in the plays whose authors are discontented with him all seem to have been lower-class tradesmen with a great many (misguided) convictions.

Mortimer's father also elicits sympathy from the audience by the fact that he is blind, and that no one—the father, his wife or son—ever mentions it. What especially attaches West End patrons to the elder Mortimer is his beguiling eccentricity and humor.

The effect of this filial tribute is enhanced by the serene and relaxed craftsmanship of Alec Guinness' acting in the title role. I have no objections to this unassuming play, but I must confess that its agreeable simplicity interested me less than did the earlier and more irritating father-berating works. If a dramatist is to be sweetly mild he must display something more than good nature. I call attention to *Journey Around My Father* chiefly because it differs in mood from most of what I have recently seen in England.

John Osborne's newest piece, *West of Suez*, is another of the Royal Court Theatre's provocative productions. The central figure, Wyatt, is a successful novelist, the father of four daughters, the eldest being a permanent resident of an island, "west of Suez," where she has settled down with her husband, a retired military man. These two have "given up," being content to go to seed under the sun. Another daughter is an "intellectual"—Osborne devotes little time to her except to indicate that she is well-informed but inconsequential, because her mind does little with what it feeds itself. The youngest daughter is pretty, chubby and, through lack of pronounced attributes, comforting to her schoolteacher husband who dislikes his job.

Most representative of Osborne is another daughter, possessed of eye-catching legs. She is acidly honest, cold, barely loving and barely loved—bitterly satisfied to remain safely undisturbing to the despised social structure within which she lives. Nor does she much trouble her husband, a pathologist who tolerates his wife and life though he never expresses affection or genuine interest in either.

Incidental characters include a flagrantly gay hairdresser and another famous novelist who is also queer. (At one time it was forbidden even to mention the existence of homosexuality on the English stage; now there is an obsession with it.) Among other characters is a "good" American who has left his country and settled on the island (is that what all good Americans are supposed to do?), and some silly American tourists who, the good American assures his British friends, are harmless. The brown and black natives, when they are not being patently hostile, are quietly disdainful of the white settlers. There is also a handsome hippie—unshod of course—who has been invited by the hairdresser to the hospitable household and is received for dinner.

The most deftly drawn character, superbly played by Ralph Richardson, is Wyatt himself. He is witty, civilized, skeptical, egotistic and disaffected from all faith or passion. He is committed to nothing but writing, particularly his own. Wyatt embodies the best that Osborne can say about those of his countrymen whom he has chosen to depict in his recent plays.

West of Suez, which for the most part is discursive (as is usual with Osborne, the discourse gratifies the ears), ends in shock. Provoked by a pass from the hairdresser, the hippie bursts into a violent harangue in which, barely articulate, he damns the whole crew as empty, futile, worthless. It seems here that Osborne has blown his cool: the language becomes mere vehement obscenity, conveying little more than disgust and a desire to destroy. The desire is fulfilled by the sudden and unexpected eruption of masked natives who, shooting at random, kill old Wyatt. This world ends not with a whimper but a bang.

Osborne *hates*. One cannot view his resentment as vitalizing indignation, the denunciation of a corrupt society. It is instead the sick and self-vilifying product of that society. The audience may not be troubled by this at the present occasion because *West of Suez* is intelligently entertaining. Richardson's own charm, amused and a little sad, regretful and puzzled, gives the evening a quality superior to the play's textural content.

Simon Gray's *Butley* does not trouble the audience at all: it delights it. The comedy proliferates funny verbal twists, a medium for irreverent levity. It also enjoys the advantage of Alan Bates' easy and expert performance in the name part. But if one chooses to think about it a moment (the audience apparently doesn't), one must realize that it is even more devastatingly nihilistic than the Osborne play. Harold Pinter, who directed *Butley*, was surely aware of this.

The English theatre public will let a playwright get away with anything if his text flashes with humor and is cultivated in texture. *Butley* has little dramatic core. It is the pen portrait of a college professor (his specialty is T. S. Eliot), a man who has forsworn all concern for education and his pupils, for whom he evinces nothing but scorn.

Butley drinks. He is altogether pleased to do so; the audience in consequence does not worry about him. He neglects his person—is in fact a slob. This also amuses. He is predominantly homosexual, though given to wounding remarks about homosexuals. He has been married, has a child, doesn't like his wife's divorcing him, resents her marrying someone he says is a bore, and does nothing to prevent either move. His chief victim is his homosexual consort, formerly a student, whom he has contrived to have appointed to the faculty of the same college. At the end, even this weak young man quits him.

What is it about Butley that, apart from his jokes, "gets" the audience? He despises everything with which it has itself become disenchanted. Everything, even sex, bores him. Butley is dismally tired. He will die from exhaustion with his own viciously corrosive banter. But there is a certain relief from spiritual depression in *Butley*. Its protagonist makes inconsequentiality, disinterestedness, deliberate folly appear acceptable through laughter—and not only acceptable but somehow damned clever.

In contrast to such fare is Maxim Gorky's *Enemies*, admirably produced by the Royal Shakespeare Company, an organization which in recent years has covered itself with ever more merited honors. Written in 1906, immediately after the suppressed uprising of 1905, *Enemies* was forbidden performances by the czarist censorship and was not staged until 1933 in Leningrad and at the Moscow Art Theatre two years later.

Gorky was socially prescient. At a time when most of his literary cohorts, disillusioned by the 1905 debacle, were writing works of dejected mysticism or of a turbidly desperate sexuality, Gorsky predicts in *Enemies* the ultimate triumph of the oppressed. That alone would not cause me to like the play; a dramatist need not prove himself a political seer. The play is absorbing through the compression of its characterizations which are subtle, rich, compassionate and instinct with social insight.

Almost the whole society is limned in brief strokes. There is the doggedly brutal boss, determined not only to squelch all signs of independence in his subordinates but also to take over the factory from his more refined partner. (The play's action is sparked by the murder of this bourgeois ruffian by a worker whom he has kicked in the stomach during a labor dispute.) There is the soft and easily swayed liberal owner of the factory, who wants to be fair to all parties and cannot understand the reason for the fierce hostility which surrounds him.

His brother has taken to drink because he has sensibility and understanding without specific talent or a capacity for action. The man's wife is an actress who is drawn to the rebellious workers—it is she who foresees their ultimate victory—but who, despite her sympathy, makes no positive move on their behalf. She is a bystander, a witness, an artist. Her deepest concern is to be cast in plays that will be earthshaking or ennobling.

The most winning portrait in the play is that of the liberal boss's orphan niece. She is ardent with love of decent people and causes. Gorky had a special empathy with such young girls who, in the midst of moral desolation, strive toward a radiant future. Of this particular eighteen-year-old girl the actress says, "If you begin asking yourself questions you'll become a revolutionary. . . ."

Then there are the workers, some craven, some brave, some consistently loyal, others innocently trusting, and a few supported by peasant shrewdness. When the actress asks the oldest of the men what remedy he would apply to the evil of their lives, his answer is "we've got to do away with the kopek . . . once the kopek's gone why should we push each other about? . . . " The actress challenges "And that's all?" to which the old man replies, "It's enough to begin with."

I found myself positively refreshed by this play. The fact that the revolution it presages has led to a new tyranny does not diminish my accord with its spirit. There is heart in Gorky's "politics." It epitomizes the warm humanism of the Russian intelligentsia in its purest phases—something which still remains inspiring and exemplary.

Adding to the pleasure I took in Gorky's "script" was my admiration for the acting company; many of the players were the same as those who had performed with so much physical agility and gaiety in Peter Brook's *A Midsummer Night's Dream*. Especially notable in this respect was Mary Rutherford. In the *Dream* she was Hermia; in *Enemies* she plays the fervent answer-seeking Nadya, seen by her friend (the actress of the play) perhaps rightly as being overwhelmed and finally crushed by future eventualities. The entire company is excellent, projecting by its own special means the essence of this eminently Russian play.

56

Old Times
(New York)

[December 6, 1971]

To CALL Harold Pinter's *Old Times* "a great play" in New York at the present time is simply a means of priming the theatrical pump. The fact is that for a large number of playgoers it is a difficult play, from which most of them come away bewildered.

Old Times is Pinter's most poetic play. It is an extremely concentrated expression of mood rather than "story." Another writer might have attempted to convey that mood in a lyric or mystic manner. Pinter's mystery is wrought without "mysteriousness." Another writer might have projected the play so that the audience would immediately recognize it as fanciful. Pinter writes as if his mystery were cold fact, a literal and specific report of actual occurrences. In other hands, the play's idea might be transmitted with warmth; Pinter's artistic demeanor is tight, glacial.

What Pinter seems to be saying is that memory merges much of what has happened to us into things which we only imagined or dreamed as having happened. The reality of the past fades and memory transforms real events into shadowy remnants of experience which are no more substantial than reveries. "There are some things one remembers even though they may never have happened," one of the characters says, "but as I recall them so they take place." In other words what happens in people's minds is as true as what has happened in the objective world, while clouded remembrance of actual events may become dim to the point of nonexistence.

Deeley, the only man in *Old Times,* has married Kate, but after twenty years he meets Kate's friend Anna, whom he recalls as also having been a girl who attracted him at the time he met Kate. Kate and Anna speak of their intimate relationship in the old days—they lived together—and exclude Deeley as they indulge in recollections. Indeed they speak as if the old days were present and Deeley not there at all. The two women fuse in Deeley's mind as if they were part of a single experience: they are two and one.

The female figures then are either two women whom Deeley's desire has made into one never altogether fulfilled desire, *or* they are two different aspects of the same desired woman. Some English critics have maintained that neither one has ever existed, but that Deeley's imagination has conjured them up as part of a deep and forever frustrated sexual yearning. Whatever reading one may ascribe to *Old Times* is less important than the anguish of sexual longing which many feel at the extinction of the past, with all its pleasures, hopes, ambitions and adventures. Hence an experience is both real and unreal, never fully possessed. Reality is remote. There are enormous gaps of darkness in our consciousness; with the passing of the years what we live through is buried in obscurity. Only the mirage of life is constant.

That at least is Pinter's feeling. But he does not *say* it. He will not be forthright, assertive, ratiocinative. All such attitudes might bespeak a theory, an ideology. Though there is longing and a quiet weeping in *Old Times,* there is no outcry; there is even humor. It is a frozen dream of life, conveyed as lucid and transparent. Life, finally, is puzzling and frightening, a wonder and a "slight ache." Pinter's "face" is fixed to avoid any indication of perturbation or plaint.

His craftsmanship is masterly. The expected visitor, Anna, is already present in shadow from the first. In the midst of what seems a casual conversation the characters veer without transition to a conversation out of the past so that past and present are undifferentiated. The old-time songs the characters remember are carefully chosen to set the play's atmosphere: "When a lovely flame dies, smoke gets in your eyes" or "Oh, how the ghost of you clings."

Deeley speaks of taking his wife's face in his hands and "it just floats away." He is struck by words no longer in common use like "lest" and "gaze." Speaking of where he sat in a movie house Deeley says in typically Pinteresque fashion—ambiguously pointed—"I was off center and have remained so."

Every stage device—the indicated silences, the turning on and off of lamps, the arbitary dimming and brightening of the illumination —all sum up to an eerie sense of past and present as a unity of time which makes for timelessness, a flow which is also static, "forever."

Hardly a word is wasted. The compact writing is integral with the "message." It is local (London) English directed toward universals. "My work concerns itself with life all over . . . in every part of the globe," Pinter has Deeley say. "I use the word globe because world possesses emotional, sociological and psychological pretensions and resonances which I prefer as a matter of choice to do without . . . to steer clear of . . . to reject." Later in the same vein with the same intent, Deeley says, "I have my eye on a number of pulses, pulses all over the globe, deprivations and insults."

In reviewing the play from London (pages 286–288) I suggested that Pinter's "inscape"—particularly in this play, which is one of his best—is somewhat alien to me but that I nevertheless admire it as a consummate expression of Pinter's view of life, an emotional tendency that is taking hold in today's overcrowded, claustrophobic civilization in which we gasp for the air of contemplation and inner privacy. Because of the double vision inherent in *Old Times*, coupled with the duality of my reaction to it—high esteem and involuntary refusal —I advise that it be seen twice to be properly appreciated.

The New York cast—Robert Shaw, Rosemary Harris, Mary Ure, finely directed here as in London by Peter Hall—finds itself in John Bury's original settings which capture ideally the tone of the play. The acting here is softer and seemingly more "natural" than in London. The effect produced is therefore perhaps more conducive to acceptance by an American audience. The London cast is more unyieldingly hard, of a more restrained heat, and thus more congruous on the whole with Pinter's style.

57

The Screens

[December 27, 1971]

"HELLO! I'm laughter—not just any laughter, but the kind that appears when all goes wrong." That is a line from the Mother's soliloquy in Jean Genet's *The Screens* at the Chelsea Theatre Center of Brooklyn.

The Mother's greeting may well be the open sesame to a sense—I do not say "understanding"—of a play which may be set down as a terrible masterpiece. Its running time is four and a half hours, and if you seek strict coherence, you are lost. The scenes are scattered, confused, frightening, absurd and ultimately no more nefarious than a nightmare. The play's very explosion constitutes its meaning. "Everything wicked in the vegetable kingdom," the Mother goes on to say "was won over to me." That is Genet's insignia, his contribution. If evil and hatred must have a conscious voice in drama, let it be Genet's.

The outraged patrioteers who rioted in Paris at the Roger Blin–Jean–Louis Barrault production of the play several years ago, because it insulted the French army fighting the Algerian rebellion, were quite mistaken. The French presence in Algeria is not the butt of Genet's venom, nor is French officialdom the object of his mockery and wrath. His real target is civilization itself—all of modern civilization. He despises everything that it has spawned; he is no more pro-Algeria, as a social interpreter might read him, than he is anti-French. His scorn is all-embracing; it aims at universal devastation. The agony within him and the residue of a profoundly Gallic cultural heritage are wrenched from him in immense gusts of grotesque laughter. They echo like reverberations from Rabelais and Rimbaud.

As long ago as 1915 James Huneker wrote, "Foul is fair in art today." If, as some assert, we are entering a new dark age, it will surely produce its saints as well as its victims. Sartre has called Genet a saint. He is a saint who would purge us in a reversed morality which scours our hypocrisy, deceit and violence in an acid bath of loathing. (The play's title is not a reference simply to the screens that are used as "scenery" but to the symbols of the false front behind which we hide our villainies.) Evil be thou my savior is Genet's prescript, an outcry which has in it almost as much mephitic irony as anguish.

The play's "story" is a springboard for an apocalyptic vision which contains the essence of Genet's *esprit*, and makes it more stage poetry than dramatic narrative. The pivotal figures are Saïd, an Algerian youth, and his mother, both at the bottom of the social scale. Saïd is so poor that to earn some money he marries the most hideously ugly girl (her face throughout the play is covered by a hood), a girl whose father pays a pitiful sum to get her off his hands. Saïd mistreats her; for sexual satisfaction he frequents a brothel (a prominent and telltale locale in this play as in *The Balcony*). But Leila, Saïd's abject wife, develops a slavish devotion to him, apparently thriving on his cruelty. She follows him like a whipped dog and joins him in his every misdeed. To escape Algeria, where he works as an abused farmhand under international capitalist ownership, he steals and Leila abets him in his thefts. Both are frequently jailed.

Saïd turns traitor to his countrymen. It isn't clear whether he does this because of a desire to escape the misery of his condition as an oppressed worker or because he has become a stooge of Genet's ideological bent. He says, "What can I sell out on, so as to be a complete louse?" When finally he is hunted down and the French authorities want to make a hero of him—with song, decoration and statue to celebrate his betrayal—he refuses the "honor," with his mother's blessings, and allows himself to be shot down. He is an adherent to no political cause, a patriot of no land—in which respects he imitates Genet himself.

In and around this bit of plot is a vast panorama of scenic flashes in which the foreigners' orange groves are burned by the natives, the elegance of French military splendor is burlesqued, together with the stupefying decadence of the *haute bourgeoisie*. Then, too, one glimpses the hilarious unconcern of the afterlife, the demystified exchanges between the living and the dead, one hears voices from "nowhere." There is always the return of the whores—who know everything, for in their company men reveal their true feelings.

Through all the long parade of vicious insult, scatological rhapsody and infernal scurrility, Genet provides such keynotes as: "I want you to plunge into irrevocable grief. . . . I want you to be without hope. I want you to choose evil. I want you to know only hatred and never love." A local sibyl, now deceased, calls out, "Saïd, Leila, my loved ones. . . . You realized that in evil lay the only life." Then, addressing the others, she asks, "What have you done for evil to prevail?" Then, too, we hear the Cadi confess: "All I brought from life is my trembling. If it's taken away from me, I lose everything."*

All this builds to a strange, often bewildering and always arresting eloquence. Unlike his imitators (how I shun them) Genet, through the world's early rejection of him and through his subsequent suffering, has earned the right to his epic nihilism. He bears his humiliation like a defiant badge. And yet I find his outrage somehow cleansing, almost an alleviation in a world of half measures, cautious distinctions, "reasonable" remedies and timid compromises.

The very vehemence and savagery of Genet's ribald imprecations have something unutterably comic about them. They transform the insane turmoil of modern society, of life itself, into farce. Now everything has been said, every condemnation, every superlative of obloquy has been voiced; now we know how bad, and badly off, we are. We are shamelessly unmasked, but on beholding our shamefulness we can emit a roar of relief that we have been told the worst. Pushed beyond the edge of despair, we may realize all that has been left unsaid, all that is still good in the Gehenna in which we dwell. Genet

* These quotations are from Bernard Frechtman's translation (Grove Press, 1972). The Chelsea production credits its director, Minos Volanakis, with the translation it uses.

flagellates himself and us into a new purity through the excess and sullied grandiloquence of his derision.

Only a true poet, a man possessed of verbally imaged artistry, could write such a play as *The Screens*. In one of his earlier pieces, Genet spoke of "a truthful idea born of an artificial show." The use of the screens in the present play to obviate all traces of realism, the instruction he gives for devising weird masks, costumes, sounds, reveal a fabulous theatrical imagination, a joy in the creation of stage hyperbole. And when one acknowledges the joy in spectacle added to the thrills of language—colorful, adventuresome, astonishing and dense in allusion—it can no longer be maintained that the end result or even the purpose of the whole enterprise is to depress or destroy. Genet is one of the few creative dramatists of our epoch. From the holocausts of the day he lights his own flaming torch. It illuminates what we are, what we have wrought, what we must renounce.

Minos Volanakis' direction is admirable in its fidelity to and understanding of the script, its treatment of the actors, its skill in the use of the limited technical resources available at the tiny Chelsea quarters. Speeches and scenes, which in reading one might suppose unplayable, become clear; no intention or nuance of action is left recondite, as literature. Everything is theatrically visualized. Watching the play, I speculated on how much more tricky and costly Tom O'Horgan would have made the production if he had been given the opportunity: there would have been more lavish expenditure with much less point. I also wondered why, if we dare cut Shaw and Shakespeare, Volanakis did not venture to abbreviate Genet. But perhaps without the license of length Genet's play would lose some of its dynamism.

The cast too merits much praise. The list of players who warrant compliments is too long to be included, but some words of special commendation are due Julie Bovasso for her shrewd humor and bite in the acting of the Mother; to Grayson Hall for the acrid clarity of the play's emblematic prostitute Warda, and to Joan Harris as Malika, who seconds Warda; to Robert Jackson for the tortured fervor of his Saïd; to Martin Garner for the canny and touching skepticism of the Cadi; to the physical and vocal versatility of Barry Bostwick's showoff sergeant; to James Cahill as a Mouth for the dead; to Janet League for the accomplishment of her arduous task as Leila; to John Granger for the pathetic fatuousness of his French lieutenant.

Robert Mitchell has used every possible foot of space and remarkable ingenuity to accommodate the multiple effects called for by the play. Especially gratifying are Willa Kim's costumes, among the best of the season; they speak of something more than the money spent on them.

58

Envoi: To the Young

[November 19, 1969]

On Receiving an Honorary Degree at
Boston University

I AM MOST GRATEFUL for the honor you have conferred on me today. It is called "Doctor of Fine Arts." It has a splendid sound even if it does not cure all ills.

I cannot say like Puccini's Tosca in the aria *"Vissi d'arte"* that I have lived for art; my own belief is best expressed in the Brechtian aphorism "Every art contributes to the greatest art of all: the art of living." For me life is enough.

The arts may be described in many ways: they are antennae in the world's maze; they are the recorders of the earth's quakes; they are prophecies in the darkness of our ignorance; as play they are also a testimony of our soul's freedom, the superfluous, as Voltaire said, which is so needed. They are surely the flowers of existence.

The purpose of the so-called humanities is to render us more human, more aware of the adventure and challenge of being men and women. We know only too well these days how difficult it is to make whole persons of the beast in us. The artist is engaged in that effort.

For the greater part of my life I have devoted myself to the discipline of the arts—I do not speak of the theatre alone—and I have always resisted the idea that the arts exist apart as a separate

309

entity in the world for a special breed of people. "Nothing comes from nothing." The arts are rooted in the very stuff of life. They are not meant to make us aesthetes, connoisseurs or critics. Only through the pleasure, the probing experience of contemplating and dealing with the constant drama of living do we achieve full stature as humans. That is the action and function of art.

At certain moments I have been inclined to call this quite simply and plainly "having fun"! It is not a goal reserved for the professional artist. It is something we must all aspire to, teach ourselves to do. It is a capacity we may all attain.

In return for the tribute you have paid me this morning I offer you my own rallying cry: let us all become artists unto ourselves; let us all think of our lives as works of art. It is a prescription to heal many wounds.

Thank you.

Index